THE TRIAL OF MAXIMO BONGA

THE STORY OF THE STRANGEST GUEST HOUSE IN SOUTH EAST ASIA

JOHN HARRIS

THE TRIAL OF MAXIMO BONGA

Summersdale Publishers Ltd
46 West Street
Chichester
West Sussex
PO19 1RP
UK

www.summersdale.com

Printed and bound by CPI Group (UK) Ltd, Croydon, CR0 4YY

ISBN: 978-1-84953-723-0

For my Maximo Bonga, whose storytelling ability and imagination I inherited. I miss you, Dad.

CONTENTS

1

I knew it was going to be a strange place the moment we entered the village. It's not every day you see a man nailed up on a cross. A real man, a live one, his head hanging limply to one side, blood from the crown of thorns on his head dripping into his fluttering eyes. Just as I stood up to get a better look, the bus driver put his foot on the brake. In a squeal of metal everyone shot forward. Young mothers dropped their crying bundles, old ladies lost their composure and dismissed the transport system as going to the dogs, and the youngsters on board grinned wider than ever. I headbutted the seat in front.

A cloud of dust smothered the bus before being blown onto someone's roadside washing. I used the foggy moment to wonder whether what I'd just seen through the windscreen was real.

After all, it had been a back-breaking 17-hour journey over a dirt road that wound its rutted way along one side of the island. Bus journeys of this magnitude tend to make the mind wander. Seven hours they'd told me when I bought the ticket the previous day. The bus collapsed halfway. 'Seven hours, you said!' I appealed.

'No wheels!' the driver replied, pointing at the snapped axle. A half-day trip turned into an overnight epic. Seven hours, my arse.

My body was heading north, up the coast of a large Philippines island in the South China Sea to a place called El Refugio. My mind, blurred with on-off sleep in a dusty heat haze, was still on Hong Kong's cross-harbour ferry, gazing down hypnotically at the rubbish; the little polystyrene icebergs in the water.

My personal reasons for leaving Hong Kong after six years were painfully inescapable to me, despite all attempts to lock them in the past. But why come here, the Philippines, and why El Refugio in particular, I couldn't quite recall. I think I just needed chaos.

Everything works with the well-oiled precision of a BMW in Hong Kong. Everyone's life is regulated, no one breaks the law except the triads, and even they only chop each other. I was fed up with order in my work and my social life. Everything I'd been looking for in the wild East had been replaced by the very things I'd originally run away from in the tame West.

I'd replaced the routine of one with the other. Exchanged England's afternoon tea with dim sum, Sundays at Greenwich flea market with visits to Stanley Market, and midweek football with horse racing on a Wednesday night at Happy Valley. And then there was the work, the nine-to-nine. If I'd known my bosses in Hong Kong were going to be just as anal as the ones in London I wouldn't have bothered.

So run away I did, once again, trying to shake the shackles of destiny as they chased me halfway round the world and found me hiding in China. I was giving it all up again; a familiar partner and the regular sex and love it provides, the security of a permanent income from a safe job, and the comforting circle of friends. The loving, stable partner, the security and friends were the problem.

And I guess all this put together added up to the Philippines, that extra mile: 'The land of not quite right,' as a friend put it. Or, more precisely, a huge island far enough from the mainland to be different. They had 7,000 of them, so getting lost should be a doddle. OK, so a few people had been kidnapped by Muslim fundamentalists but so what? With any luck they'd kidnap me.

And when the dust cleared in front of the bus and the man on the cross at the head of the Easter procession materialised again I began to see just how different this place was going to be. A real Jesus. Jesus. I knew the Philippines was the only Catholic country in Asia, but this was good. He was wearing basketball shorts.

I yawned and stretched out the early morning cramps from the long journey. 'Is this El Refugio?' I asked the driver, praying it was.

He wasn't listening. Instead he leaned out of the window, spat on a passing dog and impatiently gave the parade permission to pass in front of the bus. An old man next to me wearing a cowboy hat said it was El Refugio and I sat down again, wondering what was going to happen next. The driver yanked up the hand break and rested his elbows on the wheel, resigned. A group of Filipinos dressed as Roman soldiers, with plastic swords and skew-whiff helmets, appeared from between the houses.

'What's going on?'

'Look at them,' the man next to me said.

I looked at him.

'Re-enacting the crucifixion of Christ. Every Easter it's the same. Christ. No wonder our country never gets anywhere. It was better under Marcos.'

The crowd stopped again, the man strapped to the cross opening one eye to see what the hold-up was. Bus versus Jesus in a stand-off, the Lord looking out the corner of his eye at us.

The driver leaned forward, pressing on the accelerator. Want some of this? It may be Easter week, mate, but I've got a schedule to keep. I've got a bus full here, and if I don't get them in on time there'll be all hell to pay. Vroom! His hand moved slowly across the face of the steering wheel as he reached for the horn, eyes fixed on The Man.

'Get this bus moving,' the cowboy next to me shouted, wiping another layer of dust and sweat from his face.

The driver pressed his hand down. *Beeeeeep!*

A cheer went up between the houses. The crucified man was hoisted aloft again and his head lulled back onto his shoulder, smug. The procession moved out from the side street, dancing, chanting and holding multicoloured Virgin Marys and crucifixes. The drunk-looking centurion at the front gave Jesus a whack with his plastic sword for good measure.

Lining the street, old women dressed up in their best lace looked happy that someone was suffering more than them. Young careworn mothers, knowing they still had decades of suffering left, looked tired. They held their little statuettes with barely concealed bitterness, as if they wanted to clunk the old girls over the head for being so superior.

On one side of the street were the doilied dinosaurs, on the other, tired child-rearers. And in the middle, young girls looking brand-spanking new in their crisp dresses, squared shoulders and erect backs.

Circling the whole crowd, running up and down the lines on this bright morning, were the boys, bursting with energy. They poked the girls and received coy brush-offs, which the older women could see was all heading in a vicious circle of innocent games turning into more teenage pregnancies.

Church bells clanged somewhere. I stuck my head out the window and looked up. A flock of pure white birds flew across the blue sky. The tinny recorded voice of a repentant woman chanting Hail Marys echoed off the crooked limestone cliffs that circled this small fishing village they call El Refugio: The Refuge.

I looked back the way we'd come in, squinting into the rising sun; a natural canyon in the landscape just wide enough for the dirt road to squeeze through. On both sides fissured limestone rising to 50 metres was picked out crisply against a clear sky.

Lining the road each side of us were tatty shacks with storefronts where entrance doors would normally be. Eateries with trays of butchered animals, fried fish and rice. Shops with dangling blue and red plastic Chinese products, each one selling exactly the same as its neighbour. A bakery displaying radioactive-looking cakes, and a table with some shrivelled vegetables on it. All unattended as the crowd grew and grew until the bus was floating in people.

The driver slumped back onto the steering wheel as the 3-metre crucifix passed in front of the windscreen and made a right turn. Another cheer went up. The frenzied procession turned into our road from the side street, a collective bounce starting somewhere in the mass. It was a bit like jogging on the spot, everyone shuffling forwards, framed pictures of the Messiah held out. Up and down they went, the man on the cross bobbing precariously at the head. Then it happened.

The straps holding Jesus to the beam unravelled, his feet slipped, and he did an arms-in-the-air fall and forward roll on the dirt a Premiership footballer have been proud of. Right in front of the Hard Rocks Videoke Bar.

This time the roar came from inside. Drunken, shiny-faced men rushed out of the pub and went down on their knees to administer a tonic to their fallen idol. Was he all right? Would he live? A bottle of rum went to his lips. There was a moment's uncertainty as he milked the once-a-year attention for all it was worth, remaining stiff as a board, eyes defiantly closed.

I was on the edge of my seat. I was out of my seat, and so was everyone else. Even the jaded old cowboy next to me was leaning forward, hat off, mouth open. A fly went in.

'Perhaps he is injured,' a concerned woman said.

'He only drinks San Miguel,' the old man dismissed.

The bottle of rum went back to his lips and everyone held their breath. There was a flutter of eyelids, a pained frown and smacking of dusty lips before his eyes opened fully. 'Oh my God, where am I?' his expression said. He grasped the man's wrist in a death-like hold, sucked on the bottleneck and guzzled.

All the men cheered and began piling back into the bar. All the women sighed with despair, resigned to yet another show of their men unable to get a grip on life. Unable to steer even Jesus from temptation.

And when the Roman centurion saw the only foreigner on the bus and came on board to get me I tried to say no. I had to find a room. I needed a shower to wash off the hours of dust that had stuck to me. I felt like a stinky pair of underpants. I needed food, water, rest.

'You like drinking beer?' the legionnaire said.

Everyone on the bus stared at me.

Look, I thought, as he dragged me – not exactly kicking and screaming, it has to be said – from the bus, Jesus ain't the only one who's suffered. If you'd spent six years stuck in Hong Kong you'd want to get pissed as well.

2

The village of El Refugio reveals itself pretty quickly. There aren't more than half a dozen dirt streets and the whole place nestles inside a snug, square kilometre. The surrounding cliffs on the landward side and the open sea on the other make it impossible to walk for more than 10 minutes without either repeating a street, slamming into a cliff face or walking into the sea. I felt as though I was at the end of the line, literally. It all seemed to make sense. The place matched my mood perfectly. Any further and I'd have been drowning, in every sense.

When I'd arrived at Manila airport two days earlier the woman at customs had asked where I intended to visit. When I told her where I was going she looked up from her stamping duty. 'Why not Boracay? The place you're going is...'

'The end of the line?' I completed. 'Perfect.'

But that wasn't far enough away for me; I needed the end of the end of the line. And as I stood there that morning on El Refugio's little beach, surrounded by shagging dogs, defecating pigs and drunk fishermen, I knew I'd found it.

Dropping my bag and squinting through the wood smoke drifting from the village, I gazed out over the flat calm of the bay. Running my eyes over the pregnant belly of a large dome-shaped island just offshore, I could see the end of the world.

I closed my eyes and floated above the earth, picturing thousands of islands and focusing in on this one. I could see the road from the state capital and its end here, as it ran between the cliffs and dropped into the sea. I could visualise myself as an 'X' on a map. I drifted, the beer I'd just drunk with Pontius Pilate and Co. warming my stomach nicely.

'Goot mornink to you.'

I opened my eyes and stared at a fisherman pulling nets from a beached outrigger just in front of me.

'I say goot mornink to you!'

I spun around. A very short, pot-bellied, middle-aged white man with a handle bar moustache and wearing only a G-string was marching along the beach. I thought I was hallucinating. He waltzed past, his stubby little legs scissoring to and fro, his buttocks wobbling and rotating around the tiniest strand of red material.

'I am Ziegwalt,' I just about heard him say before a mad pack of dogs came racing out between the palm trees and chased him down the beach.

The fisherman watched the bum speed away before coming over. He plonked a bucket on the sand next to my foot. 'Lobster?'

I blinked, looking from him to the galloping pack chasing the pink arse.

'Him live here,' the fisherman said, as if that clarified things. 'Dog not like him.'

I crouched and looked into the bucket at the lobsters. They were massive. Only a week before I'd paid thirty quid for one half this size in a dim sum restaurant in Hong Kong. It was tasteless. 'How much?'

He weighed it. 'Two hundred pesos.'

Three quid. 'I'll take it.'

'You want I cook him?' He pointed to the boat where a woman was off-loading a little stove.

'Help! Zhese dogs! Zhey are not goot!' Ziegwalt ran back the other way still chased by the salivating pack.

'Yes please,' I said.

The fisherman picked up my bag and we sat on his boat's outrigger while his wife boiled the lobster.

They seemed so content with their lot, and I really envied them what they didn't have. Here I was, pockets full of cash, money in the bank and totally bloody miserable. And there they were; one crappy wooden boat, a tatty fishing net, a few sticks of dynamite, and they were smiling. I felt like doing myself in there and then.

The lobster boiled up nicely. The fisherman's wife jammed a knife into it and served it to me on a plate. 'Salt?' I nodded and asked if she had pepper. She had. And calamansis (tiny native oranges the size of marbles), and rice, and more ciggies.

I felt all right with the world after that. The vomity feeling I'd been experiencing had gone down, along with the suicidal tendencies. There's a lot to be said for a full stomach. I think it might be connected to the heart.

'You need room?' the fisherman asked, chucking the scraps to the pack of dogs, who'd got bored chasing Ziegwalt. A fight broke out, tails between legs, lips curled over top teeth. I briefly thought about the discos in Hong Kong, and how similar the packs of gladiatorial women behaved when they sensed a bulging wallet nearby.

'Yeah.'

'Him have rooms,' he said, and I followed his arm and pointing finger down the curving beach.

There was someone standing further along, past the burning coconut husks. An old man dressed in... I blinked... battle fatigues? Second World War US by the looks of the helmet. He was standing on the shore facing out to sea. I stood my ground for a moment, squinting into the sun-streaked coconut smoke.

Slowly, ever so slowly, the old man's right arm came up and he saluted.

'You need a room?' a female voice called.

I turned.

An old Filipina woman with candyfloss for hair came to her garden fence and cracked a rug like a whip, drawing her head to one side to avoid the dust.

I looked back at the mirage then at the old lady again.

'You need a place to stay?' she barked. 'I have rooms here.'

The sign above her read 'Gladys's Cottages. Hot and Cold showers & More'. I looked back down at her, wondering what the 'more' was. She reminded me of the Tai Tais in Hong Kong, a species of wealthy, grasping elderly ladies I'd learned to hate over the years. It's not good to judge people on first encounter but sometimes gut instinct is right on the money. The sun was striking her pink rinse and I could see her scalp. She wore a thick mask of make-up and I could just imagine it sliding down during the heat of the day to transform this gargoyle into a real monster by evening. I was already sweating like crazy, so God knows how she felt in that dressing gown. This must be Gladys.

The prospect of a shower and bed right there and then was tempting, but if that old soldier had a place to stay I could be in for a real treat. Like I said, I was after weirdos and chaos. Although Gladys wasn't exactly the epitome of sanity standing there on the beach in her mules, that old boy beat her hands down.

'Well... um... I think...'

'Two hundred and fifty pesos a night,' she said, draping the rug over her picket fence. 'Including Milo. Take it or leave it.'

'Can I have a look,' I said, trying to find a reason to leave it and wondering who the hell Milo was.

'That one there.' She pointed to a wooden shed behind her.
'Does it have a shower?'

'Well if you want to look I suppose I'll have to go to my store and get the keys.'

What a dragon. She should call it Gladys's Lair.

'But I don't want visitors. No hanky-panky, no drinking – there are too many drunks in this village already, he's one of them – and no pets.'

Her voice trailed off as she looked back down the beach. The old man was gone. All that stood in his place now were two dogs going at it like the clappers while kids threw stones at them. One of the children stood and mimicked them, thrusting his groin back and forth in the air. Another kid copied him and soon all of them were standing in a line. It looked like they were doing the conga.

'Never see their parents in church on a Sunday,' Gladys huffed.

'What, the dogs?'

She didn't laugh. Instead she turned and growled at a girl who was polishing the veranda of one of the cottages with half a coconut husk. The cleaner had begun to sing very lightly while swinging her hips to and fro, using her foot to move the buffer. She went down on her hands and knees and smiled through the balustrade at me.

Gladys's face turned to stone. Her English was impressive. 'You'd better start polishing, my girl, otherwise you'll be laughing on the other side of your face.'

'I think I'll take a look around,' I said.

'You won't find anything else. This is holy week. Everywhere is full.'

I looked over her shoulder at the deserted beach huts.

'The only reason I have any space is because I like to keep some rooms for foreigners. I'm like that. It's my downfall. I know you've travelled far and need a bed for the night. There's always room at this inn,' she said, and tried to look bountiful.

'I haven't seen any tourists. There was no one on the bus coming here.'

'Locals. From Manila, the provinces... They like to visit our wonderful place. Everybody wants to come here. Huh.' She patted the back of her adamantine perm, as though it was her everyone was coming to see.

'I think I'll go and get some breakfast,' I lied.

'Suit yourself.' She took her rug off the fence and turned to go. 'But you won't like Bonga's Guest House, I can tell you now. Maximo Bonga...' She was lost for words, shaking her head and walking towards a small water tank where a terrified plumber was laying out his tools for a repair.

'Maximum Bongo?'

'Bonga,' said the fisherman's wife as she cleaned up my bowl in the sea. 'It means flamboyant.'

I was smiling inside. Gladys had given two words too many. And as she bore down on the poor plumber I rolled my shoulders and let the grin work its way up onto my face.

Maximo Bonga. Even his name was mad.

3

The guest house was a little way back from the beach, but that was OK. I didn't mind giving up the view in favour of what might turn out to be a very unusual stay. A sea breeze, the gentle plop of waves in a bay full of the most spectacular islands I've ever seen, limestone rocks pushing up out of the sea and towering majestically over the inhabitants of El Refugio... pah, overrated.

As I walked through the village I asked a few people where the guest house was and always received the same response: 'Bonga? Maximo Bonga? You mean you want to stay at Bonga's Guest House?' When I said yes they all seemed puzzled and said the same thing: 'Why don't you stay at the beach? Gladys's or Mama Den's? They have nice rooms. Bonga's?'

And it was weird how everyone knew of him but didn't know where his place was, as if they'd completely forgotten he existed. They seemed to know the name but frowned and cast about for the recollection. It had obviously been a very long time since anyone had asked.

Eventually two kids on a home-made go-kart were given an order by a store owner to take me. The whole thing was building my anticipation nicely. So much so that I'd completely forgotten my fatigue by the time we reached the end of the dusty track and I was standing at the front garden gate.

The kids asked for money so I told them to get lost. The truth is I was about to give them a few pesos for some penny sweets, but because they'd asked I changed my mind. They walked off and threw stones at me.

I barely noticed; my eyes were now welded to the sight laid out before me. The bag slid off my shoulder and fell to the floor. I just stood and grinned.

The sign above the gate read Bonga's Guest House in wonky letters made from spent brass bullet cartridges covered in green patina. There was a small sunny garden beyond and a neat flower-lined path which ran up to what can only be described as a living museum. An encampment. It was like one of those exhibits where a period in history has been painstakingly recreated. The Battle of the Alamo, say, or the World War One trenches of France.

The small two-storey wooden house looked normal enough, but the veranda was enclosed with a battlement, a wall of sandbags, beyond which sat a small open-air restaurant. Sticking out through the defences was the barrel of a very large machine gun; the kind that comes from a tank or rear defence of a bomber. A cannon.

I picked up my bag, pushed open the gate and stepped inside.

'Halt!'

I froze, scanning left and right. Nothing, no movement except the silent flap of butterflies playing in the red frenzy of hibiscus. I took another exploratory step forward and waited for a voice. Then another and another until I was midway down the path, still holding my breath. The bushes to my right moved. Someone was in there. Someone camouflaged. What should I do? Should I play along, pretend I hadn't noticed?

'Ouch!' There was the snap of a twig and a rustling sound.

I hid the smile creeping across my face and looked at the rest of the garden, anywhere but those shaking bushes. I could even see the top of the helmet, the sun striking the chipped matt finish of olive green as its wearer stumbled and snagged on the branches.

'Ow!' And then 'Uch!' and 'Oof!'

I decided to give him a hand. 'Is anyone home?' The breaking of branches and owching got louder. I bit my lip harder. 'Hello? I need a room.' Out the corner of my eye I could see the old man as he sneaked out of cover, crouched over and hurried along the hedge. He crept around the rear of the house, tripping only once.

I stood dutifully on the path and waited in the sunshine for something to happen. A moment later he appeared on the veranda in full World War Two combat gear, helmet under arm, trying to look surprised but composed under a sheen of sweat.

He was a wizened old Filipino man with wispy grey hair, damp and flat with the sweat of the steel helmet, and a thin, pencil-like Spanish moustache. He looked 80 years old but stood like a younger man. Perhaps it was the starched army uniform that was holding him up.

'You American?' he asked, and puffed out his narrow chest, looking sceptically down his nose at me.

'English,' I said.

He looked disapprovingly down at a rooster I just noticed was standing to attention beside him, at heel exactly like a dog. Had this man trained a chicken?

'English,' he repeated, and something in his memory seemed to register. The head turned just a degree and the rheumy old bloodshot eyes narrowed a little. 'What regiment?'

'Regiment? I'm not in…'

'You air force?'

'No, I...'

'Name, rank, serial number.'

'Um... Harris. John,' I said with appropriate military protocol. What the hell was this?

'Give me five, soldier!' He stood bolt upright and pointed to the ground. I hesitated. 'I said give me ten push-ups!'

'Ten? You just said five!'

'Sol-jah...'

Without realising what I was doing I dropped my bag. The cockerel raised its head and crowed. I felt mocked: 'Cock-a-doodle-do-it soldier!' No wonder people frowned when I'd asked the way to this place. He's mental. I knew I should have stayed at the bloody beach.

I went down on hands, just for the fun of it I told myself, and began humping the ground, drips of perspiration from my head cratering the dust. The last three I did one-armed. That'll show the silly old sod.

'Can I have a room now,' I said, brushing the dirt off my hands and trying not to show the exertion.

'You want to barrack here?' He put on his helmet and looked back down at the bird, still at heel beside his left boot. 'What do you think, MacArthur?' he said. The rooster had a bloody name! It pecked the air once, ruffled its feathers, turned its head to one side and looked me square in the eye. Unnerved, I looked back at the old man. 'Four dollars a night, cold shower, reveille at zero-six hundred,' he said.

I took a step closer, up onto the porch next to him, feeling like I'd passed some kind of test.

He looked me up and down once, nodded his approval at my physique and shorn scalp, and held out a hand. 'Sergeant Major Maximo Bonga. Cavalry.'

'John Harris, tourist,' I replied, shaking his hand and trying not to laugh as he gritted his teeth and attempted to crush my fingers. 'What roo... barrack should I take?'

His glazed eyes had halos around the irises, like rings on a tree stump, each one a memory. They watered a bit, like all old people, but these ones were alive and suspicious, if a little boozed. I got a whiff of yesterday's alcohol.

'Putting you in bunk four, Harrison, next door to me, so we can communicate. This country ain't what it used to be. I used to be in the US Army, you know,' he said, his voice suddenly taking on an American lilt. 'That was back in the... um... forties. Me and Vick... Vick, um...' he drifted, trying to remember a name. 'Anyhow, Vick and me. We used to drive tanks. They called us the aces, Vick and me. I remember once, we were posted together in... um...'

'I'm just gonna have a shower.' I showed him the dirty palms of my hands.

'You freshen up... um...'

'Harris.'

'Harris. And then we'll talk. I got things you need to know.' He tapped a nostril. 'See that cowling up there?' He pointed up to part of a plane that was hanging from the rafters.

'Christ!' I ducked, smartly stepping to one side, wondering how on earth it was held there. It looked like the only thing stopping it crashing down and killing someone was a threadbare length of ancient rope.

'Zero. Shot that down over the err...'

'Pacific?' I suggested, cowering to one side.

'No no no, the um...'

'Atlantic?'

'No, the... the...' he tapped his foot, impatient with his memory.

'South China Sea?'

He looked at me as if I was mad. 'Course not, man. Over the um...'

'Over the mountains.'

'No. Over the... over the... summer of forty-four! That's it. Knew I'd remember. Huh.'

I picked up my bag.

'Where are you going?'

I pointed to the corridor that looked like it led to the rooms. 'Shower.'

'I haven't given you the rundown. Positions. Now then, Jarvis...'

'Harris.'

'Tell you what, you freshen up and we'll talk later. Ten-four? I've got some things to do.' He clapped me on the shoulder and poked out his chin, stretching his turkey neck in the worn collar of the jacket.

'Key.'

'To what?'

'Do you have a key to the room?'

'Huh. New in town, uh? Let me tell you, no one gets into my place without my permission. I'm guarded on all sides against all comers. Not only are we fortified around the perimeter but I've got the beach assault covered too. You know what I mean?' He looked left and right before leaning very close. I could smell the pomade on his hair. 'Explosive charges,' he whispered.

'I'd better not smoke then.' The joke fell completely flat and he glared at me as though I'd just suggested sex with his granddaughter. 'I'm gonna freshen up. Ha ha.'

He shook my hand again.

I breathed a sigh of relief and blinked through the tired, burnt skin and grime that was holding me together. My second wind had all but blown away. I'd been on the go without sleep for three days now and I could hear the bed calling me. But first that shower.

'You freshen up. I'll be out here if you need me,' he said. 'You got soap? Course you have. Go on then, man. The well's just out the back by the pigsty.'

4

I woke up in a pool of sweat, my face stuck to the nylon pillowcase. It was late afternoon but there was no electricity to work the table fan. I'd been told that the power came on after four and went off at midnight. Sure enough, just as I was counting my money the fan swung into action and blew pesos all over the room.

When I went out to the little restaurant cum barricade, Maximo was slumped in an old armchair, blotto, an empty bottle of Tanduay rum grasped lovingly across his chest like a baby. He looked dead so I bent closer.

'Don't worry, he ain't dead.'

I stood up straight, startled.

'He's always gone by lunchtime. This ain't a first. You American?' said the American voice.

'English,' I said, locating the man sitting at a table in the corner. He was enormous, obese, 180 kilos of bare white flab stuck in a chair. He looked like a fridge in a cap-sleeve shirt. He was wearing shorts, his legs wide open to accommodate barrel thighs that were thicker than my waist.

Laid on his massive belly was a tiny handkerchief to catch the crumbs from the crackers he was eating. A big square family tin of them sat on the table in front along with a dozen cans of tuna. As he spoke, without looking down at the food he opened one and spooned the oily contents onto a cracker.

'Name's Frank Johnson the Third,' he said. 'I'm from the US of A.' In went another cracker piled with fish flakes. 'This here's the missus. Say hello then.'

I hadn't noticed the girl. At his feet, on her hands and knees cleaning his toes, was a petite Filipina. Without stopping the pedicure she smiled, revealing her teenage beauty. It was infuriating; I hadn't had a shag in weeks.

'I'm fifty-five years old,' he munched, as if deliberately taunting me further. 'Got me this here lady and some land upa yonder. Man, I love this country.' And as if to celebrate his good fortune further, he opened another can of tuna upside down onto another cracker, a bloom of oil spreading out on the table.

'I'm John,' I replied, wondering if Frank Johnson III was in fact all three generations in one. 'You two married?'

'Yes, sir. God bless the internet. Ain't nothin' better than a young wife to keep you on yo' toes. You single? Coz she got plenty of sisters, hek hek hek.'

'Yeah,' I said.

'Well you came to the right country, boy.'

'I wasn't really looking.'

His eyes narrowed. 'Say, you ain't queer, are ya?'

'No, I'm not.'

'Uh-huh.' He nodded and leaned forward with great effort to peer into the big cracker tin, frowning then poking around inside with a chubby hand. 'Mary, didn't I tell you earlier that I's almost outta thum crackers? Crackers, I sez 'bout lunchtime. Go git me some o' those suckers when yo' at the mawket.' His voice went all high-pitched and piping like a girl as he complained. 'Now I ain't got none to offer this here young man.'

'That's OK,' I said, wondering why on earth he was eating canned fish when we were sitting in a fishing village full of the fresh stuff. 'I'm just going out to eat.'

'Well at least have a drink, woncha?'

I looked down at poor old soldier Maximo Bonga, his false teeth sliding out every time his mouth opened to snore. The stuffing on the arm of his chair had burst and was poking out like a sudden fungus, completing the scene of being absolutely knackered.

As well as getting something to eat I wanted to find a place to drink, always the first thing to establish when entering a new town, especially as I felt I'd be staying here for some time. Boozers are always the best source of information when you're travelling. They always seem to attract people who've done everything and filtered out all the crap. Over a drink they spill all the choicest tidbits about things to do, people you must meet and those to avoid. Travellers are incapable of keeping secrets.

In fact, when people tell me they're going travelling and ask for advice, I always tell them to go and get drunk in the local. If there's a pub with a foreign landlord, so much the better.

I looked back up at big Frank and he suddenly looked like the loneliest person on earth. Someone lonelier than me.

The place really came alive at sunset with the hustle and bustle of village life. The stores and eateries along the dusty potholed streets were lit up with fairy lights for the Easter holiday and a small Easter fair crawled with kids. They even had a freak show. 'Monkey Boy!' read a sign above the entrance to a tent. There was a hand-painted image of a child covered in hair, his arms twice as long as normal.

Music blared out everywhere, from karaoke machines or acoustic guitars. I'd never seen so many people playing guitar and singing before. And when I passed the Hard Rocks Videoke again and saw the people singing together, it dawned on me for the first time the true meaning of karaoke. I'd been in Asia for years, surrounded by it, and had always hated it. Why did they sit there in a room night after night singing those songs, wailing at the tops of their voices? Couldn't they hear how bad they sounded?

That was missing the point. It doesn't matter how bad you sing, no one cares. The whole point of it is to get together with people, get drunk and be happy. Go back to England 70 years ago and every household had a karaoke. We called it a piano.

I was stopped briefly outside Hard Rocks by Francis, the transexual owner, and the red-faced locals from my earlier drink. They pointed to the young Jesus, who was now comatose in the corner, holding the microphone like an ice cream.

I managed to get away by saying I wanted to eat, and then, when they told me they had food – 'Francis will cook! He's a woman!' – that I was meeting someone. I had to say something, otherwise I might never see the other end of town.

I continued through the village towards the cliffs at the western end, dark against the twinkling purple sky. All the men called out, 'Hey, Joe!', as in G.I. Joe; a hangover from the US occupation, and a common greeting for foreigners in the Philippines regardless of nationality. How quaint and friendly, I thought.

The rest shouted 'Kalbo!', which means baldy. Wankers.

With the words still ringing in my ears, I turned towards the beach, then did a left into another narrow house-lined street that ran parallel to the shore. And tripped over two women brawling in the dirt. Dust went flying as they scrapped.

No one else seemed to pay any attention. A woman behind an outside shop counter served a customer. A man sitting on an upturned boat lit his cigarette and smiled. 'Stand back a bit, if I was you,' was all he said. He lifted a cheek and broke wind, the sound reverberating through the inverted wooden hull in a throaty growl.

I gestured to the mass of tangled hair and clouds of dust billowing at my feet. 'Shouldn't we, you know… stop them?'

'You can if you want, but the hospital's closed for Easter.'

'Bitch!' One woman brought her knee into the other's midriff, and when she doubled up used the opportunity to roll on top of her. I still couldn't quite make out their features among the mass of hair, but one looked like a foreigner, much broader across the back and with white skin. One of her breasts was hanging out of her torn T-shirt.

She sat astride the other woman, raised an arm and noticed me. The poised fist unclenched and swept the hair from her eyes. 'Hello. Were you looking for me? I will be back at the shop in a minute. I am Janet,' she said, and, by way of explanation, added, 'I run the Swiss Cafe. You will wait, please.'

I was speechless.

She turned back to the girl on the ground and thumped her right in the eye. An animal cry echoed off the cliffs. Janet stood up to admire her work, barking out a warning. 'No one tries to sleep with my husband!' She turned to me. 'You have just arrived? Where are you staying?'

I was a bit thrown by it all. The other woman was now on her hands and knees crawling away, one hand cupping her bruised eye.

'Bonga's Guest House,' I said.

'Little whore!' she shouted down the street before turning back to me. 'Let me show you our place. We have boat tours to lagoons and beaches. Only four hundred pesos including lunch!'

'Sounds good,' I said. She had a beerbottle label stuck in her hair which she was trying to peel out.

'And we have a nice girl on tomorrow's boat trip.' She nudged me in the ribs. 'Are you alone?'

'Yeah.'

'She is very beautiful. Italian.'

Italian. Fantastic. 'Not really looking,' I lied.

'Not like these whores!' She flared her nostrils and looked back to see that her message was loud and clear to the whole town. The people sitting outside their houses looked the other way. 'Fourteen years I have been here. I am married to a local man. And still they do not respect me. As soon as my back is turned.'

I followed her down the street. There was a dive shop called Bay Divers, which looked as though it had seen better days, and Janet confirmed was on its last legs. Also a bar called Refuge Bistro that looked more like a garden shed. According to Janet things were looking pretty grim, tourist-wise, in El Refugio at the moment, due almost entirely to the Muslim separatists from the south.

The Abu Sayyaf had been terrorising the Philippines for years but only recently had they really made their presence felt. The previous government had made the fatal mistake of caving in to the rebels' demand of a ransom payment for the return of some hostages, and now the floodgates had opened. Anyone and everyone was calling themselves a Muslim, tear-arsing around the country kidnapping along the way. And as if that wasn't bad enough for tourism in El Refugio, they had decided to kidnap some American missionaries nearby.

'They are just drunks. No job, nothing better to do than run around with guns,' Janet said. 'Maybe once it was about their religion but now it is only about cash. They gain, the hard working people lose. They think it is clever to drive us out. But when we are gone and everything is messed up they will see. When they are back to being poor farmers and fishermen again they will understand.'

We turned into her shop, the Swiss Cafe and Boutique. 'Now then.' She went to a whiteboard that was fixed to the wall and picked up a marker. 'The lagoon trip. What is your name?'

'John.'

'Joh-nah. You are lucky, three ladies with you on tomorrow's trip.' She elbowed me conspiratorially in the ribs again.

I looked at the other names on the list and tried to picture their owners: Brenda. She was going to be big. I had an aunt with that name and she was built like a rugby player. Jiz. She may as well have called herself Spunk. She was going to be scatty. And the third name sent a shiver down my spine: Annie. I've seen *Misery*. She was going to be fat and mad.

'Which one's the Italian?' I braced myself.

'Mmm... that would be Annie. Yes, Annie.'

Lightning, a crack of thunder and Kathy Bates standing in the doorway to James Caan's bedroom, sledgehammer held across her chest: 'It's for your own good.'

'Do you need a snorkel? They are for rent. Only fifty pesos.'

I shook off the nightmare vision. 'Yeah, and fins.'

She went to mark my rentals on the board but her manic dog came bolting out from behind a rack of beachwear and started rolling around at our feet. Janet got on all fours and started to play with it. 'Are you on heat? Who have you been with, eh? You little whore.'

'I'm just going for a drink at that bistro place,' I said. 'What time should I be here tomorrow morning?' The beer label was still stuck in her hair and one of her boobs was hanging out again.

'You naughty little whore. Yes! Yes! You are!'

Who, me?

'Go on, go out with your dogs, you doggy. Go!'

Was she talking to me or the dog?

She stood, parting ragged hair from her face. 'Upstairs in the cafe at eight-thirty. Boat leaves at nine o'clock.' She stamped her foot playfully at the dog lingering in the doorway then sniffed her fingers before extending her hand to me. 'Welcome to El Refugio.'

COCKFIGHTS AND KYBOSH

1

I surprised myself by being back at Janet's cafe at eight-thirty on the dot the next morning. I felt a bit rough, hung over from a night of drinking at the bistro, but I was there. My breath was pure alcohol, I had a splitting headache, and if it hadn't been for the cockerels I wouldn't have made it in time.

The dawn chorus had started at five o'clock. In fact, despite popular belief, it had never really stopped all night, but the main racket kicked off an hour before sunrise. And once one mangy bird started the others had followed until the whole village was in uproar. I woke up wondering if one of the bastards had flown into my room, it was that loud.

Then, as the room lightened an hour or so later and the mayhem began to subside, just as I began to drift back to sleep, Maximo had started, right in the hallway outside my door. I wanted to strangle the old git. I'd been having a dream that I was in a hotdog eating competition and everyone else was a naked female. 'Go away!' I shouted.

'No!' he'd replied, and clanged what sounded like a saucepan lid even louder. 'It's six o'clock. Get up.'

'I'm sleeping.'

'I don't care.'

Putting the pillow over my ears did nothing so I got up and opened the door. He was gone. I looked left and right. 'I'm not going to stay here if you do that again!' I bellowed down the corridor.

A distant voice shouted back, 'You have a tour of duty that starts at zero eight hundred hours, soldier. Now drop your cock and grab your socks!'

I went back into the room baffled and got dressed wearing a frown, wondering how on earth he could have known about the island-hopping tour I was booked on.

It had been a strange night indeed, and I'd met some very odd foreigners who now called El Refugio home. They even had a little band, The Refuge Trio. When said quickly it sounded like The Refuse Trio. It consisted of Ziegwalt, the German dwarf I'd seen, on accordion (he was only just over a metre tall and it looked like he was being attacked by a square serpent); a ragged-looking, though very well-spoken Englishman on bongos called Jim, and Janet's nice Filipino husband Taddi on guitar and vocals. He was the only sane one of the three.

But the most interesting of all was Bernard, the wacky French owner of the bistro, who had insisted I should get up to do the boat trip. He'd called it 'the best introduction to the whole area, and El Ref in particular'.

I thought back to Bernard's story, of his incredible life, and how you never meet people like him back home. He was in his sixties and had been living outside of France for 40 years. At first reluctant to talk, as the night wore on and the rum flowed, so did his words, pouring out of his head cathartically.

He'd trained as an anthropologist and had originally worked in South America, mostly under the Pinochet regime in Chile. Bored with academia as a 20-year-old and flush with a sense of adventure, he'd been persuaded by the people in power to use his skills to financial advantage; both theirs and his.

Basically they wanted him to hunt for treasures. The deal was simple; they'd provide resources in the form of guides and local know-how, and Bernard, under the guise of various French universities, would find and then trade the artefacts at a massive profit in Europe. Indiana Jones without the morals.

Eventually, inevitably, the regime changed and Bernard decided to hop to the other side of the Pacific, to the Philippines, where an almost identical dictatorial government was in power. Marcos was offering anyone with a sense of adventure, and who didn't mind too much where the cash came from, the opportunity to make it big.

Originally living with and studying the local tribes on the island, Bernard soon fell into old habits and began treasure hunting. 'After all, what is archeology if not the search for buried treasure, my English friend?' Only this time it went a stage further. Headhunting. Or at least selling the heads that others hunted.

At that time there were still cases of headhunting among the tribes of the remotest parts of the Philippines. Bernard's job, with the sanction of the Marcos government – in fact Ferdinand himself, according to Bernard – was to collect 'artefacts' and find a market for them abroad. Bernard found highly decorated, dried human heads, and ready buyers in Europe and the US.

It may be difficult for your average person like me to comprehend, but there are billionaires in this world who want for nothing. They have every conceivable toy, possession, sexual pleasure, antique and work of art money can and cannot buy. They're bored with everything and are always looking to get something new, something their competing multimillionaire acquaintances don't have.

In a world where trophy buildings, trophy girlfriends, Rolls Royce cars and Lear Jets are the norm, where heads are firmly in the clouds and their grasp of reality is seriously skewed, one purchases a real human head to mount above the drawing room fireplace, old chap.

'Think about it,' he'd said when everyone had left his bar and we were alone, his face lit dramatically by the kerosene lamp, 'any rich man can buy a Ming Dynasty vase. Just go to Sotheby's.' He leaned in. 'But how many people know where to buy a decorated human head? Eh? Eh?' Once again, inevitably, people power brought in a change in government and Bernard was left holding the head, so to speak.

He'd been married seven times over the years, had numerous kids scattered about the planet and, unlike most expats I've met who've been abroad for years, wasn't boorish or bitter. Elsie was his latest love, an acquisition from a Manila bar, and she had flirted shamelessly with me all night long.

All interesting stuff, I thought as I stood outside the Swiss Cafe and watched Janet's husband Taddi load up the outrigger on the beach. But what really concerned me most at the moment was the quality of the three women on the tour with me. And why Janet's dog had attached itself to my bloody leg.

'Gerroff,' I shook my leg. It didn't budge. Looking around nervously I tried again, this time harder. Still it was glued to me, looking up, its tongue lolling. I traipsed up the flight of stairs to the restaurant with the dog attached.

I reached the top landing and turned into the restaurant. Just in time to hear Janet, sitting at a table with her first customer, a stunning woman with cascading blonde hair, say, 'Whereabouts in Italy?'

It wasn't until we were out at sea half an hour later, the deafening clatter of the boat's engine echoing off the surrounding cliffs, that I was finally able to speak to her.

Annie, that is, the beautiful Italian who looked nothing like a psycho and everything like the sanest thing I'd encountered since arriving in this village. She was completely out of place, like an alien from some far-off world, the Planet Perfection, dropped here by mistake. A visitor from a different galaxy where everyone had gorgeous hair, immaculate, unblemished skin and the latest Versace swimwear. She didn't even look like a backpacker.

Of course, the other two women sitting in the outrigger bolstered the illusion. They looked like bizarre, eccentrically carved bookends each side of her. One of them, Brenda, was a very well-built, brick shithouse of a Belgian, an amateur wrestler, she said, and had one leg in plaster. As soon as she'd limped into the little outrigger boat we nearly capsized.

The boat boy stood behind her ankle deep in water while she hopped along and swung her leg up into the boat. Using the arm of an outrigger she'd tried to hoist herself in but the whole lot came away. 'Oh no!' All I saw was her white leg and torso disappear over the side followed by the broken outrigger. She lay in a foot of water, grinning and blinking. 'It is so warm!'

The other punter in the boat, Jiz, was a scrawny Australian woman with verbal diarrhoea. 'Hi, there! I'm Jiz!' and she held out her face, waiting for me to fill the one second of quiet. When I didn't, she jumped in with a monologue that was still going now, half an hour later. It was exactly like watching someone on speed, all hyperactive, the air around her full of hands and words; all complete bollocks.

When I wouldn't answer any more she started on Brenda, and when Brenda turned out to be hopeless at conversation – 'I am a semi-professional wrestler! I have broken my leg nine times!' – she turned to poor Annie.

We cleared the headland, Jiz in heated competition with the deafening outboard, and the true beauty of the place was spread out before us. The blue sea danced with light, broken only by the razor-sharp limestone islands rising up, and the non-stop yapping of Jiz.

Annie looked across at me. I smiled and turned to Taddi. 'Which island are we going to first?'

'Top Hat Island,' he said, and kissed the air instead of using his finger to point, the way all Filipinos do.

'Is that–'

'Why is it called Top Hat Island?' Jiz barged in.

'It looks like a top hat.'

'What about that one over there then?'

Taddi explained that the one she was pointing at was an exclusive five-star resort owned by El Refugio's plutocrats, the Lam family. I used the moment to look at Annie as she craned her neck to see the island in the distance.

The boat boy, a handsome 20-year-old with a cigarette constantly clenched between gleaming teeth, noticed and leaned towards me, still gutting our fish lunch. 'She is very beautiful,' he whispered.

Jiz was listening, I could tell.

'You must have lots of girlfriends,' I replied to the boy. 'There are many beautiful girls in El Ref.' I didn't have a clue about local girls but it seemed like the best way to deflect his eyes from Annie.

'Ha. They do not like me.' He rammed the knife spitefully into a gill and pulled out a blob of jelly. 'I have no money. Girls in this village do not want to marry a fisherman.'

'They want to go abroad,' Taddi added.

I began to prickle with embarrassment, waiting for the inevitable 'They only want to marry foreigners'.

'They only want to marry foreigners.'

'You mean they just marry for money?'

Taddi shrugged, skilfully manoeuvring the boat around some corals, perhaps remembering that he'd married a Swiss woman. 'They love you for what you can provide. A stable life. A nice home. They will love a man for taking care of them. Is that not love?'

I thought about big Frank the Yank and his young wife.

'You must not blame them,' Taddi went on. 'Until ten years ago no one came to El Refugio. I do not remember seeing a foreigner when I was a child. We fished and played together, boys and girls. Maybe once a month a German came by in a yacht. But what do the teenage girls see here now? They see foreign backpackers with expensive clothes and computers.'

'I'm not rich!' Jiz protested.

'You are here.'

'I don't have a lot of money; I'm on a budget. I'm staying at Bay View Guest House for a hundred and fifty pesos a day!'

Taddi deliberated a moment, calculating. 'That is four and a half thousand pesos a month.' He lit a cigarette and one for the boat boy, skilfully using the silence to let the maths sink in. 'That is double what he earns. And that is just your lodging. Out of two thousand pesos a month most Filipinos have to pay the rent and feed a family of eight. It is a hard life.'

'But a rewarding one!' Jiz insisted. Up went her finger. 'You have many things that we don't have. You're happy. People in my country are not happy.' Her face turned unhappy.

I looked at Taddi's face. I couldn't help thinking that he wanted to push her over the side.

'And,' she concluded, having run out of things her society was devoid of, 'you have spiritual depth.' At last she hunched her shoulders, cupping both hands. Annie leaned away from her as if she might explode.

Taddi, one hand on the tiller, listening intently with a face that said he'd heard all this a thousand times before, flicked his ash over the side and asked the inevitable. 'So you will stay here?'

'Well, I can't,' said Jiz. 'Obviously, I don't have a job.'

'Most locals don't have jobs.'

'Yeah, but I've got a return ticket. I can't really give that up.'

Taddi nodded, guiding the boat calmly between the ragged rocks of our village on one side and a large island on the other; a wide channel with a racing current. The only other boats out were drawing in empty nylon nets, the fishermen adding insult to their injury by showing us that they couldn't even catch dinner.

The boat boy flung some guts over the side and smiled at me, flicking his eyes at Jiz. At least I hoped it wasn't at Annie.

'I think the Australian likes you,' I whispered to him.

He looked at Jiz and she blushed, studying the wake of the boat earnestly. He leaned in close to my ear. 'Do you think so?'

'Yes.' We were covered by the noise of the engine, so I thought I'd kill two birds with one stone: help the boat boy and get Jiz away from Annie. Not lie, just keep her preoccupied throughout the day. 'White women like dark men,' I said. That wasn't a lie. 'She's soft, you're tough. They like that.' Neither was that. 'And–'

'But I like the other one. She is more beautiful.'

What! 'No no no, she's... The other one is married. The Aussie, Jiz, she's the one.'

'But she is not looking at me.'

'She's teasing you.'

'Ha. Same like village girls. So tricky.'

'All girls do it. When we get to the island, ask her to go out with you tonight.'

He put both hands on his head in embarrassment. His innocence was pure magic, and I felt nostalgic for my youth. What I would give to be his age, with those looks, but know what I know now. This kid had a body carved out of ebony.

He leaned in again. 'She is very angry.'

I looked across at Jiz. She put her nose in the air and swished her tangled mane flirtatiously.

'That's because she likes you. She's trying not to show it.'

He clucked his tongue. 'What I should say?'

'What do you say to local girls?'

He went into a fit of embarrassment again before suggesting he ask her to church on Sunday. I could barely keep from laughing, and wondered what approach would work on a girl as frustrated as Jiz.

'Just tell her you want to boom boom her.'

His eyes lit up.

I didn't want to give him the wrong impression of foreigners, but in my experience as a traveller the direct approach usually worked. Whether we admit it or not, most of us when we get away from our own country want to get laid as quickly and frequently as possible.

And we don't want the usual, that's why we go away. Flowers and chocolates and all that wooing is for back home in cold, miserable England. When you have the tropical weather, beaches and moonlight, all the serenading has already been done for you. Isn't nature wonderful.

'Don't worry, she'll ask you probably. Just be yourself. Remember, he who hesitates masturbates. But no church.'

'She is a heathen?'

I wasn't sure how to answer that. In a country where Catholic missionaries had ruined everything by condemning pleasure I had to pick my words carefully. 'She believes in God but doesn't go to church. In her country it's OK to have sex before marriage.'

'I like Australia.'

I don't normally go on tours but all in all it turned out to be a pretty eventful day. We stopped at a couple of deserted islands for a few hours of exploring and snorkelling, each of us taking it in turns to shout out, 'Come and look at this!' before putting our heads under again and marvelling at the mad shapes of the fish.

Brenda had to make do with hanging off the side of the boat's outrigger so as not to get her plaster cast sodden. Taddi held onto her foot while she strapped on a mask and dipped her head under. From a distance it looked quite comical, and I mentioned it to Annie in between trying to sound knowledgeable about the things around us.

Annie and I floated together and I exploited her fear of the underwater world to the fullest, holding her hand and, just before lunch, getting an arm around her slender waist when she lost a fin. I retrieved it manfully from the rocks, making a great show of the effort before the current swept it to China. Actually it had only floated into some seaweed just out of sight, but I wasn't going to tell her that.

Apart from barbecuing some fish on the beach, the boat boy spent most of the time racing hermit crabs with Jiz. At first she seemed to be humouring him, slightly dismissive of his childishness, intellectualising everything. But as the day wore on and she reddened under the sun, nature worked its wonders. By the time we went to visit the hidden lagoon in the afternoon she didn't even want to swim in, content to sit in the boat with him and flirt. She said she was too tired, but we know what she meant.

The lagoon was breathtaking, hidden from passing boats, only a small dark cave revealing its location to the trained eye.

To get inside we had to stop in very deep water and then swim through, timing the swell so as not to get bashed on the razor-sharp cliff face.

Coming out seemed worse, and there was a minor catastrophe when Annie mistimed it and grazed her exposed chest. For me it was a blessing in disguise. There were no plasters on the boat and, rather than mucking about at the Swiss Cafe when we returned, I took her back to hers (Gladys's unfortunately) and got to plant a plaster on her left tit. Such a gentleman.

All in all a pretty eventful day, as I said. It looked like Jiz was going to get laid by the rugged boat boy (they went off hand-in-hand when we came ashore) and I had arranged to meet Annie the next day. I didn't want to rush someone who was in no hurry themselves.

Taddi had told us there would be an Easter fiesta of cockfighting and boxing at the village cockpit the next evening, promising an annual event not to be missed. 'Bring your camera. Everyone will be there, including the mayor. He's called Elvis!'

Boxing in a cockpit with a mayor called Elvis. For some reason it seemed like the most normal prospect of an evening's entertainment in El Refugio. It wouldn't surprise me if Elsie, Bernard's flirtatious girlfriend, was the French boxer and Janet represented Switzerland. Or, for that matter, that Ziegwalt would venture into the ring in his G-string and do a bit of Greco-Roman wrestling. And what about Brenda? Surely she wasn't going to miss it. I pictured her in a leotard, getting Ziegwalt in a headlock, his tongue sticking out, eyes bulging; 'Heeargh!'

All that remained now was to go back to my guest house and rest in peace.

2

'So you've got a sweetheart.' Maximo's croaky old voice cut through the early evening warmth as I marched through the garden gate.

The air was full of insects going about their business in the last of the light, and swifts darted in and out, dogfighting and spiralling into plummeting, feathery pairs. The shadow from the cliffs that loomed over the entire village split the garden right down the middle. The sun sets at breakneck speed in the tropics, and as I stood there trying to locate Maximo I could feel the shadow creeping over the ground like a burgeoning ink stain.

There was a rustle of bushes to my right. Got you. I crouched tiger-like and crept to that side, going on all fours. I'll teach him to be such a know-all. Crawling carefully up to the hibiscus I waited for a sound.

'Where is she from?' came his voice from the other side of the hedge. 'Better not be a Jap.'

Keep quiet, I told myself, and pounce at the last moment. Scare the living shit out of the interfering old codger. That'll stop his nonsense.

'Can't find me, can you, soldier? Ha! You need training. Living with those damn communists in China done that to you. Got you all fat and bloated. Call yourself a detective?'

Christ, how on earth had he got that information? I sat on my haunches for a moment wondering about the few people I'd encountered here, and the even fewer I'd had a long conversation with. The only people I'd told about living in Hong Kong were Annie and French Bernard, and I think only Bernard knew I'd briefly worked as a private investigator in China. Village mentality. Hmm, I thought, I'd better watch what I say around here in future.

Suddenly I felt myself rising to a challenge, something different from the usual mundane life I'd led where everyone I knew was the same age, did the same job and behaved exactly the same way. I began to feel good about him, about this whole idea of battling wits against an 85-year-old veteran.

I'd already gleaned some info about Maximo's past from Taddi during the day's boat trip. According to him, Max really had been a soldier in World War Two.

The Americans had been in the process of liberating the Philippines from the Japanese towards the end of the war when Max was in the army. As customary during conflict, sympathetic locals were attached to the foreign divisions as guides and traders. Maximo was apparently one of those who found himself placed alongside the Yanks, acting as an invaluable source of info when it came to all things indigenous.

The huge might of Uncle Sam's war machine would provide the iron-fisted clout when it came to air, land and sea bombardment, young Maximo and his pals would provide anything else that would be needed on the ground; from translation to finding and arranging recruits.

As well as the mundane, however, he had been allowed all those privileges that came with the territory, so to speak. He'd fired the latest weapons, smoked Lucky Strike cigarettes (pre-packaged fags were virtually unknown in the country at that time), and watched the latest Hollywood movies where sex sirens had kissed on screen. He'd eaten milk chocolate, shaved with a safety razor that trimmed bristles without taking off a layer of skin, listened to Glenn Miller and splashed on Old Spice.

He got to share in the endless supply of women that were allowed to set up outside the American bases (a legacy the Philippines is still having to live with to this day; just go to Angeles). He'd listened to the wireless, danced to gramophone records, and got to drive jeeps. Imagine getting to drive motorised vehicles in a country where the top speed was bullock miles per hour.

And to top it all off, the crème de la crème, he got taken up in the sky like a bird. Not in some boring passenger plane like the rest of us, but in the real thing; a fighter plane. Raking low over fields and through valleys in a P-51 Mustang, victory-rolling and sucking the hats off astonished farm folk.

For Maximo Bonga it was a past he just could not forget. A golden time that nothing, not marriage or the raising of children or grandchildren, could possibly top.

He did not want to let go of it for the mundane, boring present, so he didn't. His life had become a time warp, like so many people with a glorious past. If he couldn't go back to those good old days, when men were men and he'd been in charge of million-dollar equipment, then he'd bring those days to the present.

And that's what this guest house was; a time machine. In his mind this was 1944. It was the world outside his garden fence that had jumped into the future. Who was I? Who were these aliens walking past in strange clothes, talking suburban babble on mobile phones? He wanted no part of it.

A mosquito buzzed in my ear and I slapped it, deafening myself. The shirt on my back clung to the sweat and the dust stuck to that. I needed a wash. But first and foremost to bring this old foe crashing into the future. Ask me about Annie, would you, you cheeky old twat.

'You've dropped your bag,' the voice taunted.

I wasn't waiting any longer. Gathering my strength, I tensed and leapt over the metre-high hedge. I felt like a pouncing tiger but probably looked more like a hopping frog in my green beach shirt.

Sprigs and dust flew everywhere as I cleared the bushes and sailed through the air. I did a sort of parachutist's roll on the other side and came up perfectly on my hands and knees, just as the little loud speaker was yanked through the dust.

'Ha ha!' it said, a shower of red hibiscus petals falling like embers around me.

I couldn't believe my eyes. Or my ears for that matter; it didn't even sound like a real voice now I could see it wasn't. It sounded more like a goose down a tunnel through that battered old 5-watt speaker.

I stood up in a rage. 'You stupid old git!'

'I may be old, private, but I fooled you,' it honked. 'Now then...'

I went to kick the black box and made even more of an idiot of myself when he tugged it out the way and I kicked air.

'Now then.'

I was so embarrassed at the drubbing I crashed back through the flowers to retrieve my gear without a care for the gardener's feelings.

'Where are you going? We've got training to complete.'

'Sod training.' I picked up the bag pretending not to be interested, but still wondering where the hell he was hiding. 'I'm going for a shower.'

'There's no water.'

He's bluffing. Don't fall for it.

'The well's empty. See for yourself.'

Then, out the corner of my eye, I caught a flash of him as he went past an upstairs window. I stopped and looked at the garden. All the flowers and potted plants had just been watered, the soil dark and muddy. That's it. I'll make a mud pie and chuck it at him when he pokes his head out. I packed a nice sludgy lump together, listening to his heavy breathing through the speaker.

'I can see what you're doing, man.'

I drew back my arm and jumped up quickly to lob the missile.

'Drop it, soldier!'

He was gone. The window was empty.

'I said put down that grenade.'

I lowered my arm and line of sight. He was now crouched behind the sandbags, dressed in flak jacket and helmet, the rusty old machine gun trained squarely on me.

'Now gimme fifty. On the double.'

'I'm a guest!' I said in a right whiney voice. I dropped the mud cake and walked towards him. The gun barrel followed me.

'Where are you going? Don't you want to hear my story about how we took it in turns to blow... um...'

I climbed the stairs to the veranda. 'Blow up the Japs?' I offered.

'To blow...'

'Blow up the Germans?'

'No. To blow... um...'

I stopped next to an old manikin that stood guard over the rooms at night as Max let go of the twin gun grips and frowned in thought.

He removed a pair of binoculars from around his neck and tapped a lens impatiently. 'To blow...'

'To blow up their battleship?'

'No no no. To blow... on the fire!' His eyes narrowed. 'We were stranded in the Cordillera mountains, surrounded. Our only source of heat was a small wood fire that was dying by the minute.'

I started to walk to my room again. 'Tell me later. I've got to get some sleep.'

'Where are you going?'

'Shower then bed.' God, it was like living back home with mum and dad.

'Bed? Then be careful,' he said, 'there are some very strange people around here. Better take this with you.'

I stopped and turned.

He stood there, this wizened octogenarian soldier, and held weakly in his right hand was a massive, almost forearm-long combat knife.

3

After breakfast the next morning I was confused, partly because of the 12-hour sleep I'd had but mainly because of the sight before me. There was something wrong, there had to be. Either he'd gone completely bonkers or this was some new kind of trick. And seeing as how he was clearly already mad, it must be a trick.

I was standing at the front gate of the guest house in my underpants, my belly warming nicely in the morning sun, my stomach glowing on the inside from the breakfast Frank's wife had cooked. Maximo was standing at the veranda steps dressed in a suit and tie.

He noticed me staring. 'What?'

I couldn't find words. He was washed and shaved (a blob of shaving foam was bursting out beside an earlobe like a tuft of cotton wool), his turkey-wattle neck and small head looking strangled and devoid of blood from the starched collar and tie. He looked handsome in the chalk-stripe suit, standing there surrounded by the divergent sandbags and machine gun.

I grinned. 'You look very handsome.'

'Huh. I'm going to church. It's Sunday.' He reached into the inside pocket of his waist coat and withdrew a pocket watch on a fob, frowning and giving it a tap. 'Zero nine hundred. Got to go. Can't stand here chatting with you.'

I was sceptical. 'You mean,' I began looking around for the leaf-covered pit I was meant to fall into, 'you're not going to do anything?'

'What are you talking about?'

Suddenly I felt foolish. He didn't look remotely like a half-cocked soldier now.

He buttoned the jacket over the waistcoat, rolled his coathanger shoulders and came down the path towards me, looking this way and that nonchalantly. His patent leather shoes winked in the sun, along with his waxed hair. 'Now don't forget, the well is nearly dry but there're plenty of buckets out back.'

A powerful stench hit me. He was wearing aftershave.

'You've got a date!'

'Don't be ridiculous.' He barged past me, refusing to step onto the dirt, then went through the gate but stopped and turned. 'Well go in then. Don't just stand there, go and have your shower.'

'You go first.'

'How childish.' He turned and began to walk, so I did the same, smiling at the old boy's ways. Yep, he was all right in my book; just the right mix of eccentricity while still maintaining a little sanity. Crazy behaviour is all very well providing it's part-time, rooted to the ground on occasions. He may be old and mad but it's only six days a week, and on the seventh day he puts the guns and ammo away.

Frank was still sitting on the veranda. He'd already started on the tins of tuna and crackers, despite having just eaten bacon and eggs with me.

'Hey, buddy,' he said, briefly pulling his face out of a can. 'You like boxing?'

He'd already asked me this. 'No, not really, but I'm going.'

He looked out the corner of his eye at me. 'Hey, you ain't queer, are ya?'

'No, Frank, I'm not. You've already asked me that.'

'Anyhoo, there's a tournament tonight. Boxing. Everyone who's any good in this here island's coming. I'm sponsoring one of them. Sweet kid. You can too, if you want.' Then he remembered something. 'Say, Mary,' her head popped out from under the table, pedicure clippers in hand, 'you git thum candies I axe you git?'

'You don't arse me get nuttin,' she said.

'I'm going for a shower,' I said, sensing a protracted argument. 'See you ringside.'

I turned and walked down the hallway toward my room, relishing the thought of a refreshing cold bucket shower and a visit to Gladys's Beach Cottages to see Annie. I'd slept like a log and dreamt about her all night.

I opened the door to my room. Placed neatly on my bed was a fresh towel, and on top of that a bar of soap. I couldn't believe my eyes. How sweet of the old boy to do that for his guests on a Sunday. God, why couldn't English B&Bs be like this?

I checked the time, collected my shaving gear and grabbed the bar of soap.

And received an enormous electric shock up my hand. I jumped back, flinging the pink Lux block through the air. It hit the side table before swinging to and fro against the wall, dangling on the end of two wires that ran out the window. 'Shit!'

There was a wheezy laugh and I quickly looked out the back window just in time to see Maximo's unmistakable dark blue suit as he scurried out of sight, cackling all the way.

'Some detective you are!' he shouted, then tripped up. 'Oof.'

'I'll get you for that, you…' I shouted back, wringing my hand. 'You could have bloody killed me! You better not go to sleep tonight!'

He'd inserted the stripped ends of two lengths of wire into the wet soap. The other ends ran out into the backyard and were attached to the poles of a 12-volt car battery.

Using a flip-flop I flicked the soap out the window and tried to compose myself, looking around the room to see if there were any other items that were new, or had been moved. Perhaps a booby-trapped loo roll – that could be painful – or a toothbrush wired up to the mains. Ouch.

He'd raised the stakes here, and it was time to get my own back on him, old man or not. He could not be allowed to taunt me like this. I was on holiday!

I'll shower, I thought, go to see Annie in case she's forgotten about tonight, and then devise some form of revenge. Meet Annie, that's the priority.

I pulled off my pants and looked down forlornly at my own electrically charged member. Shit, I can't go out like this, Annie will think I'm some kind of ravenous beast. It just would not go down, it hadn't for days. I wondered if it was something to do with the village. Bernard had warned me that it affected people. Everything in this village seemed to be at it; the people, the dogs, even the fish in the sea we'd goggled at yesterday were going berserk, darting in and out of corals shagging.

By the time I got to Annie's half an hour later I was beginning to wonder if Maximo had slipped some of his Viagra in my food, my erection was that permanent. Annie was in the front garden dipping biscuits into a coffee while swinging gently to and fro in an enormous bamboo hammock. I stood to one side so that the bulge in my shorts was hidden by the bamboo sling she was in.

She smiled and shuffled to make room, patting the hammock next to her affectionately.

I cast about for a reason not to lay down with her. We were in the front of Gladys's Cottages, the mid-morning sun just high enough to be hot but still too low for the trees to provide any shade. I was beginning to sweat.

'Gladys,' I said, leaning against the tree at a bizarre angle. 'She might not like it.'

'I don't care. I will go with you tonight, but please lay beside me, John.'

'Ha-ha-ha,' I laughed gaily, suddenly needing to pick up shells. 'Look at that one. Look at those amazing colours!'

'You English. Come on, Gladys does not mind.'

'What don't I mind?'

I stood bolt upright and hit my head on a branch.

Gladys came out between the huts in curlers. She seemed more omnipotent than ever, her plastered-on face mask making her look like some ghoulish clown. She was wearing a big top.

My erection shrivelled so quickly it almost reversed. When I put a hand in my pocket to check it felt like an acorn sitting atop my nuts.

'So you've changed your mind. Well, we're pretty full here at the moment.'

Annie and I looked around at the crowds of tourists that weren't there, then at the maid waxing the wooden veranda.

'I'm sure I can fit you in. You'll have to wait until I come back from church to sort out all the details. The girl will show you which one. Rose, make sure you show this young man a nice room. He's already been to Bonga's and not surprisingly doesn't want to stay there. He is going to make a transference here,' she said in a strangely upper-crust accent, surveying the whole bay she personally owned; sea, islands, cliffs, sky, air, the lot. 'Well, isn't it a beautiful morning. Praise the Lord for such blessings, and may He–' Her face suddenly froze as she noticed something down the beach.

It was Elsie, French Bernard's girlfriend, the one from the Manila night club, still wearing a very sexy, very revealing evening dress, her hair a wild medusa shock, and, God forbid, barefoot. She looked wonderfully out of place, as if flown in from a cabaret show somewhere in the red-light district. Which I suppose she had been a few months earlier.

Gladys was furious. 'Here we are, trying to make a decent little life for ourselves, and foreigners bring in RUBBISH LIKE THAT!'

The nearer Elsie came, the more pronounced her wiggle. She said hello to everyone, especially the ogling fishermen, who looked as though they'd never seen anything like it before, and petted every stray dog.

'Hi, John!'

I went to wave but got scared and pocketed my hand.

'People like her should beware. Someone might STICK A KNIFE IN HER BACK!'

'Live and let live, Gladys. Love thy neighbour and all that,' I said timidly.

'Neighbour? If she moved next to me I'd leave the country. *PUTA!* IT'S SUNDAY, YOU KNOW!' she shouted. 'OR DOESN'T THAT MEAN ANYTHING TO YOU!'

'Jesus does not want me,' came the reply. Elsie ran her fingers through her hair provocatively. I noticed she was sporting a lovely black eye. For all the defiance, I could see by the look on her face that she was really wounded by the comments.

She must have felt so alienated in this village. And yet she was no worse a person then anyone else here. The only difference between her and most of the other residents, as far as I could tell, was that she wasn't hiding behind the pretence of Catholic respectability. And I think that's really what bothered people like Gladys. She was too hung up on morals to do the thing she most needed to do; have sex. Instead she took it out on others, like the poor housemaid or Elsie.

And I really wanted to say that to Gladys, as I cowered there behind Annie, but she scared the shit out of me. What an ogre. You see, I told myself, that's what becomes of people who don't get any. Perhaps I could do her a favour and get Maximo interested. Kill two birds with one stone; get Gladys laid and have my revenge on the old duffer. What an awful prospect, having carnal knowledge with this woman. I'd rather have my nuts wired up to Maximo's battery.

And then, to top it all off, to add insult to Gladys's injury, Ziegwalt the little German came marching down the beach in his thong. He looked wonderfully out of place. All Gladys could manage was a grim shake of the head before turning in disgust and leaving. 'On Sunday…' I heard her say as she disappeared.

'She needs sex,' I said, and wondered if I sounded too insightful.

'She has a boyfriend,' said Rose the housemaid. She peeped around the corner to check that Gladys had gone, then continued. 'But they do not have sex. He is the father in the church.' She smiled and went into overdrive on the wood, singing as she worked.

This place just gets better, I thought. 'The local vicar?'

'She like him, he not like her. She buy new Bibles as gift for the church.'

'Ahh,' said Annie, 'she wants to buy her way into heaven. She makes good deeds.'

'No,' Rose said. 'She want to boom-boom the father. But she is ugly. He is handsome.'

What a way to live, I thought, all she had to do was go and get drunk with the old fishermen at the Hard Rocks Videoke. Someone would poke her. If she didn't she'd self-destruct. Or else destroy the poor maid.

'So,' said Annie, 'I meet you at the cock-a-pit tonight, yes?'

'Yes,' I said, having well and truly killed all sexual urges with an image of a coy Gladys in a fisherman's embrace, and finally slipped into the hammock beside Annie.

4

Everybody who is anybody in El Refugio was there at the Holy Week Cock Box Derby, as it was billed, plus everybody who was nobody. The entire population of the village under one corrugated-iron roof. The entire male population, anyway, from five-year-old boys who couldn't sit still, climbing up and down the wooden terraces, to their drunken fathers, who used the event as another excuse to get away from nagging wives. As usual the women had stayed away in droves, too busy to bother watching chickens, and then men, tear each other apart.

As well as rigging up a sound system – 'It's the final countdown! Duh-duh duh duh' – Ziegwalt also had an old brass car horn. God knows where he got it from. God knows where the Philippines got him from. As I approached the arena through the dark paddy field he let rip – Honk-honk! – his handlebar moustache breaking into a huge colonial German grin. A German businessman with considerable wealth, according to Bernard, he'd originally come to the Philippines to do business with the large offshore oil rigs and, like so many, had got stuck here. He split his year half in tropical paradise, half in the cold world of German commerce. Half in a thong, half in an overcoat.

The open-air cockpit cum boxing arena was surrounded on all sides by tiered terraces that rose up 6 metres. The whole lot was covered by a tin roof, open on all sides, and in the centre was the cockpit itself.

A perfect square, exactly the same size as a conventional boxing ring, except with an earth floor, the cockpit was hemmed in by a chest-high chain-link fence where the red and blue ropes would normally be. To stop the chicken chickens running away. Every centimetre of space was taken, from ringside right up to ten rows higher, into the termite-nibbled rafters.

Kids were running everywhere, wide-eyed and excited at seeing so many people in one place for the first time this year, while up and down the rows hawkers sold bags of chicharon (crispy pork). There were bookies everywhere, waving their arms in the air and shouting across the pit, convinced that they had that extra morsel of inside info on a fighter. Smoke from a hundred puffing cigarettes rose and filled the underside of the pitched roof like a humid London fog.

In the pit itself a man was busily picking up bits of flayed chicken from the previous gladiators. Half a feathery wing here, a beak there, the occasional claw dangling from the wire fence by a sinewy tendon.

Honk, honk! Ziegwalt, looking like Sneezy with his red cheeks, began waddling around the ring throwing handfuls of sweets out to the crowd. The kids went wild, waves of them, like ants swarming from every direction. They leapt onto his back, clinging on like a bunch of grapes while he struggled to stay upright under the weight.

Meanwhile, ringside, the eight fighters were massaged by their trainers. Bistro Bernard was there with his boxer, giving him a pep talk which seemed to involve copious amounts of rum straight from the bottle. The fighter, who looked decidedly tired compared to the others, needed no persuading. When

Bernard tried to take it away he wouldn't let go, like a baby with his dummy.

Bernard wore a maroon sequined dressing gown that barely covered his bum. On the back it read 'Refuge Bistro, Bon appétit!' All very classy, I thought. These French, they don't muck about when it comes to grub.

Next to Bernard was big Frank. He wore only shorts and sat there puffing and blowing while his sponsored fighter circumnavigated his bulk, mopping up the sweat running off the rolls of fat. At his feet was a carrier bag with his food supplies in, and to his right his mail-order bride, looking young and bored. I suppose in the long run it would be worth her while. Frank wouldn't live forever.

Down the line and spread out around the ring we had another half a dozen fighters and their sponsors, none of whom I recognised. Only two of the fighters wore anything other than tatty basketball shorts. They didn't need glamour; they had bodies carved out of wood.

Should I place a bet? A bookie caught my eye. No, better not, I thought. Cocks had a mind of their own but men could be bribed. I stood on a bench trying to spot Annie and got told to sit down by an irate fisherman (they carry the smell of fish guts everywhere). 'I'm looking for someone!' I said.

'So am I!' he replied.

As interesting as it all was I'd rather be in bed with an Italian woman than watch men knock each other senseless.

'John!'

I spun around in a circle, ignoring the complaints. Where is she? There! Yes! She's with her bodyguard, Belgian Brenda! No!

I told the fisherman to shove his precious view and climbed the stand. Annie was outwardly pleased to see me, while Brenda was just outwardly pleased. For her, watching people beat each other to a pulp was clearly better than the prospect of being in bed with anyone.

Annie held out a bag of peanuts. 'You like boxing?'

'This kind of boxing,' I said.

She looked unbelievable in a low-cut, fitted white T-shirt. A delicate perfume was wafting up from her neck, made all the more sweet by the backdrop of sweat and tobacco that hung around everyone else in the place. I suddenly noticed how many drunken-looking men were staring at her. Shit, I thought, this woman could start a riot here. There was no cooling breeze and all the men around us seemed to be at boiling point, their bloodshot eyes welded to Annie's cleavage. Never mind, Brenda would protect us.

'I put money on this one.' Annie pointed. 'In the red shorts. Is good, no?'

'You placed a bet?'

'Why not? Is so funny.'

'How about you, Brenda? Not a gambling woman?'

'I am not allowed to bet. I am the referee.'

'You're what!'

Without replying, she took out her camera, handing it to Annie. 'Take many pictures, please,' she said, and limped down the terrace with a dexterity that belied her bulk and condition.

'Did she say she's the ref?' I was still agog.

'Yes.'

'But she's got a broken leg!' As I watched her vault the chicken-wire fence into the ring, that comment suddenly seemed a bit redundant.

Brenda gave a wave and the audience went wild. She looked weird to me, so what must have been going through these people's minds is anyone's guess. Not many tourists stray this far from the usual South East Asia backpacker route, but Brenda would stand out like a sore thumb in London.

She wore a pair of denim shorts, cut very high because of the cast, on one buttock of which was a two-fingered peace sign in stars and stripes. Her top half was a Lycra leotard, fully showing off her enormous arms to any boxer who dared even entertain the idea of breaking the Queensberry rules.

Honk, honk! Ziegwalt handed the mic to Brenda.

'OK everybody. Zonder dank! Welllllcooome!'

The crowd cheered.

'QUIET!'

The crowd shut up.

'Now then,' said Brenda, 'each fight will be...' Someone tugged on the microphone lead and took the mic from Brenda. It was handed over to a man who had stepped into the ring beside her.

I asked a boy next to me who it was and he said it was Elvis Presley Lam, El Refugio's 50-year-old gay mayor, and I thought, only in the Philippines: 300 years as a Spanish colony, then all change into a twentieth-century American colony. Imagine, 300 years in a convent and then dropped straight into Hollywood. No wonder they're confused. I'd be messed up.

Elvis tapped the mic with his palm. There was an ear-splitting whistle of feedback before Ziegwalt touched some equipment, did a thumbs up and Elvis spoke. 'Hello everybody!' A cheer went up.

At fifty he was something of a wilting flower, but as he stood in that ring, smiling inwardly, I couldn't help feeling that he was totally at ease with everyone around him. In a place this small he knew them all by name.

In fact, given what I'd gleaned from French Bernard, to say that Elvis Lam knew El Refugio like the back of his hand would be a monumental understatement. The Lam family are El Refugio. El Refugio is the Lam family's hand, connected to their arm and firmly rooted to their body and all-controlling brain.

Of Chinese descent, they had come to the Philippines in the fifties, like so many migrants fleeing Mao's China, with nothing. Why they'd chosen this remote corner of the country is anyone's guess, but, in true Chinese fashion, they started to trade.

At that time the whole area just consisted of very remote fishing villages. The major difference was control of the fishing in and around the islands. There wasn't any, basically, and the Lams, being north Asians, took control. Starting off in the shrimp-paste business, they bought one boat and steadily expanded, eventually controlling the rights to fish every stretch of coast in the vicinity.

The local Filipinos, not being business-minded and content to just live life at a steady pace, were happy to accept the offer to fish exclusively for the Lams. Very soon they were the first family, sitting back as fleets of outriggers manned by locals went out and caught very valuable sea creatures; from huge bottom-feeding grupas to turtles to seahorses and sharks; all prized by the north Asian markets.

Of course, the locals back then hadn't a notion of the high prices old man Lam was getting in other countries. To them fishing was something you did to provide the evening's meal. And by the time they wised up to it decades later it was too late; the Lams owned everything. In fact, everyone.

Mr Lam had a continent-wide market view; the locals couldn't see past the trees on the hill. After fishing came bird-nest collecting (gram by gram more valuable than gold), and then the product that really made them wealthy – logging. The Lams were instrumental, along with greedy officials from the state capital, in decimating the region's primary rainforests. They also sold a stunning nearby island to a resort developer, despite the area's protected marine park status.

One way or another the Lam family are into everything, and one way or another, if you stay in El Refugio, you'll be putting money in their pockets. They own most of the land, and so, in effect, every property on the Monopoly board. They even own the one and only petrol station. Every time you ride in a tricycle, get on a bus or take a lagoon tour in a boat with an outboard engine, you're buying their fuel and lining their pocket.

El Refugio should be renamed Lamville. A town where the Lam herds the sheep.

Honk, honk!

'Thank you, Ziggy.' Elvis stood and ran a hand through his quiff. 'Welcome to this, our annual Cock Box Derby, proudly sponsored by Lams' Enterprises. Brenda will be in charge of the proceedings, and we have eight handsome men doing battle for us.' He did a twirl, sweeping an arm over the boxers on display.

The harsh fluorescent light caught his bald patch and I couldn't resist it. 'Kalbo!' No one laughed.

Elvis thanked everybody for turning up and hoped they would enjoy the display of 'masculine beauty', as he put it. 'But first the national anthem.' Ziegwalt handed him an electric guitar over the fence, did his customary thumbs up, and Elvis stroked the strings with affection. Nothing. 'The sound, Ziggy, the sound! For goodness sake, Ziegwalt!'

A few knobs and dials were twiddled before another one of his earth-shattering sonic booms reverberated around the hills. Everyone ducked as if being fired at. 'Ziegwalt. Please. Sort it out.'

'OK! OK! Vhat you vanting I do?' He fiddled for a while on his contraption; a mishmash of leads, wires and black boxes, while the mayor took the opportunity to pout to the crowd. He did look a bit like a has-been rock star, standing there with the guitar hanging around his neck, wallowing in the final farewell concert in what, to him, was only one step down from Wembley Stadium.

Ziegwalt looked up while twisting the volume control and I felt the unmistakable wave of silent power wash over me.

'Thank you.' He fingered a chord and stroked, allowing the note to ring out and get everyone settled before breaking into the song.

He sang it very well, although of course it was in Tagalog, so it was impossible for me to tell if the words were right. But it had the desired effect. All the punters, including me, stood and watched as he picked through chord after chord without a hitch. He even struck a chord with the overtly macho in the audience, bringing them almost to tears, bolt upright and gritting their teeth in an attempt to stem the flow of emotion. José Rizal would have been proud.

The whole thing was undermined somewhat by Francis, the ladyboy from Hard Rocks Videoke. Unable to stay put and miss glory in front of so many men, and convinced, since he worked in a karaoke bar, that he possessed a great voice, he decided a duet was in order. He sounded like a geriatric goat warbling.

Someone mimed cutting his throat and the mic died. Ziegwalt went into overdrive, like some hyperactive clockwork toy, trying to get some music on.

Brenda took the mic. 'Testing. Testing. Each fight will be–'

'Everybody was Kung Fu figh-ting! Ooh! Ahh! Those kicks were as fast as...'

'Sorry. Finishing, finishing,' said Ziegwalt flicking a switch to turn off the music.

'Ahem.' Brenda gave him a look and a flex of the biceps. 'As I was saying, each fight will be three rounds of one minwit. Normal boxing rules applying. Win is by knocking down only. No judges; my decision final. Sank you.'

'I wouldn't want to argue with that,' I said, pithily, I thought. Annie gave me a look.

'You know…'

'What?'

'She's big. Ha ha.' Shut up, John. Shut up!

'There is something wrong with that?'

'No. God, no. I meant that she has presence, therefore it goes without saying that Brenda's going to be in control of it.' For God's sake start the fight. Ring that damn bell!

The minute it took to get the first two fighters into the ring seemed like hours. I perspired, trying desperately to look preoccupied with the way the rafters had been constructed. Annie seemed to frown a lot. That's blown any chance of a shag tonight, I thought.

'Look,' Annie said, pointing, 'it's Elsie.'

Bernard's girlfriend, dressed in her revealing evening dress, walked around the inside of the ring with the round number painted on a card. The wolf-whistles were like daggers piercing Bernard's heart. He looked up with pure hatred as she circled again and again, before turning his back and taking the bottle from his boxer.

'I love you!' someone shouted, and she wiggled harder.

'Marry me!' shouted another, and a coin was thrown into the ring. It set everyone off.

'Low-flying doves,' I said. Annie looked at me. 'That's the euphemism here for a prostitute. It's an accurate term, don't you think?'

'I feel so sorry for her. She is trying to be beautiful, but listen to these stupido men.'

'Come on, she loves it. Otherwise why would she be up there? She's an exhibitionist.'

And then a drunken spectator, having been teased to bursting point by the mixture of heat, sweat, beer and bum, put his money where his mouth is and barged into the ring to fawn her.

For a woman with a broken leg Brenda moved fast. She dropped the mic as the man ran across and cut him down before he knew what hit him. A perfectly timed rugby tackle any All Black would have been proud of. There was a scuffle, a cloud of dust, and as if by magic Brenda was sitting on top of the man, pinning him face-down in the dirt, one arm behind his back.

Whistles turned to cheers and then silent awe as the wrestling referee picked him up, literally, and threw him out the ring. El Refugio's drunken police chief, Thomas Bacudo, thumped him on the head and frogmarched him away.

The crowd lapped it up. I lapped it up. This was better than boxing.

'I can't believe what I've just seen,' I said. 'She just threw that man over that fence!' Annie wasn't listening, too busy recording it all on Brenda's camera.

I could picture the snapshots in my head, frozen images of the event in Brenda's photo album, and her describing it, matter-of-factly to friends back home in Belgium: 'And this is where he tries to touch the lady. And this is me applying the half nelson. And finally the shlam.'

Brenda brushed herself off, spread her massive arms and beckoned the two fighters to approach her. They looked sceptical. She dwarfed these boys: a slab of white marble between two bamboo poles. No punching below the belt, she mimed, or biting, or knees. And no lip! Her arms spread, pointing this way and that, and they retreated to their corners.

Honk, honk!

I was taken aback at the fury of it. There was none of that dancing around, eyeing up the opponent and trying to soften him up psychologically. No fancy footwork. No bobbing and weaving, no shuffling and skipping, and none of that sticking out the chin 'come on, hit me' bullshit. They flew at each other like… well, like cocks. And it dawned on me that 'cockfight' is the perfect term for two men fighting it out. No wonder some women like to watch men fight.

A quick glance out the corner of my eye. Annie was engrossed, mouth open in amazement. Was that a good sign? Maybe after watching this I'd look like a poor substitute standing there at her bathroom door in my Marks & Spencer's underpants.

The two fighters were a blur of windmilling arms, neither taking a moment to step back and breathe for the minute-long round. Even when Ziegwalt's brass horn sounded they didn't cease, only separated by Brenda. As soon as Elsie had finished her wiggle and the honk went again, they simply took up where they'd left off. It was brutal.

The crowd were on the edge of their seats. Money changed hands like the clappers, bookies' arms fluttered in the air with sign language. Hawkers sold out of beer before the next fight had even begun. The chicken-wire fence was now a wall of bodies, hemming in the action on all sides, screaming at the top of their lungs.

I drifted for a moment, nowhere in particular, just looking outside under the eaves of the tin roof and drinking in the night air, gazing at the dark paddy fields and the silhouette of the cliffs against the stars. When I turned back Brenda was holding an arm aloft, the crowd booing.

Annie was cheering like billy-ho. She flung her arms around me and kissed me on the lips. 'I win! I win!' Her lips were like perfumed marshmallows.

'How much?'

'I do not know. We celebrate, no?'

'Where? The restaurant is closed.' I contemplated my next move.

My place was out of the question; there was no way Maximo could be trusted. If he hadn't wired up the bed to the mains he'd probably barge in camouflaged and truss the pair of us up like chickens. No.

What about Annie's place? The problem with that option was Gladys. Annie had told me that the old boiler sat beside her entrance at night, asleep in an armchair, guarding to make sure there was no monkey business going on in her establishment. Gladys slept with one eye open and always woke to question where Annie had been. Imagine that, being grilled by the landlady. Sounds just like an English B&B after all.

The beach? Too many sandflies. Hard Rocks? All very well, but what then? Where would we go? I supposed I could always book into a new guest house for the night, but that was hardly subtle. I'd check out of Bonga's tomorrow, but tonight I needed another option.

The next two fighters came together in the middle of the ring. Ziegwalt honked and after a whirlwind flurry of fists Bernard's fighter was on his back gazing blankly at the rafters. I wasn't sure if he was OK, KO or Blott-O. He definitely wasn't compos. Bernard's sexy girlfriend immediately rushed to him in tears. Bernard, in a mad rage, threw the empty rum bottle at her and walked off.

'How about my place?' Annie said.

I turned to her. 'What about Gladys?'

'Gladys goes out tonight. I think she meet the Father. We have one drink and then go to bed.'

The crowd went wild.

I tripped over one of the dogs outside the Hard Rocks and tried to stop myself falling in the dark alley. The electricity in the village had gone off as usual and it was so pitch black that I couldn't see my hand in front of my face. I know because I stood there swaying from the effects of the rum with both hands in front of my eyes.

Shit, why had I got bogged down here? It had seemed so straightforward: leave the cockpit with Annie, take a romantic 10-minute stroll through the village, along the moonlit beach right into heaven. How difficult could it be?

One drink, as usual, led to another, which led to karaoke, and before I knew it Francis the ladyboy was leading me around the dance floor while Annie sang her heart out to 'Teddy Bear'. Then all the boxers arrived, along with a dozen drunk spectators, and before long we had a right knees-up going. A bloody good blowout, as my old man would have called it. As far as I could tell, Annie had staggered out about ten o'clock.

Francis came out with a candle and a wiggle, shielding the flame with one hand. 'You take this. You want I take you home?'

'No.' I took the stick, a stream of hot wax running down and congealing like fat on the back of my fingers.

'You drunk.'

'I'm OK.' My eyes began to close against the warm glow and I fought the tiredness. 'Which way is Gladys's?'

'Just go straight.'

A half-hearted drunken cheer went up inside the bar and one of the boxers, his dressing gown now wrapped around his head in a turban, staggered out to toast us and promptly collapsed on a sleeping dog.

It was an image I couldn't shake, a perfect snapshot of a man's fall from grace. No ceremony, just the cold, hard reality of loneliness at the bottom of the bottle. A prizefighter, a has-been who's now relegated to the remotest far-flung corner of the world. An outsider.

There's a terrifying amount of self-pity in the Philippines, and the best place to see it in all its head-hanging awfulness is at a karaoke bar in the small hours. The few women have long since had the sense to go home to bed, and you're left with middle-aged men crying into microphones. Gone are the smiling faces and happy-go-lucky songs, replaced with woe-is-me power ballads and tunes that long for repairs for broken hearts.

All this flushed over my mind as I stood there wondering about my own reasons for being here. Could I be like that? Perhaps, in my own way I already was. A loner, an outsider.

The hot wax burned into my wrist and my Hong Kong girlfriend and my previous life stood in front of me. The contrast couldn't be more stark: on one hand the concrete and glass of Central Hong Kong, full of brisk busy bodies, on the other a dirt path and a comatose boxer. Might as well be a different planet.

The candle flickered and I followed Francis between houses onto the beach. Once we were at Gladys's fence I thanked him and slid the bolt quietly across, once again in total darkness. The only sound was Francis's footsteps crunching on the shells that littered the beach, then silence.

A shell cracked under the shift of my weight. Then there was a sleepy moan as Annie turned over in her hut and spoke Italian in her sleep. The only other thing that registered in the dark was a strong smell of men's aftershave.

My hand came in contact with the hammock strung between trees. My breath came back all at once, along with all the fatigue, and I slumped in the sling. I felt better outside. After six years in Hong Kong space was what I needed most, not another box.

I dreamed I was being chased down a street by a hooded man. Someone let off a spine-chilling, blood-curdling scream and the next thing I knew I was being cuddled by a very warm woman's body.

5

Mornings are lovely in the tropics. In El Refugio they are pure magic. The cliffs hold in cool air and sea mist, and the silent bay is millpond flat.

I opened my eyes and found myself in the hammock with a cracking headache and a gorgeous Italian curled up next to me. I dared not move in case she vanished, in case this new dream evaporated. The sun wasn't up over the cliff, but the whole curved beach was alight in the orange of early morning. A gentle opaque white mist hovered over the bay and clung to the cliffs at both ends, wedged in, and I was sugar-dusted in fine dew.

Gladys's maid, Rose, came down the beach and crunching through the gate quickly. She glanced at me before rushing into the main house in a panic. She was still wearing her pajamas.

Then I noticed something going on further down the beach. I could see someone looking down at their feet, at something. A large fish, I guessed from its size. Then the sounds came in; first dogs barking as they stood off from the scene, then gentle crying. A person ran out from a house, stopped and ran back again. Then another, followed by more. I slid my arm from under Annie and she woke, blinking at me and grimacing. Blimey, I thought, I hope that's not from seeing me first thing in the morning.

The maid came back out with Gladys, hair in curlers, feet in mules, puffy-eyed and bloated without make-up. Her pink towelling dressing gown had a ripped pocket and string for a belt. She didn't notice us slung beneath the tree, thank God, and quickly followed the girl out and down the beach.

Annie asked me what was going on. I said it looked like a dead fish on the beach.

'Wait. I get my clothes.'

I watched her go, her athletic legs and her bottom in white D&G knickers. A second later she came out in a long dress, her hair tied in a band of strung cowries.

'OK,' she said, and held out her hand for me to hold. 'We go.'

No sooner had we turned than Brenda stepped onto her veranda rubbing sleep from her eyes and tying a sarong around her bust. Behind her, in the darkness of her hut, I noticed a figure peep out from inside her mosquito net. It was the boxer from the first fight, his gloves hanging from the corner of the net like a trophy. By the look on his face and the fatigued way he moved, Brenda had got the better of him in round four. He looked absolutely knackered. Brenda looked... well, Brenda. She was the kind of person that looks healthy no matter what the circumstances, day or night.

'And then what is all this commotion? Why is we all up early?' she said. The boxer coughed up some phlegm and she pulled the door to, glancing at her diver's watch. 'Only six-thirty, but I already hungry.' She fished through a carrier bag hung up on a washing line on the veranda, then said, 'Huh. Only bread and jam. I very hungry,' and laughed like a moose honking.

'There's something going on down the beach,' I said. 'Looks like a dead fish.'

'OK, I come. Wait.' She went inside and before I could protest to Annie that by the time we got there it'd all be over, she was back with her camera and a Swiss Army knife. 'Maybe chance of sushi,' she said firmly, and shut the door on the poor boxer who was just about to walk through it. I could picture him humiliated on the other side, staring blankly at the back of the door.

'Right, let's go,' I said, and turned to leave.

'What's going on?' We all spun around. Jiz, her scrawny torso poking out through the flimsy bamboo window of the other hut, totally naked and proud of it, took one look at the other two and said, 'Wait, I'll get dressed.'

'Oh, God almighty,' I sighed. 'By the time we get there the fish will have recovered and swam off again. It's like a bloody school outing.'

Annie let go of my hand. I looked at her, trying to backtrack. 'I only meant…'

'Just go if you cannot wait for one minute.' I felt like a kid being given a bollocking on the school outing. 'I will wait for Jiz and see you in un minuto,' she said and shooed me away with a flick of the wrist. Funny how people revert to their own language when they are angry.

Bloody hell, why do I have to wait for this lot? I might be missing something juicy, a bit of the old El Ref gossip. I don't mind waiting for one woman, especially if it's one I like, and I'll even wait for her mate, but three. On top of that Jiz was a right pain in the bollocks.

I turned and went through the gate, glancing back quickly to see if Annie was watching me. She was, so I continued triumphantly.

Word travels fast in the Philippines. Within minutes people were pouring out of every pathway that led onto the beach. Men, women, hordes of kids and dogs in packs of five dashed out to see what it was all about. It seemed hard to believe that a fishing community could be so absorbed by the sight of a dead fish. Perhaps it was a rare specimen, something unknown in these waters. A great white! I quickened my pace and saw Ziegwalt march out between huts onto the beach.

He was wearing Lycra cycling shorts this morning, bare barrel-chested, moustache bristling with anticipation. Both arms were bent at the elbows, fists clenched, punching the air for that extra bit of speed. 'Coming on!' he shouted at me. 'Thumsing goes on!' He popped a cigar in his mouth and lit it. 'Ahh, El Refugio.'

Next to appear was Frank, on the beach early as usual, trying to walk off the leg cramps he suffered with (he rarely slept well), helped as usual by his young Filipina wife. He looked as though he'd never trodden on sand before, afraid it wouldn't hold his weight. He rested an elbow on Mary's head and she buckled beside him. He stopped on the sand, looked around, drawing breath for a moment, saw me and waved his walking stick in the air. 'What's-a cookin'?'

'It's down there, Frank,' I said, surprised at myself for already starting the gossip. 'A shark, I think.' I paced on, hoping that he wouldn't ask for my assistance.

Francis from Hard Rocks was already there, so were Janet and Taddi from the Swiss café, along with their boat boy and all the waitresses from the restaurant. In fact every person I knew was there with the exception of Maximo.

I raced on until I reached the gathering crowd, stopped at the edge of the circle of people briefly, glancing behind at the advancing, limping figure of Brenda and the other two, then pushed into the throng to get a better look.

A car horn sounded and the whole crowd turned and looked up. The police chief (he runs a force of two in El Refugio; himself and his female deputy, nicknamed Ten, apparently after her IQ) attempted to drive onto the beach in his decrepit jeep. Ten was shouting through a loudhailer.

He brought one wheel gently down onto the beach and the whole thing tipped sideways, sinking up to its axle. Ten was thrown comically out head first, still holding her megaphone, while the chief fought to control the vehicle. He put it in reverse but the car just went in further, bouncing up and down and juddering what was left of the poor man's pride. He loved that police jeep more than his wife, they said.

'No one touches the body,' Ten shouted in English.

Body! I pushed closer in, wondering what kind of fish would be so big they'd call it a body.

French Bernard was standing in the middle of the circle of people gazing nowhere, his face a blank, emotionless mask. He looked like someone who had just lost something but can't quite place what it was. As if caught in those seconds before the memory's jogged into place.

'Everyone keeps back,' came Ten's tinny, electrified voice.

I pushed in and looked down.

Lying at Bernard's feet on her back, head turned to one side – my side – still wearing last night's dress, still looking sexy, was Bernard's girlfriend Elsie. I snorted, thinking she had passed out drunk from the night before. I wasn't the only one because Janet, then Taddi and some other men tried shaking her awake. Why would we think anything else?

And then it suddenly hit me. She's dead. 'She's flipping brown bread!' I blurted.

Her skin wasn't grey, like they say dead bodies are, but kind of transparent on the front, facing up, then going sort of multicoloured purple as it went down her sides. It was as if the blood had drained from her front into her back, which I suppose it had. She looked exactly the same colour as the tequila sunrise she'd served me in the bistro.

Her red-lipsticked lips were parted slightly, her hair its usual wild mass, only now matted with seaweed. Her eyelashes had collected tiny dewdrops from the morning mist.

My eyes passed along her body to the feet with only one stiletto shoe, then back up the slender legs and over her stomach, picked out beautifully by the thin, wet cloth, to her chiselled, tattooed shoulders and finally her neck. A large open gash as thick as my finger ran around her throat like a choker. No blood, just a perfect gaping blue slit.

Placed neatly beside her hip at an unnaturally parallel angle was a massive combat knife. 'That's Max...' I almost said, recognising it instantly as the one Maximo had offered me but shutting my gob at the last minute. Everyone looked at me. 'That's mad,' I corrected.

Everyone looked back at the body.

'Is she dead?' I said, and everyone looked at me again before gasping and taking a step back. It was as though saying the word 'dead' had suddenly killed her.

The police chief barged through, bent down, felt her pulse and said something to his deputy in Tagalog. He then said something to the crowd I didn't understand. No one moved.

Annie's arms encircled my waist from behind and I suddenly felt a bit disgusted with the place. Brenda and Jiz had their hands to their mouths.

And that's how it was, it seemed for ages, all of them, tourists and locals alike, just standing there, waiting for something to happen, staring at that poor lifeless girl. All except me. I was staring at that huge combat knife.

A PRIVATE EYE

82

1

Does anyone really know their friends? Close friends even? Can you really say, hand on heart, that you know what your pal's thinking, even if you've know them intimately all their life?

The answer, I decided, was no. In the same way that perfectly level-headed, community-spirited, hard-working people can become dribbling, helpless alcoholics for reasons unknown to their friends, so apparently charming, eccentric old men can turn to murder. The brain is a mysterious organ indeed.

Some people, under the weight of circumstances, turn to the bottle over time, while others do insane things suddenly, like school kids turning up to school with a machine gun and spraying their classmates with bullets.

The trouble with this was that Maximo didn't seem to fit into any of it, mainly on account of age. Venerable old men just don't go on the rampage. Who ever heard of a geriatric, even one obsessed with the military, going on a murderous shooting spree? The headlines: 'Tea Rooms Blood Bath! Pensioner Slays Thirteen!' Or 'Meek Grandfather Snaps, Blows Up Retirement Home!'

He may be an eccentric old soldier (that's stating the obvious) but could he really be a closet wacko with that knife? I know he'd laid some booby traps for me but those were pranks. OK, so he'd deliberately electrocuted me, but cutting someone's throat? Apart from anything else, I couldn't see him having the strength to do it.

Picture him, creeping up on Elsie, slithering along the sand on his belly, knife clenched in his teeth commando-style, the moon glinting off his Brylcreem. He gets to within metres of the target, 'pounces' to his feet and... doubles over with backache and goes into a coughing fit.

And she was a young, very agile woman. Even if he tricked her into believing he meant no harm, it must be hard to pull a blade across someone's neck. I've never skewered anything tougher than a Christmas turkey before, but even that's hard to do with a blunt knife.

I know Max's knife was blunt because I tried to trim my backpack strap with it a few days earlier and it wouldn't cut hot butter. As if all that wouldn't be difficult enough, she'd have been trying to get away, thrashing about.

It was his knife, no mistake. How many weapons like that could there be in this whole country, never mind this little village? While we all stood there that morning waiting for the Keystone Cops to pull their finger out, I had plenty of time to study it. Same size and shape, same worn leather hilt, and most importantly the same steel pommel with the crossed US cavalry swords logo engraved on it. It was the one Maximo had offered me, no question about it.

My mind pinballed all through the following week. I couldn't sleep, wasn't hungry, didn't want to talk to anyone and, when Annie asked me to share her place, I said no. I went out with her but spent most of my time wandering alone, usually east along the other beaches beyond the village.

I just didn't know whether or not I should tell anyone. What I really wanted was for someone else to say that they recognised the knife and get me off the emotional hook I was hanging from.

I had to tell someone to relieve the pressure. But who? Frank and Mary had gone to visit her family 2 hours away (Filipinos are very superstitious and Frank's wife said she'd seen Elsie's ghost). Annie? She was the person I'd spent most time with since arriving here but, being a woman she'd probably tell her friends Jiz and Brenda. Apart from French Bernard at the Bistro and Francis, the owner of Hard Rocks, neither of whom seemed like a safe bet for a secret, there was no one else. Francis didn't seem that level-headed, and Bernard was the prime suspect. Apart from anything else he was now residing in El Ref's one and only prison cell.

In fact it was an old brick shithouse at the back of the police station. In fact the police station was only part of a long building attached to the municipal hall. In fact the municipal hall... Well, you get the picture: El Refugio's barely a clearing in the jungle. So when they decided Bernard dunnit, Ten was ordered to clear out the piles of rubbish that had accumulated over the years and make room in the disused bog for El Ref's ripper. Or so I'd been told by Janet at the Swiss Cafe. The village rumour mill had gone into overdrive.

I tried to picture poor Bernard squatting in a dingy little brick cell, scratching a calendar on the wall with a rusty nail, but for some reason couldn't see his face. It's easy to recognise someone you know in a crowd full of people, but to try picturing a person in your mind, their actual features, it isn't easy. I could see him standing there that day, looking out to sea, but he seemed faceless, blank, not there. If I'd known he was going to get locked up I would have looked harder.

I'd had plenty of time to look, as well. The chief of police had spent nearly an hour trying to get his jeep out of the sand, using everything from lengths of Gladys's picket fence placed under the wheels to a team of tricycles. Eventually a poor farmer was summoned under order of the Philippines National Police, along with his bullock, and things started to happen. Slowly.

Of course, by the time the farmer finally appeared around the headland and lumbered the length of the bay, leading the bullock by a rope through its nose, the water was licking at Elsie's blue feet.

It was awful watching that body get dragged up the sand like the dead fish I'd first thought it was. When the chief finally came over bristling with authority I wanted to kick him up the arse.

Instead, a tearful Jiz looked at the bull, said 'Bullshit baffles police brains', and we all watched as a wave of nervousness swept over the portly policeman. Suddenly his bluster vanished and he seemed aware of the crowd's mood. Used to having the entire village turn a blind eye to his petty corruption (Janet's info again), it had taken him no time at all to sense the hatred in the circle. Policemen have that instinct.

There was a long silence in which everyone, even the dogs, seemed to be waiting for something to happen. It did: Bernard walked into the sea. Ziegwalt shouted, 'Burn-hard! Burn-hard!' but he was in another world.

'You! Mr Bernard!' shouted the chief, and hopped from foot to foot at the edge of the water, unsure what exactly to do, but knowing full well he wasn't going to get his shoes wet. Bernard may be a murderer, but it wasn't worth getting his polished brogues sodden. After all, to quote most of the townsfolk, 'she was only a Manila whore.'

Bernard had waded in deeper. No one moved.

'Stop or… or I will shoot!'

Everyone looked at the chief in utter disbelief. Bernard stopped, washed his hands and face, then turned and came back in, oblivious to the commotion.

The chief grabbed his wrists and put them behind his back but seemed at a loss without handcuffs. Bernard said nothing, just playing along and walking off the beach, flanked by the chief.

Ten, his hopeless deputy, was left with the job of crowd control. Putting the loudhailer to her lips, she watched as some people collected a blanket and covered the body. 'Cover the body,' she boomed after it had been done. And after two metres of picket fencing from a nearby garden had been converted into a stretcher and Elsie had been put onto it and lifted, 'Now let us move this body,' she crowed.

We all followed the bearers up the beach and down the street toward the little hospital. 'We will take her to the hospital,' Ten's distant voice said. I think I was the only one listening.

Past the Hard Rocks, still knee-deep in drunks, turn right at the junction and down the only paved road towards the municipal hall. Ten had her work cut out. By that stage we'd picked up just about every kid and his mangy dog in the town, and what started out as a sorrowful march turned into a circus.

Boys were running up and down trying to get their first glimpse of a dead body, dogs yapped and ran around in frenzied circles as if sensing the ghost, and the curious townsfolk jostled and gawped.

At one stage there were so many people at the bottleneck by the junction that everything came to a standstill, and a stand-off. Ten barged into the crowd with sharpened elbows. 'I am police,' she blared in my ear. She turned menacingly, saw one of her suitors and gave a coy sideways smile.

Getting the body up the steps and through the entrance doors of the little hospital was like trying to push a fish through a net without losing any scales. With so many people pushing and shoving and standing in the way the inevitable happened. Someone lost their grip, or stumbled, or was pushed, and Elsie was dropped. A scream went up and the crowd bolted for their lives. I'd had enough of it and went back to Bonga's.

A week later I was still walking around in a daze, wandering and wondering. It should have been cut and dried; Bernard had been found by the body, and, as far as I could tell, had willingly been taken into custody. God knows, during the boxing he looked as if he could have killed her for prancing around up there, lapping up the jeers and wolf-whistles.

All the evidence seemed to suggest that she played up to it. Turns out it was her I'd seen scuffling in the street with Janet that first day, accused of tempting Janet's husband. And, though I hate myself for saying it, she was an ex-prostitute.

Maybe she could have stopped sleeping around, but aren't people like Elsie, with all their showmanship and hair-flicking, amorous ways really in it for the attention? You can't be an ex-flirter. Once a show-off, always a show-off. Clowns, singers, any kind of exhibitionist; show them a stage and their body gets a mind of its own.

And the knife? Bernard stole it. Cut and dried case, I'd say. So why was I strolling around day and night, unable to sleep, unable to think about anything other than that bloody knife? And why did I still think that Maximo had something to do with it? Simple. When I went back to the guest house that morning he wasn't there, and hadn't been seen since. Old Maximo Bonga had vanished from the face of the earth.

2

'Hey, buddy. Somebody's a-lookin' fo' ya.'

It was Frank, back from his visit to the in-laws, same position as usual on the veranda, tin of crackers and stacks of tuna in front of him. The only difference this time being the addition of a litre bottle of coke and what looked like a box of military badges. I stopped at the top of the steps. He got stuck into another tin so I had to wait a while before he elaborated. Mary's head popped up, said hello, and went back to the leg-fat massaging.

He licked the tuna oil that ran down his wrist and studiously nibbled at the remnants of his disgusting snack.

'Annie?' I asked, impatient. 'Blonde. Italian.'

'Na na na. What's her name, from the Swiss thingummy. Janet. Says she wants you to go round her place tonight. Cooking up a feeding. Me too. Yeeha! Gonna get us some proper eatin' tonight, yes boss.'

'What time?'

'Said about– Ouch! Now you mind that there biggun, m' lady.' He wagged a finger at Mary. 'You knows I got a problem with that one.' He tried to lean forward for an inspection but his barrel stomach got in the way and he slumped back, exhausted. '…'bout seven.'

'What time is it now?'

'Six-ish. Hey, where you bin? I ain't seen you around.'

In fact I hadn't slept at Bonga's since the body was found. The first night I hadn't slept at all and the last few had been spent in the hammock at Annie's place. Annie was now sharing with Jiz out of fear for their safety. Typical, I thought; two single birds and a single bloke and the girls sleep together. I'm seconds away from getting Annie into bed and some nutter has to go and murder someone. Annie said that Jiz was alone and scared and didn't want to be the next on the killer's list. I felt sure Jiz was doing it out of spite. She hated me, I could tell, ever since I'd called her 'that Aussie nightmare' and she'd overheard.

With Brenda living next door I couldn't for the life of me see how any of us had anything to worry about. No psycho in his right mind would tangle with that woman. If the killer had been to the boxing tournament – and it seemed likely considering the whole village had turned out – he would have seen her in action and wouldn't go within a mile of Gladys's place.

'Been with a friend,' I said.

'Hey, you seen Pop anywhere?'

I froze.

'Man, there's something going on here. You gawn, he gawn. And you know what? There's a damn suspicious looking fella been walking about this place. Odd lookin' dude. Like... I dunno... ' He reached for another cracker. 'Rasputin. Yeah. Like that Ra Ra Russian with the beard.'

This one baffled me. 'You mean a white man?'

'Course a white man. You ever see an Asian with a beard? I ain't. Sep one o' them wispy ones like Ho Chi Minh. Nah, I'm talking about a real beard.' Frank held his hand a foot beneath his chin. 'And tall. Hooee. Man, y'll think yo tall. Thus sucker goes seven feet, easy. And dirty. Shit, this guy ain't washed in months. He stinks. Came here and brought a swarm of flies as company. Look like he been living in the jungle all his life. All he had on was one of them native skirt things.'

'Sarong. Did he say what he wanted?'

'Nah. No name, nothing. Just came in here quiet as a ghost – sep for the buzzing of them flies – and slid into the shadows. Reckon he's a-lookin' for someone.'

The spit wouldn't go down my throat and I began to blink too much. Any idiot could see I was hiding something. 'Did you, um… did any police come?' Shut up, John, shut up.

'Po-liss? Here?' He frowned and shook his head, his jowl wobbling. 'What for, boy? What we got to do with this here thing?'

Me and my big gob. My bald head started to throb. I knew I wouldn't be able to keep the secret much longer. 'No, it's just that I thought I saw the chief here earlier, that's all.'

'You think this bearded freak got something to do with it?' He nodded wisely as if something had fallen into place. 'Say, you don't think this guy rubbed out that poor gal and now done in old Pop, do ya? Oh, man. You think we's in danger here, boy?'

'No, no. Course not.' It hadn't occurred to me that perhaps someone outside of the village had killed Elsie, someone belonging to her shady past. The thought came almost as a relief until I thought about poor old Maximo. What if he was the second victim? Perhaps he'd seen the mad monk take the knife and, knowing the killer's true identity, had been knocked off.

Then again, how many shady pasts must there be in this village? It was full of weirdos. All from different backgrounds but all with one thing in common: they had all migrated from elsewhere, either to escape another life or as refugees. Elvis Lam the mayor had told me that you could count the indigenous families of El Refugio on one hand.

God knows, the handful of foreigners alone were all strange enough, psychotic enough to do something like that, never mind the locals. I'd only been here a couple of weeks and had seen things most people don't see in a lifetime. Coming from well-ordered worlds such as London and Hong Kong obviously compounded the feeling of contrast but there was no denying its uniqueness, its eccentricity. I'd been living abroad in many different countries for many years but never had I come across a place as mad as this.

El Refugio, it had dawned on me more than once, was a very incestuous place. Small town mentality exists all over the world, but very few places are as cut off from reality, as trapped and enclosed by cliffs as this place. The people here are a bit like the iguanas of the Galapagos Islands, cut off and evolving differently from the rest of the world. I felt like Charles Darwin. I looked at Frank. He reminded me of an elephant seal.

Perhaps this was a yearly occurrence here. Perhaps every so often, unable to vent their frustration in any other way, a local feels the rocks closing in and just erupts into a violent rage. Maybe that was the reason for the chief's blasé attitude; he'd seen it all before.

For all I knew the village was full of dormant loonies, volcanoes that had blown their top once and then gone back to normal, sedate El Ref life. What secrets did this place hide within its limestone walls? Could the whole townsfolk be a party to it, covering it up and hoping that outsiders would never be in town when one of the machines blew a gasket?

I'm not one for conspiracy theories, well maybe just a bit, but it was easy to see how a place like El Refugio could be a law unto itself. It had its own police force – if you can call two people that – a reasonably effective administration, even a mayor. It had a hospital (only a day clinic really) that delivered its babies, and very little contact with the outside world.

Why wouldn't they cover things up? They liked the money tourists brought in and the last thing they needed was interference from the government in Manila, or even the provincial capital for that matter. Bring in one nosey parker who starts to dig around and it's easy to see how these people would have a lot to lose. Incest (there are a lot of very odd-looking kids in the village), police corruption, local government collusion involving the Lams and fishing rights, illegal logging and resort hotel building in a Marine World Heritage site, the list goes on and on. It would be like trying to keep the lid on a box of frogs.

I wondered how a place that looks so normal, so peaceful and idyllic on the surface, could be so abnormal underneath, but perhaps it's always that way, always that twisted in small communities. I was born and bred in London, so don't really have that insight, but it made sense. Despite the obvious problems of metropolitan life, inner-city people always seemed to me to be better adjusted. I'm prejudiced, but that's the way it seems.

Or maybe it's simply because small communities are less open about the problems they face, refusing to acknowledge fissures in their precious social structure, sweeping them under the carpet, while city folk have a couldn't-care-less attitude. There's very little feeling of collective, community spirit in large cities, so who cares if someone decides to pull in a different direction to the rest; the urban environment as a whole can stand the tension. A small village would simply fall apart, cohesionless.

Frank yawned and rubbed his belly in a circular motion. 'Man, I'm tired. You tired, girl?'

Mary said she 'don't tired'.

'You wanna come with me and John here to dinner at the Swiss Cafe?' Mary said it was up to him. 'It's now quarter after. Take me a bit of time to get there on account of my weight, so we'd better get going soon. Pass me my stick, girl.' She handed him the walking stick and he stood with great difficulty. The floorboards creaked and groaned under the sudden shift in load.

'I'm gonna have a shower,' I said, my mind all over the place. 'I'll meet you there.'

'Ain't no water, boy.' He shrugged uselessly. 'The ol' man didn't show us how the pump works.'

You're too lazy to try, more like. 'I'll use a bucket,' I said. I knew where the pump and switch were but thought the effort of drawing water and a freezing bucket shower from the well was exactly what I needed to bring me round. I'd been in a daze and had to snap out of it, think straight. I had a feeling that tonight's party at the Swiss Cafe was going to be more than just a casual get together. Perhaps answers would begin to reveal themselves.

3

They'd been busy in the week since the murder, I could tell. As soon as I climbed the stairs to the top floor of the Swiss Cafe, Janet's dog inevitably trying to screw my leg senseless, a hum of whispers filled the air. Any concerns I'd had about this get-together being just another El Ref expat nagging forum were demolished when I peeped around the door.

'He is here,' said Ziegwalt, bristling with anticipation.

I looked over my shoulder before realising he was talking about me. I smiled weakly. Janet's head popped through the serving hatch like a Swiss cuckoo clock, she tapped her left-hand wristwatch and went back in. She always wore two; one set at Swiss time, the other local.

'Come, come. You will sit here.' Ziegwalt pulled out a chair at the table and I limped across, the dog still hanging on. He raised a hand in warning to the mutt, and when it didn't budge gave it one swift karate chop. The dog went boss-eyed and staggered out the door.

I sat and looked around the table. Ziegwalt the German, Jim the tatty looking Englishman with the posh accent from The Refuge Trio, Frank, and Janet's Filipino husband Taddi. All residents of the village. So why me, the only tourist? Did they suspect it was Max's knife? Had they known all along and needed me to join their cosy little group so that I too would hush things up, be part of their cover-up, trapped within these limestone walls forever?

Suddenly I thought of that film *The Wicker Man* and the way the main character played by Edward Woodwood is gradually lured into a false sense of security before being strung up. Didn't he play a detective in that? A bead of sweat broke out on my bald head. A prickling, irksome little globule. I sat still, afraid to raise a finger and scratch it, allowing it to itch more and more. Everyone was looking at me, their faces distorted into twisted, gargoyle grins, eyes popping.

Frank's rolls of neck fat were piled one on the other like coils of an anaconda, quivering and shiny. I watched as a mosquito landed, raised its hind legs and pierced the skin with its proboscis. I could see his pulse pumping blood. In slow motion Frank raised a hand and brought it crashing in. The shock wave sent ripples cascading around his whole body. He looked at the palm of his hand and daintily picked out the parasite between chubby fingers, inspecting it before flicking it over the balcony.

The Wicker Man. I'll run out now, catch them off guard before they could put something in my drink. But what if they'd already planned ahead? I'd run out the cafe straight into the townsfolk, all gathered outside, wielding pitchforks and laughing maniacally.

'Pizza!'

I nearly jumped out of my skin. Janet leaned over me and placed some large pizzas on the table, sliding the plates expertly down her generous forearms. She smiled. 'You are three minutes late, but that is OK.'

'What?' I blinked, picking up a fork and scratching my forehead with it. 'Three minutes?'

Her husband gave her a look that said, 'This is El Ref, the slowest place on earth, not Switzerland.' Janet gave him a look that said 'I don't care'.

She placed a motherly hand on my shoulder and said, in a creepily even voice, like a long-serving mortician talking to a corpse, 'But we could not start this without you.'

Oh my God! I'm going to be sacrificed!

'Burn-hard needs you,' Ziegwalt said, and placed a chubby hand on my knee, pinning me in position.

'Burn?' I managed to squeak.

'Yeah. I told 'em. Hope you don't mind,' Frank slid a whole pizza to his side of the table. ''Bout what you told Pop. 'Bout y'all being in the bidnid.'

What on earth was he going on about?

Frank eyed the large disc in front of him, turning it this way and that as if inspecting a newly acquired vinyl album of his favourite bygone band, savouring every groove visually before allowing it to play on his other senses. 'You know what I'm talking 'bout.' I watched as he used his knuckles as a thermometer, pressing down on the topping. He sucked air through his teeth. 'Dick.'

My heart slowed to somewhere near normal but my brain was in fog. Ziegwalt was no help, his face an inane childish smirk, expectant, as though awaiting a birthday present. And as for Jim the English toff sitting next to him, well he was clearly stoned.

I looked back at Frank. 'No, Frank, I haven't got the faintest clue what you're talking about. What's "Dick" mean?'

He winked at me, said matter-of-factly, 'You know, 'bout y'all being a private dick 'n' all,' then rolled the whole pizza into a log and stuffed the end into his fat hole.

Private Dick? I thought. A gigolo?

Janet came back from the kitchen, placing a tray of San Miguels on the table. 'Frank told us that you were a detective before. Maybe you can help us solve this crime.'

Ziegwalt leaned in and, I think trying to make me feel comfortable with my new responsibility, whispered, 'Sherlock Holmes. I have read him. I can help you.'

'Detective? What the hell are you all on about?'

'Ng.' Frank swallowed a wad of barely chewed dough. 'You told Pop you used to be a detective in China.'

Suddenly the penny dropped and I recalled the conversation I'd had with the old soldier about my previous life in Hong Kong. An insignificant, I thought, chat we'd had over a beer about both our pasts. He'd told me about the good old bad old days under Japanese occupation, and I'd told him about my previous jobs in Hong Kong, one of which had been a temporary effort for a private detective agency. A stand-in job between proper jobs that lasted barely two months. I'd needed the cash and the distraction.

'Whoah! Hold on a minute.' I held up both hands. 'You've got it all wrong. When I say private detective, don't get an image of Humphrey Bogart in your head. It ain't like that. I worked for a company that spent 99 per cent of its time closing down factories in China.'

'They were ein detectiff agency, no?' Ziegwalt said, peeping over the edge of the table.

'N... well, yeah, strictly speaking they were, but...'

'So that is that. You were ein detectiff.' He unfolded his chubby arms emphatically and took a beer.

'No,' I said even more emphatically, 'that's not that. In fact it's not even close to that. We chased down people who made fake Gucci handbags. That's that. That's all detective agencies do these days. Or at least the one I worked for.'

'But you were a detective,' said Janet, another person sitting around the table who apparently had misplaced her brain. Either that or else the salt sea air had corroded her eardrums.

Since doing that job six months before, the face of every person I'd told had lit up in the same way. No matter how hard I try, and however hard the person nods understandingly, I can see the inescapable notion of glamour and excitement glinting in their eyes. Just mention the words 'private detective' and they're fixed. No amount of explaining how mundane the work is brings them round.

'Bernard is innocent, John.' Taddi opened a beer and handed it to me. 'I have known him for years. He would not kill anyone.'

'He had motive enough.' I took the beer and swigged.

'Motive,' echoed Ziegwalt. 'See.'

'See what? I only said motive.'

'You know the words. That will help mit Burn-hard. When we go to court.'

'Court!'

Janet put some pizza on my plate and a hand on my shoulder to stop me running away.

'What are you on about, court?'

She wrapped an elastic length of cheese around a finger and licked if off provocatively. 'You can represent him. It is easy here.'

'What! Listen,' I got up to leave, 'I'm a construction manager. That's it. End of story. I was out of work and a friend put a stopgap job my way. I only worked there two months, for God's sake. Two months! My job, like everyone else there, was to find out where fake products were being made. Chanel, Microsoft, Super Glue 3. These firms discover counterfeits flooding the market – mostly from China – then pay law firms in Hong Kong to close them down. The law firms pay cheap little dogsbodies, 'private detectives' as you call them, to root through the rubbish bins. Work that the law firms can't be arsed with because it's so crap.

'We investigate, write a shitty little one page report, send it back to the lawyer and six months later they close the factory down. One week after that the factory re-opens down the road and the whole pointless cat and mouse game begins again. It was bullshit.' I sat back down and took a well-earned swig of beer. I thought I'd put my case across quite well, belittling the whole notion of glamour in private detective agencies once and for all. That's all, m' lud.

Ziegwalt looked at everyone before looking at me. He rolled his shoulders and pushed the whole of his uneaten pizza in front of me. 'Zo, you know how to einveshtigate.'

4

The next day I found myself explaining it all over again, this time to Annie as we went on a day trip to climb the hills. I could hardly get the words out, drawing in air as I climbed hand over fist up the rocks. It was still only nine o'clock in the morning but as usual the temperature had climbed with us. In fact it hadn't dipped very much at all during the night. I'd lain awake on a soaking bed sheet staring at geckos through a blur of sweat.

Annie wanted to know why I was planning to stay here in the village and help them instead of leaving with her the following week as planned to backpack around Vietnam. I looked at the shifting bum centimetres from my face and gave it the full answer. 'Because that's what I decided. It seemed like the right thing to do.' Smiling at Annie's bottom as it shifted in the hotpants, and then looking past it at Brenda's dump-truck arse and Jiz's bony backside, my grin slipped, mainly at my own ridiculous obsession with perfect look; a legacy of years spent living with chauvinistic high achievers in Hong Kong. 'Why did you have to bring those two?'

She ignored me. 'But what do you know about law in the Philippines, John?' She put one foot on a root and deftly took three quick steps up and over a fallen tree. I did the same and slipped. My flip-flop strap popped out.

'Hold on a minute.'

Annie looked back, arms folded but said nothing. She'd warned me not to wear these when we set off but I'd dismissed it. What did she know? I was the veteran traveller. She was a partner in a company that made ceramic tiles.

I sat on the log and pushed the V part with the little flattened button back through the hole in the sole. *Rubber Soul*, I thought, and marvelled at the general cleverness of that album title.

We hadn't climbed far but the rooftops of the squatter settlement at the western end of the village were already laid out beneath us. Rickety old houses made of driftwood stood on stilts above a small tidal mudflat, all connected by a maze of raised wooden walkways.

Probably originally a mangrove inlet, El Refugio's poorest settlers had taken over that part of the bay, sandwiched between the concrete jetty and the limestone cliffs where the swifts nested. Jammed in between the riches of the Lam family, with their petrol station and massive pink house, and the natural wealth of the place from which all the money was generated.

Also moored below was the MV *Buena Suerte* (*Good Luck*). A 20-metre rust bucket of a ferry with hammocks for beds and a wino for captain, it did the 36-hour journey to Manila every other day, often conking out midway. Good luck indeed. Zeigwalt had once shipped a BMW over from Manila on it, the car strapped down and taking up the whole deck. That had upset everyone, locals and foreigners alike. Expats because it destroyed their illusion of seclusion, locals just out of plain jealousy. But mainly it had upset the boat, literally, which had rolled over just offshore. They said it capsized then immediately righted itself minus the BMW, which had become one of El Ref's premier dive spots, 'Beemer Reef'. The MV *Roll On Roll Over*, as it was now known, sported the salvaged BMW badge on the ship's wheel.

'I'm not saying I won't regret it,' I said. 'I probably will. But if I can help I'm going to.'

'I think you no get involved. Mafioso. So dangerous.'

'Oh, come off it. Here? Anyway, I've already told them I would help, and I can't really go back on my word,' I said, studying the split in my soul. I mean sole.

In fact I hadn't told anyone I'd help. At least I don't think I had. Last night's chinwag in the Swiss Cafe had started off as an earnest discussion about Bernard's well-being, but by ten o'clock all righteous thoughts and notions of maintaining moral standards had gone over the balcony. It's amazing what a couple of crates of San Miguel can do to a group of right-thinking people.

One minute fists were being banged on the table at the injustice of it all, the next we were all singing 'Hotel California' ('You can check out any time you like but you can never leave') and falling over the dog, poor Bernard out of sight and out of mind in his little six-by-ten craphouse.

Maybe I had told them I'd help, but only when I was completely plastered and Janet was hanging off my shoulder, begging. She wouldn't remember, she was more drunk than I was. By midnight her husband had passed out on the floor, guitar still clutched to his chest, and Janet was trying to get in the hammock with the dog. One of her waitresses was so pissed she pulled up her singlet, revealing her 38Ds, and asked me if I liked them or not. So much for morals in The Refuge. I said I liked them very much.

Anyway, I don't recall telling them I'd help. It was only now, having climbed up the hill and looked down for the first time on the shimmering bay that I'd decided to. Sometimes physical perspective helps mental perspective, it increases vision. I could see for miles.

And what had I done to help anyone recently? I'd spent years in Hong Kong helping myself. Not that I was under any altruistic illusions about my sudden change of heart. No one does charity work for someone else's benefit; we do it because it makes us feel good. I wanted to feel good.

I slid my foot back into the rubber sandal, flexing my toes. It held.

Annie smiled mischievously at me. She took a step back down and looked over her shoulder. 'Al fresco?'

I blinked and tried to swallow. Was she suggesting what I thought? I stumbled quickly over the rotten roots like the starved animal I was. All this getting drunk and agreeing to get involved in some half-arsed murder investigation was only masking the fact that I was desperate for sex.

I honed in on the target up ahead, a bullseye in hot pants and a Versace T-shirt. We met in the middle and kissed hard and sweaty. I let my hand fall home, cupping a perfect breast in one hand.

'Hey, slowcoaches!'

I froze.

'What are you two doing? We've found something. Come quick.' Jiz's screeching voice cut through me like a schoolteacher's on a field trip.

Our lips were plucked gently apart and we looked each other in the eye. Annie looked down at my right hand and raised an eyebrow.

'Does she do this deliberately?' I said. 'Coz that woman's really getting on my wick. I mean, neither of them has even been to this secluded beach before. They don't even know the bloody way.'

The point of today's excursion was to get to the beach Ziegwalt and Jim shared. The previous night the pair of them had me in stitches listening to their comic daily life.

'What are you two doing?' Jiz shouted. There was a crash of twigs and some cursing. 'You're taking ages down there.'

'Looking at the birds and the bees,' I shouted back, removing my hand. 'Even educated fleas.'

'Well you two should come up here. We've found a… a thing.'

Annie looked at me and shrugged. 'Tonight, I promise.' She kissed my nose.

I watched Annie's buttocks again as she climbed. One of them had a large mosquito bite on it and I made myself feel disgusted by it. A consolation.

When we finally reached Jiz and Brenda they were standing, hands on hips, outside a small cave. An alcove really; just a dent in the limestone cliff face. On the floor were the remains of a campfire and a skewered, half-eaten animal that looked like a rodent.

'Bird's nest collectors,' I said authoritatively. 'They work the caves taking the nests. They sleep up here sometimes.' Annie stood closer to me, further away from Jiz. Put that in your pipe and smoke it, Miss Know-all Jism. I might have even rolled my shoulders, just for good measure.

'So what's this for then?' Jiz asked, holding up what looked like some twigs tied together. She handed it to me. It was a little doll, about the size of a Barbie doll made out of tree roots; arms, legs, a bundle for its torso and a small root bulb for a head. A face had been carved into the gnarly grain. 'Looks like you,' she said, and Annie took an infinitesimal – but I felt it – step away from me.

I almost let it get to me. 'Yeah, I'll have to stop shaving my head.' I rubbed my scalp. 'To ward off evil spirits. The locals believe in the *aswung*. Can you imagine how spooky it must be up here at night. All those bats.' Annie leaned in again, her arm going around my waist.

'What's an *aswung*?'

Well done, Brenda. 'It's their version of a vampire. It's a person that changes at night into a kind of bat. But only the wings. They still have a human head and body. Except they lose their legs when they take off. Funny, eh?' I shivered inwardly. 'The locals really believe it.' I handed the effigy back to Jiz. Beat that if you can.

'These locals, well educated, are they?' She picked up a battered copy of *Seven Pillars of Wisdom* by T. E. Lawrence from a rock and handed it to me. I blinked, trying to look unphased even though I'd been blown completely out of the water. Annie looked at me.

Jiz started to say something but I wasn't listening, instead looking around the little camp and trying to pick up sounds above her nasal whine. One of the strange things about El Refugio is the lack of birds. I'd noticed it before. In fact, the absence of any animal life on the mainland during the day. Bizarrely enough, it was different on the outlying islands.

A total lack of anything other than bats and swifts. No tweeting or twittering that you would normally find in the countryside. No leaves rustling in the trees as animals hop from branch to branch, and nothing in the sky except the occaisional white bird passing over us. Dead.

Jiz put the book back on the rock and we moved on up. Or rather they did. I stood for a while wondering about this little camp and the book. A military man's memoir. Could it be him? I turned and looked out over the land. It was a perfect lookout spot, I could see through a gap in the trees over the whole village.

'John.'

I could see the Hard Rocks, the junction, turn right and boom; a perfect view of Bonga's guest house. From here I could see everything and everyone coming and going from everywhere. That crafty old git. All he'd need are binoculars.

'John. We are at the top. The view! Is so nice.'

I turned and began to climb up, smiling to myself and trying to remember exactly where I'd seen his binoculars. They were in perfect condition. Worn with use but a beautiful example of 1940s Carl Zeiss workmanship.

What was the first thing Maximo did when he got behind the machine gun? He pulled out the binoculars. Next to the bunker was a beaten up old tailor's manikin with one eye, dressed in a moth-eaten US Army uniform. Sergeant Chipstick, he called him. The binoculars were always around its neck. If the bins weren't around the dummy's neck they'd be around Max's. And tonight he'd be sitting right here in this cave.

'Ha!' I stepped over a log with renewed vigour. What a day this was going to be. Maybe I'd make a detective after all.

5

We didn't get back to the village until early evening. Bats were beginning to blink nervously in the caves and swifts were finishing their evening feeding sorties, looping and spiralling on the wing. Aswungs were beginning to wake. The four of us, burnt to a crisp and filthy from the day trip, hurried through the village before it got dark.

What a day it had been at Ziegwalt's beach. I still couldn't quite believe what I'd seen with my own eyes; a real-life comedy. Somehow the climb made the lives of Ziegwalt and Jim all the more ridiculous, all the more cut off from reality.

A friend of mine once remarked, while we were travelling through India, that nothing was weirder than real life. And until today I'd thought nothing could top the things I'd seen back then, the amusing things Indians did, but especially the mad collection of long-term travellers we'd met on the beaches.

Until I arrived in El Refugio. Just when I thought the assemblage of weird foreigners who had been washed up on Asia's shores couldn't get any weirder, their lives any more out of the ordinary, along come Ziegwalt and Jim and their beach life. The first sign that things were going to be a little, how shall we say, unusual, came when we'd crossed the spine of the hill, descended the other side and came up against a fence. Bear in mind that El Refugio is a Marine World Heritage site, a designated place of outstanding natural beauty, the beaches and reefs the jewel in the crown.

'Achtung! Private Property', the sign read. 'Keep Out!' Ziegwalt couldn't give a shit. He'd turned up on his jet ski six years earlier and staked a claim. As far as he was concerned, it was his beach.

By the time we'd jumped the fence and walked through the trees to the shore I was almost choking with laughter. At one end of the stunning crescent of white sand, built tastefully into the jungle, was Ziegwalt's house. I'd heard a lot about it over the previous weeks but seeing was believing. He'd built, or rather he'd paid people to build, a sumptuous two-storey wooden villa. It had a raised veranda jutting onto the sand and was nestled unobtrusively into the trees.

With huge, carved epilwood (illegal) sliding doors, it sported the best, most silent air conditioning and electrical generator system that German technological brains could design, and produced a wonderful cooling breeze.

There was an open-air Jacuzzi built into the rocks that was heated from God knows where, and cunningly designed so that the naked bather was hidden from the prying eyes of tourists in passing boats. And a view of all the islands from the upstairs balcony that defied comprehension.

Oh yeah, and the sun hissed into the sea every evening for his pleasure. In short, it was tropical paradise. Not a single human being or man-made object as far as binoculars could see.

Unless, that is, you looked to the right, down to the other end of the beach. Down past the idle jet ski, past Ziegwalt's juvenile Filipina girlfriend washing clothes. Over the pile of collected firewood and up to the fallen-down shack where, you guessed it, Jim the posh Englishman was sprawled out stark bollock naked on a bamboo platform. It consisted of four driftwood poles, a split bamboo floor and a palm-leaf roof.

On the one hand we had Ziegwalt, a brash, 50-year-old German businessman with a taste for young girls, for whom, apparently, money was not an object, living in splendour. On the other Jim, a quaint, very well-spoken (I'm talking *Jeeves and Wooster* English here), 50-year-old Englishman living the way nature intended. An executive in excellence next to a toff in tatters. New money versus old. New money versus none.

The fun had really started when Jim decided to go swimming. We'd just been given a tour of Ziegwalt's place and were sitting on the balcony minding the views, drinking his ice-cold beers. Suddenly he bellowed at the top of his lungs. 'Hey! You have been on my side of zhe beach!' I nearly dropped my beer. 'Yes! I see your footprints in zhe sand,' he shouted.

At first I couldn't work out who he was talking to. I looked up and down the beach but could only see the girl. She'd stopped working and was squinting at the turquoise shallows. Then, when I looked closer at the water I noticed him. There, only his bare bum sticking up, was Jim, snorkelling. He looked up and lifted the mask. 'What?'

'And now you in my vater!'

'Oh, poppycock.' Jim turned around and began snorkelling the other way.

I asked Ziegwalt why two people with such different characters had chosen to live on the exact same beach when they had so many to choose from. 'We are goot friends,' he replied. 'I am here first and he wants a place in zhe paradise too. So I say yah. Why not? When I am in Germany for six months he looks after zhe haus. Es ist goot, no?'

They fed off each other in different ways, much the same as couples with different characters, one weak, the other strong;

Ziegwalt off Jim's *laissez-faire* attitude to life. He saw Jim as a kind of pet, I think, someone he could boss about, like the little girls he kept. Control freaks always befriend disorganised people.

Clearly Jim was broke and Ziegwalt provided a secure place to live and eat without being bothered by the law. No rent to pay, no food to buy (he pulled a lobster out of the reef before our eyes), and who knows, maybe even sex with Ziggy's girls. Ziegwalt seemed like a man who got what he wanted and Jim seemed like a bit of pushover. A power-crazed dwarf and a very well-educated Englishman with an inferiority complex. Opposites do attract.

There was one other essential service Jim provided, and that was demonstrated in all its glory before we left. One of the large resort boats filled with honeymooning Korean couples seemed to be heading right for his beach. I asked Ziegwalt if it bothered him.

'Jim!' he shouted. Jim looked up from the fire where he was grilling the lobster.

As the boat approached the beach, Jim took off his sarong and ran naked and screaming down to the sea to greet them. The captain fought with the wheel, turning the boat around and nearly throwing the shocked tourists into the drink. Brides blushed, discreetly zooming in with telephoto lenses, and middle-manager husbands fumed at the hiccup in their three-night, four-day schedule, covering their wive's eyes with sun hats. It was one of the funniest things I'd seen.

And I was still chuckling to myself at the thought now, 8 hours later, as we walked back through the town.

'What's so funny?' Jiz asked.

'The Jim and Ziggy show.'

Jiz snorted. She had not seen the funny side at all, going on and on about how 'that stupid Nazi dwarf' had no right to foul up the place with his bullshit little empire building, 'stamping his anal graffiti on pristine natural beauty that everyone has the right to enjoy'. She was right, of course, but refusing to drink his cold beer and storming off didn't help save the planet.

In fact, I pointed out, he was probably doing a service by living on that beach; a kind of environmental security guard. He may bomb around on a jet ski and shag underage girls, but he did keep the hordes at bay. And on a beach where turtles still layed eggs that was surely worth the cost of putting up with a man like Ziegwalt. Jiz asked what the use of a pristine environment was if no one was allowed over the fence to enjoy it, and I retorted by saying that was the cost to us all. Ecotourism is a contradiction in terms.

She had stormed off earlier in the day, and the only reason she was with us now was that she'd accidentally bumped into us on the way back. She'd spent a 'like, really cool day' squatting in filth with the local kids in the squatter camp, and had taken some 'like, amazing pictures' of a buffalo giving birth in the mud. She was covered in shit now and stank to high heaven.

We went our separate ways at the junction by the Hard Rocks, Brenda, Annie and Jiz followed by a column of flies going one way, me going the other. Annie and I would meet at Hard Rocks later and I said we could go back to my room if she wanted. I felt safer with Max out of the way.

A great day, followed, I was sure, by a great night. And perhaps an even greater day tomorrow when I'd sneak up on that old soldier in his cliff-top hideout and find out the truth. Now I just needed to check on those binoculars.

As I walked towards the front garden Ten, the police chief's assistant, appeared from inside the guest house and came to the gate. She had a folder in her hand. Suddenly I felt affinity of a kind I'd never experienced before; a bond with that old man. I hated the idea of this police deputy and her corrupt boss using this whole tragic loss to their advantage in some way. They'd probably be the only winners in all of this, gaining everything from poor Elsie's death.

I went to walk through the gate but she blocked it, running fingers through her hair flirtatiously.

'I heard you are from London. Do you have a girlfriend?' she asked.

So much for police questioning. 'Not really. What's in the file?' I asked, unable to peel my eyes off it.

'Wouldn't you like to know?' She tilted her head back and swished her hair. On the cover it read Case Number BB041 in green ink. She looked at the house quickly, then said, 'Suppose I show you. What then? I can, you know, I am a policeman.'

'Woman,' I corrected. Would she really live up to her IQ-inspired name? I decided to test it, and said, 'No, you shouldn't. You'll get in trouble. That's classified information. You need permission.'

She flared. 'Permission! If I want to look at any file in that cabinet I can. Take a look at this.' She opened the cover and held it up for me to read. 'See. Mr Bernard has been in trouble before.'

And he had. I flicked through the half-dozen yellow incident reports quickly. Mostly minor offences ranging from brawling to a verbal insult of the mayor, they pointed to nothing other than a man who, though a bit of a pain in the village neck, could be considered no worse than most of the local drunks. The last page, however, was intriguing.

'Quickly,' Ten said, looking nervously around, 'chief is inside. He will kill me.'

Stamped in the top right-hand corner was a rectangular red ink box that read 'For full file see P.P. 1048'. The incident was bizarre to say the least. Under 'Incident Description' it read simply 'Grave Robbing'. I leaned in to get a better look and it was snapped shut in my face.

'Monika!'

This time we both jumped. Ten pulled the file away from me. 'Yes, sir.'

Thomas the police chief was standing in the guest-house restaurant opening a suitcase on a table. He said something to her in Tagalog.

'I have found Mr John, sir,' Ten gloated.

I walked in, immediately looking at the manikin. The binoculars were gone.

'Good work,' said the chief, then turned to me. 'When will you be leaving El Refugio?'

I shrugged. 'Don't know. Why?'

Like all policemen he ignored questions. 'How long have you been staying here?'

'Month, give or take. Since Easter.'

He wasn't looking at me, instead rifling Maximo's suitcase, rummaging through all sorts of odds and sods. These ranged from neckties that had been folded so long they made perfect right angles, to a petrified frog that must have jumped in before the lid was shut for the last time, entombed.

'Is something wrong?' I said, trying to stand casually but feeling like the manikin. No binoculars, so the old man had them. I was standing on the top step, my rear exposed to the cliffs, and did a thumbs up behind my back, just in case he was in the cave watching. I could picture Maximo up there, glued to the scene through his lenses, false teeth glinting in the sun.

The chief chucked the gear back in the case and closed it, looking me right in the eye. A pot-bellied, thickset man with bloodshot eyes and a fat head, he fit every stereotype of the lazy, bloodsucking cop, or 'crocodile', as they're known in the Philippines. Not a bad analogy, referring to the animal's penchant for lounging around most of the day, resting its bulging stomach, moving only to snap and gorge. I still prefer the Thai parallel, though: mosquito.

'This is for you,' he said, and handed me a scrap of paper.

I unfolded it. It was a note from Max. Dear Mr Harris, Gone to Manila to pick up Sgt. Chipstick's monacle. Back in a week. P.S. Switch for water pump is in electric board at back of house. P.P.S. Don't forget to feed MacArthur. Maximo.

I looked up at the chief but my eyes missed, hitting the other dummy that stood behind him. Sergeant Chipstick. I focused in on the black hole where an eye used to be. There was something stuffed in the socket.

'We found that note in your room,' the chief said. I brought my focus into the foreground. 'Who's Sergeant Chipstick?'

I frowned, pretending to read the note again. 'Search me.'

'We have.' He took the note from me and gave it to Ten, who put it in the file. 'Don't go anywhere in the near future,' he said, and tried to pull a straining trouser belt over his belly. His pale blue shirt was stretched across his front, so that each button was trying to pull out of each buttonhole, creating running figures of eight down his gut. 'We don't want another stiff on our hands.'

I turned and watched them go down the path, out the front gate and drive off in their jeep. I went over to the manikin, dipping two fingers in its eye socket and retrieving a note.

VAMPIRES, DOVES AND FUGITIVES

1

'Morning, John!'

I looked up from watching my flip-flopped feet go back and forth and waved to Francis, standing in his dressing gown and curlers at the door of Hard Rocks, then looked back down at my feet and kept on walking. I had other things on my mind this morning.

The Russian. That's all that was written on the piece of paper I'd retrieved from Sergeant Chipstick's eye socket. I knew it was a man because Taddi, that mine of local information, told me so.

Taddi said there was only one Russian here and his name was Charlie. He hardly ever came to town because he lived on the dome-shaped island, that mysterious-looking peak that emerges from the sea half a mile offshore. In fact it dominates the whole seascape.

I turned right and then left into the Swiss Cafe street and quickened my pace. It was still only eight o'clock and Janet's boat tours never left much before nine, but I did not want to miss the free ride to the island Taddi had promised.

Janet's voice boomed from the upstairs cafe. I looked up just as her dog poked its head over the balcony. The horny little pooch bolted down the stairs. I was too quick for it this time, on the beach and in the outrigger before it had even unzipped its furry fly.

'Just trying to avoid the dog,' I said to a bemused Taddi. 'Seems to like me. Can't think why.'

He continued loading the boat. 'Janet is trying to set you up with one of the girls on today's trip,' he said, looking a little embarrassed by his wife's seemingly insatiable desire to get me hitched.

'What's she like?'

'That one.' He pointed to the upstairs cafe where four girls were getting acquainted at the table nearest the balcony. 'On the right. Israeli.'

I grunted.

'Yeah, I know; they are a pain in the arse.'

'Beautiful,' I added, 'but a royal pain in the ring.'

Taddi handed me the coolbox of beer and I placed it in the boat. 'I have told the captain to drop you on that beach there,' he said, pointing to the right-hand end of the distant island. 'Charlie lives at that end of it, I think. He is usually there working. If he is not, our boat will not come back until three o'clock, you know that.'

I said I did. 'I need a day away from this place. I'll just walk about if he's not there.'

'Did you get the chocolate?'

I put a hand in my shorts pocket and showed him the bars of Cloud 9 I'd bought. Among the things Taddi had told me about Charlie the Russian was that he adored chocolate. He didn't like visitors very much so it'd help break the ice if I brought him a gift.

In fact the whole reason he lived on an offshore island was because he liked the isolation. He'd chosen the most mosquito-infested place of the lot. Malaria and dengue were rife there because it had a swampy, stagnant freshwater pond somewhere in the middle. What better way to keep people away.

Eventually, once everyone had finished breakfast – and the two Israeli girls had stopped worrying about everything from whether they'd brought enough water, to the likelihood of being shot by Abu Sayyaf, to being capsized by a sudden typhoon – we got underway.

The boatman untied us, aimed us at the island and gunned the engine. The others nattered about their journey here, each trying to outdo the other, while I stared at the peak looming ever larger ahead.

As soon as we approached the island and navigated through the exposed corals, gingerly touching the prow on the sand, the captain began to reverse. I was standing on the narrow pointed nose and was thrown off the front onto the beach.

'Three o'clock,' he shouted back, revving the engine as hard as he could and disappearing around the rocks. Within seconds it had faded round the headland.

I stood in the shallows, slowly sinking in the sand and listening to the silence. There it was again; that crackle in the air. The sound produced by a total absence of everything. No bird sounds, no insects, just the morning heat bouncing off the rocks.

'Hello–o!' My voice flew over the jungle, hit the peak and came back like a hot whisper.

'Hello.'

I turned.

Staring at me from the other end of the beach was a giant in a sarong. Over 2 metres tall, Frank had said, and he wasn't far off. A white man, though he looked like the Wild Man of Borneo and was sunburned a deep rust colour. Muscular and slender, he had a mass of long tangled hair and a very long beard. Exactly, in fact, like Rasputin, the mad monk. It had to be the Russian.

'How's it going?' I said, feeling as though I was intruding on private property.

He nodded, the morning sun stroking his chiselled face with orange, the shimmering light from the ripples dancing in his piercing eyes. Without a word he walked towards me, occasionally bending for a closer inspection of the sand. He suddenly went down on all fours. 'Sometimes the monitors beat me to it,' he said, still on hands and knees and cocking his head to one side as if listening. He didn't sound Russian. 'Here.' He looked up at me and winked before scooping out the sand with both hands. 'How d'you like your eggs done, John?'

He knew my name! Some of my closest colleagues in Hong Kong didn't know my name.

'I like 'em scrambled with shredded cheese, pepper, salt and chili. Hot,' he said, and dug deeper. 'Do us a favour and check the pot over there.'

Pot? What pot? I cast about, pulling a leg free from the sand with both hands.

'In the water. See that float?'

'That bit of polystyrene?' I took off my shirt and waded nonchalantly into the sea, trying to look as tough as him. The float had a line wrapped around it and I held it aloft. 'This?' He looked through his hair and nodded before going back head first into the hole he'd dug, down to his waist now.

I pulled on the line. On the end was a cone-shaped basket made of bamboo about a metre long and 30 centimetres in diameter. Inside was an enormous green lobster flicking its fan-shaped tail at me angrily.

'Got one!' I shouted, blinking at the salt spray. When I looked at the beach all I could see was Charlie's bare buttocks sticking up as he picked out the turtle eggs and placed them carefully on the sarong he'd taken off. His dangling cock and balls pointed down at the hole like an arrow marking buried treasure.

'Bring it in,' his bum said.

As I worked my way back in, gingerly avoiding anemones and coral, I stopped to wonder what sort of past life would drive a man to this remote kind of existence, and whether I was completely safe. Asia is full of ex-cons and criminals from the West who've sought refuge way out East. This giant could easily whack me over the head and nab my gear, I thought. But there's something about nudity that instills trust.

When I got back to the beach he was sitting on the edge of the hole counting the eggs.

'… ninety-one, ninety-two. That's it. I'll put most back.'

The pile of eggs was enormous, a pyramid of glistening white ping-pong balls.

'Grab those baskets in the bushes there,' he said. 'Too many to carry in this.'

'I thought you said you'd put most back.'

'Monitors.'

'Are there lizards on every island?'

'Not those monitors, the Philippine Environmental Bullshit Monitors. The NIPAP, or whatever they call themselves these days. They steal everything, even the full-grown turtles. They sell them to the Chinese through our friends the Lams.'

'But they're funded by the EU.'

'So they're well-paid thieves. Give us a hand.'

I suppose it didn't really surprise me. The nicest building in town by far was the NIPAP office, and all I'd ever seen the staff do was sit around playing cards. God knows what it stood for but even the patrolmen, whose job it was to zip around local waters in their brand new Zodiac boats stopping the dynamite and cyanide fishing, spent their whole time getting drunk in the Hard Rocks. I should know, I'd got pissed with them on many occasions.

We loaded up the baskets with eggs and carted them over the rocks to a tiny cove where, he said, no boats could get in past the corals, and where he'd successfully buried and hatched thousands of turtles in the past. I asked him why the boatman had seemed reluctant to stop here.

'They think I'm the devil,' he said, chuckling. He patted the sand where we'd finished burying the eggs and stood, nonchalantly untying and rewrapping his sarong centimetres from my face, like a flasher. 'I couldn't care less what they think.'

And he couldn't, I could see it in him, in his manner. So many people I've met over the years, dropouts, so-called beach bums, those looking for an alternative lifestyle, were never really at ease with their lives. They claim to have forgotten their roots but live with and feed off the constant flow of backpackers. They need them, either financially or, more usually, for the company. All these people have really done is to transport their own lifestyle to a new plot of land.

This man was different. And as we walked towards the trees, towards the shack he called home, I gently probed into the circumstances of his life. I didn't ask if he was Charlie; there couldn't possibly be another person in the El Refugio area, on this island, who looked like this.

He was Russian by birth, but as a young adult had fled the country, first trying his luck in the neighbouring Eastern bloc and then further afield. Carpenter by trade, he began to wander the earth earning cash here and there, living life to the full and, he said, screwing as many women as possible. 'It's a numbers game, John.'

He eventually ended up married to a German woman with Australian citizenship, and they settled in Australia; the north-east coast to be more precise. Charlie had tried to be normal and thought he'd unpacked his bags for the last time, going about his hippy-chippy means of earning a living, this time by working in the local boatyard. It was fatal. One look at those tickets to freedom moored in the marina and he began to get restless.

He toiled away for a couple of years, the dutiful husband, getting up and going to work at the yard every morning, coming home every evening for a beer in front of the goggle-box. But unbeknownst to his wife he'd started a little project on the side. With his boss's permission, and using his own time and money, he finished work at five o'clock every day and set about building his own boat.

The yard owner allowed him use of any offcuts, surplus materials, etc. and the use of the yard's tools and facilities, providing he put in his full day for the firm. Charlie started to get up at five in the morning instead of seven, always first at the yard gate. He worked every weekend and even at night under lamplight to finish his pride and joy.

I asked him why he didn't tell his wife. He just shrugged and said, 'most women don't understand, you know that.' I did. He just didn't fit the settled, nest-building domestic life. No man does. The fact that most men do it is testament to their fear, from the pressure society's rules exert.

Two years later he had finished it. Hidden away in a quiet corner of the yard was Charlie's boat; a home-made, single-masted junk, without electric or electronics. No engine, no pump and only a sextant to navigate by. He'd also taught himself navigational skills at evening college.

'You just set sail?' I asked as we sat in his tiny palm-leaf beach shack grinding coffee and unwrapping the chocolate.

'Yep.'

'And you'd never sailed a boat before?'

'Nope. Sugar?'

'Yes, please. How did you know what to do?'

'It's easy. Basic trigonometry. Angles.' He poured the steaming water into two chipped mugs and handed one to me. As he continued his story he began working on a piece of wood at a makeshift bench beside me.

The first thing he'd packed that night, he said, and the one thing he still had with him ten years later, was the bag of carpentry tools he was using in front of me now. 'Get a proper trade, get some good tools and you're set for life. You'll never be out of work anywhere in the world. Look after your tools and they'll look after you.'

I watched as he went through his range of blackened chisels and routers, selected one and went to work, carving and caressing the wood with the blade. Brunette curls fluttered to the floor like those in a hairdressing salon, and I fell back into the story again, picturing the night he'd left his wife.

He'd studied the weather over the previous year and timed finishing the boat with the correct trade winds. His plan; to sail north and then west through Asia and see where the wind blew him. According to Charlie he was still in love with his wife at the time, and had broached the subject of moving on to pastures new, never of course mentioning the boat. She said no, again and again.

So, one morning when the weather was just right, he packed his tools for work as usual and never came back. One bag of tools and the shirt on his back. He left her all his cash and even his passport.

'What use was it to me?' he said, refilling my cup. 'I was no Australian. I'm a nomad. It's in you, is you, for life.' He chucked another coconut husk on the fire to keep the sand flies at bay but I was being flayed alive. The itching was incredible.

I sipped the woody blend and studied the rubber sole of my flip-flops again. Shit. This is what I was afraid of. For years I'd been wandering around looking for answers and this man was telling me that there was no answer. Bugger.

I asked him what had happened next.

'Made it through Asia then onto Africa. Spent the best part of five years trading goods up and down the east coast. From the Horn to the Cape and back, or from Mombasa to Yemen and back, using the boat as a container.'

He'd find out what was needed by the wealthy in one port of the continent, jump aboard, pull up the sail and fetch it from the poorest, cheapest part of the land. Vanilla, cinnamon, cloves, cocoa, and even, once, beautiful black women who went for a fortune in Saudi Arabia as concubines for rich Arabs.

'Imagine,' he said, 'just me and seven of the most stunning ebony women you've ever seen, all in that small boat for over a month. You should have seen them swimming naked every day out in the ocean.' He puffed his cheeks. 'And I was being paid a fortune to do it. The things men do for sex.'

The word 'slavery' popped into my head but I said nothing.

He put down the chisel and picked up the piece of wood, sighting along all four edges before going to work on it again. 'Then I came back to Asia. Give or take a few years.'

Over the next half-decade or so he had sailed around Asia, this time reverting back to his skill as a woodcarver, more often than not in the wealthy shipyards of Singapore, Hong Kong and Japan. It was during one of these return journeys, crossing the South China Sea, that he had come unstuck during a typhoon. Desperate for shelter, he aimed for the nearest land, which happened to be here. He eventually smashed into the reef off this island.

'That was two years ago. Been here ever since.' He blew some shavings off the bench and sighted again. 'That should do.'

'What are you making?'

'Books.' He went into a corner and brought out an enormous tome with a carved wooden cover, leather binding and a hundred blank pages. 'Desk diary, photo album, whatever they want. My girlfriend sells them to rich people in Manila for a fortune. She's there now.'

He plonked it on my lap. It weighed a ton. I'd seen a similar, if smaller, example at the Swiss Cafe. Janet used it as a guest book. I ran my fingers across its intricately worked wooden surface, trying to detect ridges or valleys. There were none, each piece laid and joined die flat. A masterpiece of woodwork, and all without mechanical tools.

'Where's your boat now?' I asked, heaving the book onto the bench.

'In the mangrove swamp,' he said, pointing at the wall. 'She's still seaworthy. I keep her patched and ready for when the day comes.'

'What day?'

'The day they chuck me out. They always do.'

'You're not doing any harm, are you?'

'What's that got to do with it? Sooner or later someone makes it their business to get rid of me. The authorities will think of some excuse and I'll be hounded out of here.' He gulped down the coffee and picked up a pot of paint. 'D'you want to see the boat? Grab that brush over there. I hope you're not afraid of mud.'

2

'Where?' I squinted into the reflected glare.

'There.' Charlie nodded at the windy estuary and continued tucking the sarong between his legs like a giant nappy.

I gazed out at the rippling grey water. We were standing at the edge of a mangrove swamp, the sun beating down on the half-mile-wide inlet. I still couldn't see his boat. The only man-made object breaking up the natural beauty of the bay, as far as my eyes were concerned, was what looked like a black shipping container midway across, sitting at an odd angle, half submerged.

'I still can't see it,' I said, squinting.

'Right there.'

'What, behind that container?'

'What container?'

'That block box with the tree, or whatever it is, sticking out the top.'

'That's the boat. Beauty, ain't she?'

I didn't know what to say. I didn't want to hurt his feelings, but I suppose I already had by calling it a container. 'You sailed all over the world in that? Jesus!'

It was hard to believe. Forgive my prejudices, but when someone tells me they have a boat I expect it to look like one. OK, most boats are white and this, uniquely, was matt black, but I can accept that affrontery to conventional yachting wisdom.

What was beyond comprehension was the unboat-like shape of the thing. It was, and I exaggerate not one bit, a 12-metre black rectangular box. With what looked like a telegraph pole sticking out the top.

'Single-handed,' he added, raising a finger, as if that would smooth the absurdity of the vision.

'What's that thing sticking out the top?' I asked.

'That's the mast. She's a single-masted junk.' He waded into the mud and sank to his knees. 'Come on then, if you're coming. We've got to get there and back before the tide flows. She's ebbing at the moment and it comes up quickly here.'

I snapped out of the terrible vision I was having of this man in that boat in high seas with seven beautiful, but ultimately useless, women as shipmates. It was a scary and astonishing thought. This giant in front of me, now cut down to size by the mud, was either very brave or very mad.

His possible insanity had crossed my mind more than once, but his very normal, warm way of talking had convinced me that he was in fact the most level-headed foreigner in the vicinity. Now, standing there in the hot light of day, I was beginning to sway on the side of insanity again. I wasn't sure at all whether I should follow this guy anywhere, never mind into a swamp to get to a half-sunken boat.

A squadron of pure white birds flew in formation into the estuary, banked across us and landed on the highest branches of the trees on the other side. 'Egrets,' Charlie said, noticing my gaze. He was now up to his thighs, holding the pot of paint on top of his head. 'You should see it at sunset. Huge fruit bats.' He held his hands a metre apart.

I stepped out of my flip-flops and gingerly squelched my way in. Grey mud with lumps and needles oozed between my toes like vomit.

'You feel that?' he asked. 'Those little pinpricks? Lice. They're harmless.'

Oh, that's all right then. I looked down at the blooms of grey churned up with each step, and the clods of clayey silt coating my hairy legs, and wondered what else was down there. 'Any snakes?'

'No. Some of the worms aren't far short.'

Ten minutes later we were standing chest-deep in the centre of the estuary beside what, even without the tricks played by light over distance, still looked exactly like a black metal box. The only difference I could make out now was the mass of rust blotches covering it like an outbreak of smallpox. It still didn't look like a boat.

He heaved himself out of the mud and up a rope ladder, then helped me aboard, reminding me not to cut myself on the burrs. 'Don't want tetanus.'

The deck was featureless with the exception of the wooden mast; no sail, no ropes, no cleats and not even a rail around the edge. Nothing. The only thing that stood proud of the surface was a kind of tank turret towards the rear, with a hand-high lip to stop the water washing down the hatch.

'You sit in here,' Charlie demonstrated, lifting the hatch and getting in, his bottom half vanishing below deck. 'Work the sail with one hand and steer with the other. See?'

Behind him at the stern was a wrist-thick scaffold pole that ran over the back. When I looked it was connected to a rusted steel rudder. He jigged it from side to side but it was jammed solid.

'Just mud,' he said. 'She's ready to go at any high tide.' And as if to prove her seaworthiness, he popped off the paint-pot lid, dipped the brush and began to sweep grey primer back and forth over rust holes that had eaten clean through the deck.

'Can I have a look inside?'

'Sure.' He disappeared down the hatch. 'Mind the sharp edges,' he repeated, his voice echoey, 'you don't want tetanus.' He grinned up at me through one of the corroded scabs.

I climbed down. The dark interior was medieval. A bare hull with a loose-planked floor above an open bilge. A few tea chests, a varnished upright of teak upon which hung a blackened Tilley lamp and a sextant. Stacked in an ottoman were rolls of shipping charts. It was like Sinbad the Sailor's boat. And the heat! The sweat began to pour down my body in rivers.

'Tea?' Charlie asked.

'Got anything cold?'

'No electrics on this tub, droog. Candle power.' He picked up a kettle, put it on a kerosene stove and opened a box of matches. The match flared, lighting everything briefly. The ribbed walls, the floor, the cobwebs, Charlie's beard, but especially the rear sleeping platform I hadn't noticed in the gloom.

And sitting on it, rubbing the sleep from his eyes like a baby was that old codger himself, Maximo Bonga, smacking his toothless gums together.

'Where the hell have you been?' he said, blinking rapidly and trying to look on the *qui vive*. 'I hope you've been feeding MacArthur.'

3

'Did you do it?' I'd waited long enough to ask that question.
I just couldn't hold it in any more. Ten minutes of silence as I
watched him doddering about making the tea drove me nearly
mad with frustration. Rasputin was back up on deck dabbing
rust spots with a bald brush while Maximo played mother.
Every time the old man went to fetch something from one place
or another, huffing and puffing his way over planks and crates,
he forgot what it was he was supposed to fetch.

'Tea,' he said, marking the air with a forefinger. He started to
rummage through a shelf full of odds and ends.

'It's there,' I said, pointing to the kettle. 'Beside the kettle.'

He put the sugar he was carrying down on the shelf and came
back to the teapot. 'Spoon. Now where does Charlie keep 'em?'

They were beside his head in a jar. 'Three o'clock,' I said.

'Already?' He checked his watch.

'No, the spoons.'

He cast about.

'There.'

He still couldn't see them. 'There!' I said, getting up and
taking a spoon for him.

'Damn dark in here.' He scooped some tea from the caddy
in the direction of the pot but completely missed it. One after
another was heaped onto the floor, falling like iron filings.
'Three... make it four. One for his knob.'

I couldn't help sniggering. Not one spoonful of tea had hit the pot.

He held the caddy to the candle and peered inside before shouting, 'Need more tea, captain. Nearly out.'

There was the sound of the paint pot clanging down on the metal deck above my head before a distant voice said, 'What? I only bought that two days ago!'

God, I thought, it was like being with Laurel and Hardy. The one where Stan and Ollie, flush with cash from their new fishmonger business, decide to buy an old boat and do it up. Next thing I know Maximo will have his head stuck between the mast and the bulkhead. Rasputin will be on the very top painting the tip of the mast and the old man will be sawing blithely through it.

He put the caddy down and lined up three cups.

Sugar, I thought, that's the next thing. He's forgotten where he put the sugar.

'Sugar,' he said. 'Now where does he keep the stuff? Can't stomach it myself, but the captain...' With hands on bony hips he peered into the gloom, head forward, eyes squinting.

'On that shelf, Max.'

'What shelf's that?'

'There. The one you left it on.'

'Damn these candles. Bloody hopeless. Keep telling Charlie to get... Charlie!' he shouted, crossing back to the shelf, stumbling over my foot and picking up the jar next to the one he'd put down. 'Charlie! I keep telling you to buy a new mantle for that lamp. Can't see a damn thing down here!' He went back. 'How many?'

'Two, please.' This time the sugar hit the spot. At least it would be sweet hot water. He put no less than six (*six*!) spoons of sugar into Charlie's mug.

As he stood waiting for the kettle to boil the question I'd asked seemed finally to cross his mind and he stared at the bench in front of him. Next to the teapot was a large kitchen knife. He reached out and took it just as I was about to repeat the question.

'No,' he said, putting the knife down, 'of course I didn't. What do you take me for?'

I wasn't sure how to put this delicately. 'Has your knife gone missing? The big army one.' I shifted uncomfortably on the plank. It's hard to sit still when you're at a 30-degree angle. The pain in my legs from trying to stop myself sliding along to the other side was growing.

He looked me in the eyes. 'It was found next to that girl. I know.' The kettle whistled and he removed it from the heat. 'I saw her.'

'You saw Elsie that morning on the beach?'

'I'm up at five, remember. I'm always the first person on the beach.'

'But when I got there, you weren't there.'

'Of course I wasn't there! What would you do? I panicked.'

'What would I do? I'd go to the police, that's what I'd do. How do you think this looks?'

He huffed at my suggestion and, using a cloth, picked up the kettle and poured it into the pot. Half of it ran down the side before he noticed the clouds of steam billowing around him and corrected it.

'Go to the crocodiles? This is the Philippines, mister, not jolly old London town. Out here it's your knife so you did it. Lock him up, close the door and close the case. No more questions.' His bottom lip quivered with an old man's fear. He was scared.

'But someone else's fingerprints would be on it.'

'Fingerprints, he says.' He looked at me as though I was ten years old. 'This is El Refugio. And that fat idiot police chief and his poodle Ten wouldn't even know how to unscrew the top of the powder pot if they had one. Fingerprints,' he repeated to himself, stirring the water in the pot. 'Know why they call her Ten when her real name's Monika?'

'Because of her IQ?'

'No. Because it costs ten dollars to bribe her.'

I watched him stand there, stirring and thinking, even more convinced than ever that he had nothing to do with this. My eyes had become accustomed to the gloom and for the first time it struck me just how resilient this man was. How many 85-year-olds in London would still be in his condition?

There he stood in his shorts, bamboo legs and coathanger shoulders, and he wasn't even close to giving up. Most pensioners I knew could barely stand at that age, never mind get to this island, cross a mosquito-infested jungle, climb rocks and then wade through a swamp to live in a container.

'You know they've got Bernard locked up,' I said.

'Nothing happens here without everyone knowing about it. Bernard was standing next to the body, he gets locked up. That's the way the police mind works. If you'd been there, you'd be behind bars.' He put the lid on the pot and poured it into the cups. 'He didn't do it.'

A question burned on my lips like scalding tea, and when he brought the chipped mug across to me I asked it. 'So why don't you just tell them your alibi? Tell them where you were that night.'

'It wouldn't make the slightest bit of difference,' he said, putting the mug down. 'They don't care about the truth. All they want is an easy life. I'm amazed they've even bothered coming to my place for answers.'

'Well, they found your knife.'

'So what? The crime scene is altered to fit the suspect in this country. God only knows why he didn't chuck the knife in the sea himself and let Bernard rot, that's the usual procedure when a policeman finds something that might ruin his case. Captain on deck!' he shouted.

Charlie's upside-down head came through the hatch. He took the mug from the old man, disappearing again.

'You going into hiding is hardly going to help though, is it? It's like an admission of guilt.'

'You're not listening, soldier. They found someone standing over the body, so it's him who did it. Elsie was an ex camp follower, he was her jealous boyfriend. The only reason, as far as I can tell, that the case is still open and they're looking for me is because it's a foreigner in cuffs. Very inconvenient for the chief. Lots of paperwork. Not to mention a black mark on the town's name if it ever gets out.'

He rummaged through some things, found a packet of biscuits and sat down.

'And old man Lam wouldn't want that, would he?' He took out a biscuit and dunked it, frowning at the taste. 'El Refugio needs tourists and this little episode would really put the kybosh on things.'

Sometimes I marvelled at Max's English. All those years spent listening to the Voice of America and the BBC World Service on the wireless had paid off.

'Tourists?' I asked. 'There are only a dozen of us in town.'

As I leaned across, reaching for a biscuit, Charlie's voice rung out from above like a wounded seagull. 'Arrgh! It's got salt in it!'

'Not those tourists,' Maximo went on. 'You only bring in pennies, and none of it finds its way into Lam's pocket. It's the big resorts they're worried about. The Korean tourists, they pay in dollars. It'd kill the golden goose. It was the same when those missionaries got kidnapped a few years ago. You can bet your bottom dollar old man Lam had the chief round his house the moment he found out. Find a local to pin it on and keep it quiet.'

'You.'

He nodded. 'Now do you see why I ran off. When I saw that body and my knife I came to the only conclusion possible. Then I ran to the only person I could trust. The only person who trusts me.'

'There's no tea in it!' Charlie shouted. 'What the hell!'

Coming from a country where you're innocent until proven otherwise it was an almost impossible concept to grasp. But what was the point of telling him to go and tell the truth if the corruption went right to the top? If the person, or family, who ran the whole show needed a fall guy, then fall Maximo would.

And I could see his point about how much money was at stake. While the guest houses in town were making 200–300 pesos for each of the few backpackers, the resorts were charging 300 dollars per punter per night. Who cared about one eccentric old drunk? No wife, no kids. Who'd miss him?

'The very best we can hope for is that someone in the capital will get involved,' he continued. 'But even there the Lams have enormous influence. If it got to Manila we might stand a chance.' He shook his head. 'I don't know. Money buys everything in this country, including justice. Everyone has a price.'

We sat in silence for a moment and I listened to the sound of Charlie above my head, his paint pot scraping along when he'd finished a spot. Did Charlie have a price, I wondered? How much would it cost to pay off his conscience? Here he was, living in a shack in the middle of nowhere, carving out books from driftwood. Would he buckle if offered five thousand dollars? But what would it buy him? He had run away from all that. He'd escaped and now had the tropical paradise most millionaires were saving up for. And he'd done it all for free.

And what about me? What was my price? Suppose Lam offered me a suitcase full of cash to point the finger. Would I? What would it buy me? I'd had bags of cash in Hong Kong over the years and had put most of it up my nose. What a joke.

I looked up through one of the rust holes just as Charlie's face came across it, blocking the sun. He smiled. An unconditional smile that carried nothing with it but joy; no expectations, no unease and no demand for a smile in return.

'Not everyone has a price,' I said, staring into the old man's eyes.

Maximo stared back. A beautiful smile crept across his wrinkled old face and he touched my hand.

4

I didn't bother going back that night. How could I? There was just too much to talk about, with both of them, and an afternoon wasn't enough. Twenty-four hours probably wasn't enough, but I felt that's all I could risk without drawing too much attention.

Thomas the police chief was sure to be sniffing around the guest house, and he'd specifically told me not to leave. The last thing I wanted to do was lead him straight to the old soldier. One night should be fine, though, I thought. It was unlikely that the chief would wonder where I was, and I knew big Frank would play dumb.

As well as talking to the two men I wanted to stick around to watch the show. Sunset over the estuary was full of promise.

So when the Swiss Cafe's boat came back to fetch me that afternoon, bombing towards the beach, boatman ready with the reverse gear, I declined the ride. Charlie had built his own little wooden sailing outrigger. He said he'd take me back the next morning.

So that evening the old man and I sat on the rusty old deck of the container and watched the sun say goodbye, while Charlie cooked on shore.

Six o'clock he said it would start and at six o'clock it did.

'Six,' Max said. 'Told you.' He showed me his watch. It said seven.

'That says seven,' I said.

'That means six.'

It started with dribs and drabs but within minutes the sky was black with them. Bats. These things were like monsters, like nothing I'd ever seen. They looked more like flying dogs than bats, with a thick furry mane, glistening eyes and pointed ears. I could even see the veins in their metre-long sinewy wingspan. And the noise! It was like sitting in the centre of a gigantic aviary.

Ten minutes later the sky had gone purple and it was over; the bat show, that is. The sunset was beyond belief. A sky full of every colour of the rainbow, from one rim of the hemisphere to the other. A flashing, popping sunburst that gave me a stiff neck.

It was the first time I realised where the term 'sunburst' came from. As far as I was concerned it had been invented by the Fender guitar company to describe a particularly colourful finish on their Stratocaster guitar. Now I could see the whole of the heavens in exactly the same design, minus the pick-ups and knobs.

'I wish I'd brought my camera,' was all I could say once Charlie and I were sitting around a fire on the beach. Now the sky was full of stars and planets; Venus, Mars and Saturn lined up beautifully near Orion, and unusually bright.

Not that I knew anything at all about the constellations. Sitting next to me, however, was Charlie, an expert. If you really want to know about the night sky, ask a sailor, not an astronomer. A real sailor, one who has spent his life navigating by them. One who has put his life in their hands, not GPS.

Our dinner was lobster, crab and squid, all washed down with Charlie's own brew of fermented coconut milk called tuba. We even had after-dinner cigars; tobacco leaves rolled into a cone by a woman in the village. Charlie had taken her and her grandson to her husband's burial on a remote island during a storm when no one else would dare put to sea. She'd paid him the only way she could; in trade.

The only sadness that night, I suppose, was the old man's absence. I'd like to have heard the pair of them trying to outdo each other with their tall tales. Maximo couldn't make it across the mudflat. By the time sunset was over the tide had already flowed and ebbed again, and the outrigger couldn't get in. I offered to give Maximo a shoulder carry but he declined, saying he wanted to be alone.

In any case I'm not sure how much fun the old man would have been. His mood seemed to darken with the night.

And when the next day Charlie and I caught the flowing tide across to see if he wanted to go ashore before we left for the mainland, he still seemed dispirited. Charlie knew him better than most and didn't bother to reply, simply pulling the sail up in his little outrigger and turning us around. 'Ready about.'

'A beautiful day,' I said, squinting into the morning light and scratching my bitten body.

Charlie tacked into the wind and pulled hard on the sheet. The boat tilted, one outrigger now well out of the water; we cleared the estuary grey and pushed into the blue.

'Next time you come I'll show you how I catch crab,' he said, sweeping the tangled mass of hair from his eyes. 'Pearls too.'

We rounded the island and shot across the straight towards the village, its familiar smoky shore now seeming like a polluted metropolis.

There was an explosion in the distance. Not big, more like a gun firing, and I frowned at Charlie, waiting for the explanation. He frowned back. A minute later it came again and I noticed a small cloud of smoke drifting down a beach. Jim and Ziegwalt's beach.

As we passed close on a tack I could see Ziegwalt squatting on the sand with a papaya balanced on a rock in front of him. He saw us.

'Goot mornink to you! Come! Come! You vant beer?' he bellowed.

'Ready about,' said Charlie, and I ducked just as the boom passed across and we raced seaward again.

'Maybe later,' shouted Ziegwalt. He pulled the cigar from his teeth, touched it to the fruit and ran. There was a wisp of smoke and a second later the papaya blew apart.

'He's blowing up fruit,' I said.

'That is one bored midget.'

Ziegwalt wiped orange papaya flesh from his face and went back to inspect the remains, carefully studying the single piece that hadn't been vaporised. He held it aloft to Jim, who was sitting on a rock, then turned and picked up a fresh watermelon.

We cleared the headland and were on our run into shore, Charlie looking straight ahead. 'Where do you want me to drop you?'

'Do you know Gladys's?' I said, thinking how much it would impress Annie and at the same time get up the nose of Jiz, seeing me sailing in.

'Yeah. Are you sure, though? Look.'

I turned. Outside Gladys's, just as we pulled into El Ref's smoky bay, I could make out the chief's jeep, and standing on the back looking at us through a pair of binoculars was the chief himself, Inspector Lestrade Bacudo of The Yard.

5

'It is just an informal inquiry. We need all the help we can get. You want to help, don't you?' I nodded reluctantly and the chief looked over his shoulder at Ten sitting in the back seat of the jeep.

She looked well pissed off for being told to sit in the rear. About fifty kids were trying to hang on the sides and she looked like she was going to shrivel up and die with the shame of it.

One of the kids took her hat. Then a basketball was accidentally-on-purpose thrown and hit her on the head. Ten went berserk, jumping out the rear with flailing arms. The kids scattered. She picked up the ball, pulled out a pocketknife and drove it in: Psssshhh.

A fresh-faced boy with tear-filled eyes walked up to her, held out his hands, looked first at me, then in deliberate English to embarrass her said, 'I'm telling Mum.'

Ten's face looked like the sunset I'd seen the day before. 'I work for the Philippine National Police.' She tucked the ball under the seat. 'You think I have to do what mum says? Go home. Go to hell. It is illegal to play basketball in the street anyway, so mum will be on my side.'

Thomas turned the key in the ignition but there was just the sound of the alternator clicking away. He sighed and tried again. I flicked a switch on the dash and the siren and flashing light came on. The chief switched it off. 'We will get a tricycle.'

'Why don't we just walk?' I said. 'It's only five minutes.'

He ignored me, heaving his fat gut out of the front seat and waving down the road at a driver who was dozing in the back seat of his motorized three-wheeler. The man rose like a praying mantis, languidly got into the front seat and started his engine. First time. There was an audible ripple of laughter from the kids.

'Go about your business.' Thomas barked. No one moved. Gladys, standing at her gate with the maid, turned and left, and an old man went back to sleeping on a hammock. Annie, Jiz and Brenda were watching from the front yard of the guest house, along with all the kids in the street.

The Philippines tricycle (a 125cc motorbike with a sidecar not much bigger than an old pram, and meant to seat two) is a bastard to get in and out of at the best of times, but for the chief it was like trying to get a quart into a pint pot. He tried getting into the tiny carriage head first but because of his swinging stomach couldn't. In the end he reversed in, falling into the seat with his fat arse. The whole vehicle rocked from side to side.

'Keystone Cops,' I heard Jiz say.

'Monika,' Thomas said to Ten, using her real name. He poked his head out the vehicle like a chubby cuckoo clock, 'get another tricycle. I will meet you there.' He roared off in a cloud of two-stroke fumes. Ten and I and the punctured basketball followed in another tricycle. It took 30 seconds.

How ridiculous, I thought, stepping into the municipal building courtyard; a tiny village like this with taxis. To walk from one end to the other, from the point where the road ran into a dead end at the cliffs to the bus terminus only took 5 minutes. How had the locals become like this? So lazy.

As we walked through the courtyard toward the little police office, more apathy stared me in the face. Government workers slumped asleep over typewriters, drivers asleep under trees, an engineer in the Highways Department using his drawing board as a headrest. And no end of administration staff eating, chatting, dozing or picking their noses.

Lam, I thought, crossing into shade. It had to be. Everyone worked for him, and to get money from central government they had to show a resource. The size of the building alone could have handled a small city, never mind this little village.

It was all for show; just so the mayor could justify huge sums from the public purse for the upkeep of buildings that didn't exist and the people to staff them. No one was doing anything because there was nothing to do. The jungle and the sea run themselves. It reminded me of the Phantom Battalions I'd heard about, where army generals produce lists of fictitious recruits, hundreds strong, just to get money from central government into their pockets.

'Just in here,' Ten said, gesturing to a door.

'I don't see the point,' I said, going in. 'I don't know anything.'

'You may know something without knowing it.'

That makes sense.

Inside the small office were two desks, a filing cabinet and a motionless electric fan. It was stifling.

'Electric doesn't come on until four, as you know,' Thomas said.

We sat, myself and the chief at one desk, Ten at the other. A moment later an old man came in struggling with a pre-war Imperial typewriter and dumped it, puffing and blowing, in front of Ten. She pulled a piece of paper from her desk, inserted it and began clunking away.

'Is that really necessary?' I asked, scarcely believing I was still in El Ref. It felt like the tricycle had taken us back to Manila; to a less wise, altogether more crooked place.

'Two Rs or one?' asked Ten. 'Harris.'

I sighed. 'Two.'

'Ha-rris,' she hissed, hammering the keys. 'Nice name.'

'Just treat her like she's not there,' said Thomas, and launched straight into the question I was dreading. 'Have you seen Maximo Bonga?'

'He is the owner of your guest house,' added Ten.

'I know who he is,' I said, thankful for the distraction. 'Um... no. No, I haven't.' I sat quiet. And then he did what teachers in school used to do to me, what they're so good at. He said nothing, just looked and waited. He sat back in his chair, pulling a pack of Marlboro from his top pocket and a navy blue NYPD cap from his drawer. He put the cap on, yanking it down tight, and lit the cigarette.

Just keep shtum, I told myself, feeling my face burn and trying not to wipe the sweat. Suddenly I could hear everything; kids playing outside, the sound of a tricycle revving, a man selling balut (a fertilised duck foetus boiled in the shell), even the low background noise of a far-off generator. Thomas drew on the cigarette and I could even hear the snap, crackle and pop of the chemically saturated tobacco burning.

It was torment. It's the oldest trick in the book and I, stupid git, a man who'd left school behind so long ago, did what all liars do when confronted with a question followed by silence; I filled it.

'No, I haven't seen him,' I repeated.

'You have said that,' Thomas said, and turned to Ten. 'Did you get that? He has not seen Mr Bonga.'

'Yes, sir.'

'How many times did you write it?'

'Two times, sir.'

'Good. She does not miss a trick. Just imagine she's not there. Do not type that.'

Why had I agreed to come here? I could have refused. It was turning into a nightmare. One question and I wanted to faint. And why me?

'Am I the only one being questioned?'

'No.' He leaned across and flicked his ash into the nautilus shell he used as an ashtray. I wanted to slap him.

A nautilus. Of all the shells he could have picked, he'd chosen one of the rarest and most beautiful. And the one shell shape that is least suited to be used as an ashtray. In fact he'd had it stuck to the side of a large wooden paperweight, on end, just so the opening was uppermost and therefore of use to him.

The anger I felt helped me compose myself. 'Well, is that it? 'Cause I want to go swimming with my girlfriend.' I put both hands on the armrests.

'A few more questions.' He lifted the peak of his cap a little before pulling it down again. 'Why have you been here so long? Most tourists only stay three or four days.'

'I like it.'

'Is that it?'

'Yeah.'

'Don't you have a job to go back to? A wife? Family?'

'No. Is that a crime?'

He didn't like my attitude and leaned in, pulling the cap off and placing it on the desk. 'What did you do on that island for two days? No one goes there except bird's nest collectors. Did you know its full of malaria?'

'I went to see Charlie.'

'Mm, that man...' He looked across at Ten. She was focusing on a word, apparently wondering how to spell it, her tongue sticking out the corner of her mouth in thought.

'C, H, A, R, L, I, E,' I said. 'Like Chaplin but without the Chaplin. What, I can't go to visit a friend, is that what you're saying?'

'No. But someone has murdered a person in our peaceful village and I do not think it is a good idea to wander off alone. Especially not over there.' He took a deep breath. 'This is the Philippines, not America.'

'He is England, sir,' Ten said, looking chuffed.

'Well this is not England, either. It can be a dangerous place, and there are some bad people. I'm sure you know about the Abu Sayyaf.'

'Oh, come off it.' I used exaggerated body language as cover to wipe the nervous sweat running down my face. 'Don't you think you're overreacting?'

'I have lived here most of my life. People like you come and go. I know what's what in this place. I have seen it before. Abu Sayyaf, drug addicts, crazed alcoholics, and even the criminally insane; we've had them all here. We still have them. It's the end of the road.'

'It's hardly inner-city Manila.'

'You see, that is the trouble with you people. You come here with your own ideas about our country and do not learn.'

'It's a tiny village on the edge of an insignificant island, for God's sake. Why should I be worried if some local drunk goes off his nut one night? How on earth does that affect me? I swim in the sea and eat coconuts. That's about as daring as it gets.'

I sat back this time, feeling smug, and even grinned a sly little grin at my own bravado. That told him.

'Did you know that our provincial capital has the Philippines' largest open prison?'

My grin slipped.

'And that it holds many of the country's worst offenders; murderers, serial rapists, arsonists, from every province. You name it, we have them. All life sentences.'

My grin slipped further.

'Just outside the city you arrived at by ferry from Manila. Very big.'

'What do you mean, "open"?'

'What I said. Open. No fences,' he replied confidently, with more than a hint of sadistic pleasure. 'Out in the countryside. The inmates work in the paddy fields during the day and are locked in at night. They farm, or make things for sale in the market. There is a good chance you have eaten their rice.'

'But what's stopping them from escaping?' I asked, leaning forward and beginning to perspire more.

He stubbed the cigarette on the sole of his boot and flicked it out the window. 'Willpower? A moral sense of right and wrong?'

'What? Killers don't know the difference between right and wrong. That's why they're killers.'

He shrugged. 'It is not my idea. Some soft bureaucrats in Manila thought it up years ago. If I had my way I'd hang a lot of them.'

'Firing squad is better,' chimed Ten.

'Hanging's cheaper, though, Mon. No bullets, just a rope.'

'Yes, sir. You're right. And only one man needed to do it.'

'Uh-uh. Two. One man must be a witness.'

'And don't forget the priest, sir; to pronounce them dead on arrival.'

I watched the conversation go to and fro, wondering if either of them was really serious about all this. They'd just dropped a bomb on my head, informing me for the first time that I was in fact taking a holiday on the Philippines' version of Alcatraz – a fenceless Alcatraz! – and now they were discussing the best way to carry out a death sentence.

'But remember,' Ten dared to add at the risk of contradicting her boss, 'we must pay the hangman and his assistant. Wherein, sir, soldiers are already in service to the nation.'

The chief nodded and looked at me. 'She's going to make a fine policewoman. Already you can see she has the right way of thinking.' And then he gave the game away. Just like the liar in me and the fibber in the naughty schoolboy, so he couldn't shut up. 'So you see,' he went on, 'we also have good detectives here. It's not only you who can solve crimes.'

Whether he felt threatened personally, or was simply trying to scare the pants off the only person he believed capable of rocking the outrigger, it was unclear. What was obvious was that someone, probably Janet, had told him I was a detective. It didn't matter to me that I wasn't. The tables were turned.

'So who do you think did it?' I asked, feeling a little confrontational.

He got up from his chair and stretched before going to the window and doing a 'psst!' noise at someone. 'We have suspects.' A balut hawker came to the window, lifting the cloth off his basket of eggs for a quality inspection. The chief picked up a few, selected four good ones and paid the man, also taking a little bag of salt and chili vinegar. He sat down.

'So you think Maximo Bonga killed Elsie?' I said. 'Why would he do that?'

'I do not think anything. He has disappeared, that's all. He is an old man and we do not want him to injure himself.' He tapped a boiled egg on the desk and peeled it. The duck's head flopped out, dangling on the tiny thread-like neck.

'I think he can look after himself.'

He sucked out the juice and then, unusually for balut eaters, who typically consume it in three parts: The Slurp, The Decapitation and The Main Attack, peeled the whole shell, rolled it in salt and popped it in intact. 'Ou can go ngow.'

I didn't want to watch this fat pig at feeding time. It was disgusting listening to his sucking and tongue-clicking noises.

He put his feet up on the desk and I would love to have pushed him right over.

'But remember what I said,' he went on, wiping an oily trickle of embryonic fluid from his chops. 'Watch your back.'

I turned and left without replying.

Outside in the sun I felt good again, and hungry. The Swiss Cafe would be open for breakfast. In celebration I caught a tricycle instead of walking. Bollocks to the ozone layer.

'A girl been lookin' fo' ya, boy. Sweet as honey, too.' Frank leaned back, knife and fork at the ready as the plate of bacon and eggs was placed in front of him by the waitress. 'Hey, and don't you forget my...' A further plate piled high with fried tomatoes and toast that wouldn't fit on the first was brought by another waitress. 'Thata girl, hek hek.'

I sat next to the big man, first checking that the coast was clear of that bloody dog.

'I've already seen the policewoman,' I said. 'This morning.'

'Not her,' Frank said. There were seven fried eggs on his plate. I watched as he criss-crossed them with his knife and fork until the whole lot was a blend of chopped orange and white. He began spooning them onto slices of toast.

'Local?' I asked, confused.

'Ung.' He nodded while fitting the toast into his hole, just like he'd done with the pizza.

The only local girl I really knew, if you can call him that, was Francis at the Hard Rocks. Why would he be looking for me? I cast about for a moment as Frank chewed, holding up a hand for me to wait so he could enlighten.

Janet's head popped around the kitchen door, sending a waitress out with two trays of food and a stinging insult before she acknowledged me. 'Hi, John! Look how many girls we have on our tour today! Look how beautiful they are!' I shrank. 'This is John!' she shrieked at the top of her lungs. 'He is single!'

God bless Janet and her attempts to get me hitched. Why do married people always do that? Bloody annoying for a woman, fantastic if you're a man, a nightmare for both if you're already chasing someone.

'Not any more, doll,' Frank said, readying another slice. 'Got himself a perdy little thang from this 'ere bee-utiful country. Filipinas are the most lovin' women on God's earth. No offence to you girls,' he said to the few tourists waiting for their boat tour to start.

I asked Frank if he meant Francis. 'You know, from the videoke bar.'

A slither of yoke had run down one of his chins and congealed on the end like puss. As he stared out the corner of his eye at me a fly stuck to it like a magnet. 'Say, boy, you ain't–'

'No, Frank, I'm not. But I don't know any Filipina girls.'

Using a knuckle he scraped off the yoke and licked it clean. 'Well this one's a gal. Believe me.' In went the egg sandwich, followed by the fly. More yoke oozed out the corners of his mouth and down his jowl folds like orange lava from Mount Pinatubo. 'Said she wants to meecha. Said she'll be at the church for midday mass.'

Janet looked suspicious. 'What girl?'

'The one that come here this mornin'.' He made another egg and bacon feast and held it in both hands. 'That dirty one. Hoo-ee.'

Janet was mortified. 'John, you will not meet her. Do not even think about meeting her. She is a prostitute from A Better Place.'

'A better place? What, like out of town?'

'No. A Better Place. It's the name of the town's whorehouse.' She gritted her teeth. 'Damn shit, coming in here. I threw her out. They should have never allowed that place in this town.'

'El Ref has a brothel?' I smiled. 'Where?'

'What, you want to go there?'

'No, just asking,' I lied. I'd never been in one in my life but I'm pretty curious. Combine that with this whole mystery and it added up to something bordering on an Agatha Christie novel.

'Then you do not need to know where it is.'

'It's on the road out of town,' Frank said. 'Just as you pass between the cliffs.' Janet glared at him. 'Not that I've been inside or nothin'.'

She glared at me. 'Oh, John, I did not think you were like that. I am so disappointed.'

'Hang on a minute, Janet, I'd never even heard of this place.'

She wandered into the kitchen shaking her head as though her only begotten son had been caught with a common tart.

I looked at Frank. 'You going to church?'

'Mm-hm. Me and the missus. She's there now.' He shouted out for another coke.

I picked up my tea.

6

'You're going where?'

'Church.'

Annie, Jiz and Brenda, all sitting in the same enormous double bamboo hammock, goggled at one another. I think the palm tree was bending under the combined load.

'What, I can't go to church?'

'He has had a religious experience on the island,' added an earnest-looking Brenda while drawing an EU flag on her leg cast. She looked up and placed a concerned hand on my shoulder, then pulled my head into her bosom. 'Go on. You must cry now. I will hold you.'

I pulled my head out of her cleavage, somewhat reluctantly it has to be said. 'No, it's nothing like that. I just said I'd meet someone there, that's all.' They looked at each other. Jiz looked at Annie and raised her eyebrows as if to say, 'See? Told you all men are the same.' Cow.

I clarified. 'Someone who might be able to tell me about Elsie.'

'What about our day trip to Charlie's island, though,' Annie asked. 'You promised.'

'The boat doesn't leave until one. I'll be there at Janet's,' I said, taking a tentative step away to see how Annie would react. Her face said, 'If you don't get on the boat, don't come knocking on my door tomorrow.'

'We will wait for you,' Brenda said.

I looked at Annie, taking another step away. 'OK, Annie?' She shrugged and I thought, bloody hell, you could hardly blame me if I was getting it elsewhere. I've tried, God knows I have, but you're always with Pure & Simple here.

I wanted to sleep on a deserted island but part of me was asking what the point was. Sleeping under the stars was ten-a-penny in El Ref; it was sex under them I was after. I could picture myself tomorrow morning as we arrived back here; Jiz and Brenda animatedly discussing the previous night's events while I felt utterly frustrated. Apart from anything else, my balls hurt.

'We will wait for you, John.'

I turned and walked off towards the church, Annie's sigh ringing clear as a bell in the belfry.

'Sing alelu-hoo-ya. Sing allelu-hoo-ya. Sing alleluyah to the Lord!' Silence descended.

'Please be seated,' said Father Hilario reverently. The hundred-strong congregation ducked en masse to his command.

Tall and thin for a Filipino, and with a short grey beard, Father Hilario Resurreccion (only in the Philippines, where the national head the Church is called, and I kid you not, Cardinal Sin) was quite a good-looking man for his years. Mid fifties, I'd have said. It wasn't easy to see from my position at the back of the church.

He placed both hands on the pulpit and looked around his congregation, focusing on no one in particular, just sweeping the place with his bushy eyebrows. Someone coughed, and then another, before the ripples fully settled. He rolled his shoulders, this time looking stern, then waited, allowing the silence to seep into the guilty. Just like the chief, just like the schoolteachers.

'Is this normal?' I whispered to Frank, sitting next to me.

He leaned sideways. 'Yeah. Git them sinners sweating.'

I looked around wondering if anybody was going to make a run for it. The crowd was quiet, nothing outside moved in the blistering midday heat. Even this church, with its two-storey open sides and free-standing pitched roof felt airless, like an oven.

'He who has not sinned cast the first stone.' Hilario's voice, amplified admirably by Gladys's PA system, drove into everyone's head. He said nothing more, once again only looking around and allowing the well-chosen words the time they deserved.

'Is she here?' I whispered.

'Yeah. Over there. One, two... six rows from the front. Red dress.'

'You mean that flowery one? It's not really red. More like burgundy.'

He looked at me as if I was taking the piss.

'She's Rose, the maid at Gladys's. She's not a pros... a you-know-what.'

'I never said she was, did I? All I sez was...'

'And the adulteress lay before Jesus, her sin laid bare for all to see.'

'All I said was there's a gal lookin fo' ya. That's her. Now hush!'

Perhaps Janet had been mistaken, mixing Rose up with a girl from A Better Place. Then, just as I looked back at her she looked at me. Her rosebud lips, red from her once-a-week lipstick allowance, stretched into the faintest of smiles. I smiled back. A part of me was attracted to her directness. Most of my relationships had been with complicated women. I reckoned she had plain old-fashioned sex appeal without the post nookie nagging. 'Did she come in with anyone?' I asked Frank.

'When I gits here... Say. Wait a minute. Is this part of yo' investigation? It is! Damn! I knew it! Huh!' He turned to his wife. 'Din I tell ya, blossom? Din I? Huh!'

'Yeah,' I said, 'sort of.'

'Well now, when I gits here she… um… Say, Mary, was she with anyone when we gits here? Thatun yonder, the one who's here for John.'

'Shh, Frank. Yes.' Mary pointed to the front row.

'Ah yeah, that's it,' he said, leaning right in and whispering so close that my ear was filled with spittle. 'That old hen Gladys in the first row there, with that poodle on her head.'

I leaned into the aisle. Front row, pink rinse. Gladys. There she was, gazing up lovingly at Father Hilario, hanging on every word, virtually hanging onto the pulpit. She was the first to stand for every song and the last to sit for every sermon, just trying to be noticed.

When Hilario wrapped up the sermon and everyone had to stand for a hymn, Rose quickly slid out the row. I remained seated, waiting for her to pass by. As she did she dropped a tiny piece of paper into my lap and bolted for the sunlight, her silhouette swallowed by the brightness like an apparition.

Gladys turned sharply and glared at me. I put the note in my pocket and quickly left the church, fully expecting all the exits to suddenly slam in my face, and for Gladys to drop from the sky on her broomstick, cackling manically.

Rose had gone, the main street was empty. Midday, parched, dusty. I looked left and right then unfolded the piece of paper. 'meT mE mUng Bonga hosE', it read. I looked back up and there, standing only a metre away, was Gladys.

'What's written on that piece of paper?' she demanded.

'What piece of paper?'

'Don't "What piece of paper?" me. That piece of paper in your hand, young man. The one that idiot girl gave you.' She took a step closer.

I squeezed the paper in my palm. 'Just a phone number.' She wasn't buying it and folded her arms matronly, her sagging breasts lifted temporarily, dangling over her forearms like dough. Keep quiet, John. Stare her out, you can do it.

She'd obviously run from the back of the church trying to cut off the girl's retreat and was losing her composure. Her nostrils flared as she desperately tried to suck in enough air. The sun beat down relentlessly as we stared each other out in the street at high noon, with only a mangy dog and the singing townsfolk as company. A plastic bag blew down the street like a tumbleweed.

She took the last step, only centimetres from my face, her pink lipstick-lined mouth opening and closing like a cod out of water. Her lips slid up over her false teeth and plastic gums, and a wave of stale alcohol washed over me. She wheezed like the church organ, her face a pained grin, globules of perspiration breaking out on her powdered top lip.

'You should take more exercise,' I said. It was a mean-spirited thing to say, and I really don't know where it came from, but it felt good. It tormented her not knowing what was written on the piece of paper.

She held out her hand, gritting her teeth, totally out of breath. 'Give it to me.'

'No.' Without thinking I put the note in my mouth and ate it. Her face went black with rage.

'You fool.' I turned and walked away, her voice ringing in my ears. 'Don't you know she'll cheat you! You don't know her! Listen to me! Don't do it!'

Realising I was giving the rendezvous point away by walking directly to the guest house, I turned and walked back past her, as if towards the other end of town.

'John,' she said softly, thinking I'd changed my mind, 'you're a good boy. We need people like you. But you must…'

I walked straight past her.

'She's rubbish! Don't do what she wants! Come back here!'

The second I turned the corner I ran, right around the block, past the school and doubled back to Bonga's, hurdling his hibiscus like an Olympian.

Rose was standing behind the sandbags. 'You have been running,' she said.

'Yeah, from Gladys. That woman's a maniac.'

'She knows?' Her eyes were suddenly wide with panic and she turned to leave.

'Wait.' I grabbed her arm. 'She doesn't know you're here. She didn't follow me. She's too old.'

She hesitated, looking out at the street, then at the hallway that led to the rooms. 'Inside.'

I didn't need to be told twice. I marched down the hallway, pulling out my door key like the sexually frustrated dog I was, aiming it at the keyhole from six paces.

'No. Here.'

I looked at the key. 'You sure? I mean, it's a bit exposed,' I said, trying to make her out in the gloom. 'Where Mr Maximo?'

'Maximo?'

'Mr Bonga. You are stay here. Him your friend.'

'I don't know where he is.'

She looked at me with her gorgeous brown eyes, and dared me to remain silent. Oh no, not another one. What is it with these people and silent stares? I could handle Gladys, and maybe even the chief with practice, but these sad sparkling eyes...

'I don't know where he is. How should I know?' Better turn it around with a question of my own, otherwise I'll crack. 'Why?'

'He not kill Elsie,' she said, looking up.

I had to be careful here, it might be a trick. She couldn't know about the knife.

'Elsie my friend. We work together.'

How should I put this? 'So you were a...' I fumbled in the dark in every sense of the word. 'You used to... work in A Better Place?'

She nodded. 'With Elsie. Maximo–'

'Maximo what?'

'Someone's coming!'

'No one's...' And then I heard it. A tricycle's high-pitched whine coming up the road. 'Wait there.' I went to the entrance, got on my hands and knees and crawled over the sandbags, peering out.

Coming down the street towards us was a three-wheeler. Through the front windscreen I could see the driver twisting the handlebar throttle for all it was worth. Sticking out the side, buffeted by the wind, was the unmistakable pompous pink rinse of Gladys.

Rose was behind me now, terrified. 'Please hide me. If she find me here...'

'Quick, in my room.'

We ran back down the hall. The sound of the tricycle seemed to fill the whole corridor with its two-stroke buzz, echoing off the bare walls. I fumbled in my pocket for the key. Not that pocket, the other one. Eh? Right pocket again. No!

'Quickly!' She was pinching my side with exasperation.

I could hear the trike getting closer, like a giant mosquito filling my head. Even Gladys's chilling shriek as she bellowed orders at the poor driver.

'It's not there! I put it in my pocket a moment ago but it's not there!'

The girl's face went slack with worry.

The tricycle revved twice and cut out. 'Wait here,' Gladys's voice said. She insisted on speaking to everyone in English, even other locals.

I grabbed the girl, looked around the corner and saw Gladys struggling to get out of the vehicle.

'But ma'am,' the driver began to protest, 'I have to take my wife—'

'Wait!' she barked, and the driver flinched and quailed like a cornered dog.

The hallway was a dead end and a rear escape was impossible without being spotted, so we doubled back to the restaurant. Next to the gun emplacement was a large wooden dining table that Maximo used for his props; gas masks, box brownie camera, side arms, a uniform. That would do.

Choosing my last chance carefully, just as the old gorgon got out of the tricycle arse first in her floral tent, we bolted for the table. Drawing the trouser legs of a uniform across the front like curtains, we tucked ourselves beneath and held our breaths.

The wooden steps creaked, then the floorboards under Gladys's laboured weight. The footsteps halted briefly as she pooh-poohed the disarray of Max's place.

I could hear her, sigh after disapproving sigh, huff after belittling huff, as she stepped further into the restaurant and took a look around. She picked things up, saying, 'My God,' or, 'What kind of man...' or simply murmuring to herself in Tagalog, repeating the same word, '*Nakakadiri*' (nasty), over and over again.

Through the trouser legs hanging down in front of my face the pink and blue floral dress swept into view on the other side of the room.

'Is anybody home?' Gladys picked up one of Maximo's teacups, examined it, then put it back down with total abhorrence. 'Disgusting. Hello. Is anyone home? Mr Bonga? Anybody?'

Then she changed direction and came toward the table. I shivered. Shit, this was it. What was I going to say to her when she parted the legs and looked under the table at me?

Something warm closed over my hand and I looked down then up at Rose's face. She was holding my hand in hers, still looking straight ahead, not trembling.

Gladys picked up something right above my head then put it down again, saying the same thing as before. It must have snagged on her billowing dress. As she moved away, unhooking herself and cursing, she bumped into the bunker, dislodging a sandbag. It fell right in front of me, kicking up a cloud of dust.

The particles filled the air and a sneeze rose in my head. Not now. Please, God, not now. Gladys went off down the hallway. I couldn't hold it. I buried my face in a trouser leg, blasting out a sneeze that sounded like a buffalo farting.

This time the girl grabbed me, yanking me out from the table and dragging me down the stairs into the sunlight. We ran down the garden path, through the gate and past the driver.

As we bolted around the corner at the end of the street I glanced back just in time to see Gladys, as quick as she could, stumbling out of the house. Within seconds I heard the tricycle engine pop into life.

Still holding hands, Rose and I hurdled the hedge and ran across the school playing field towards the road that led out of town.

'Where the hell are we going?' I panted.

She held on to me tighter. 'To A Better Place.'

7

'Ahhh.' I savoured the sublime feeling that reached from the soles of my feet, through my every sinew, into and out of my soul and right up to the uppermost bristle on my head. Elysium comfort laid itself on me like a quilt.

What a night. What an amazing night. And what a woman! Never had I been made to feel like this before. Never had sex straightened me out like this; untangling every knot and bend in my body.

Rose had taken me in and, knowing what I needed more than anything, had taken me to heaven, a better place indeed. And now, the next morning, after hours of heart-stopping shagging, where I'd given myself to her to do what she wanted, like a schoolboy in expert hands, I felt loved. Funny how easily I can mix up my feelings when I'm desperate for sex, how quickly lust turns into real fondness for someone and I can kid myself that it's reciprocal. I always imagine I'm the one in control.

This was living, I told myself. This was life; giving myself to someone who's giving their all in return. Someone who wanted only to give an equal but opposite passion.

A cockerel crowed outside and even that made me smile. The day before I'd have got up and chucked a brick at it. Now I wanted to kiss it for being alive, for singing and letting the world know.

I opened my eyes. Shafts of white sunlight stood at angles from the holes in the bamboo roof to the floor. I turned over to cuddle the exotic woman next to me and ended up kissing the bamboo mat. 'Rose?'

Probably making breakfast for me, I thought. Lovely. I looked at the bead curtain that led to the karaoke room of the brothel. We'd slept together in the back room, all the other Better Place girls on the main floor. They were probably all soundo. I pulled on my shorts.

During lulls in our lovemaking we had talked many things over: El Ref, its people, the meaning of love in Asia and love in Europe, her family, mine, food, women, men, and of course, Maximo.

Come to think of it, the most revealing topics of our discussion had been pretty one-sided. She'd told me of her family, including the terrible way her father had treated her, but had not answered a single question I had regarding the old man or Gladys. Stupidly I'd spilled the beans about Maximo's whereabouts.

The curtain into the main room was yanked back and Rose was standing there in a boob tube and denim shorts. 'We go,' she said, all business, apparently having completely forgotten the previous hours of acquiescent adoration she had extruded from me.

'But…'

'Shoes.' She pointed to the flip-flops and walked out.

'But…' I squeaked, sounding all weak and defenceless.

I caught up with her on the path into town. 'Where are we going?'

'Maximo. You say him out there,' she said, pointing to Charlie's island.

Why the bloody hell does she keep banging on about Max, I wondered. 'Yeah, but…' the strap on my flip-flop pulled out of its hole again and I hopped after her. 'But what about last night? I mean…' How should I put this without sounding too wounded, too cast off. 'We made love five times!'

She marched on single-mindedly.

'But we need a boat to get to the island,' I said, hanging off her right arm, still hobbling along. 'And we have to be careful in case someone sees us going there. We don't want anyone to know where he is.' She thought about this and stopped, and it made me feel better, a little stronger. Sod morals or dignity, I thought, I'll just withhold information as a way to keep her obligated to me. 'And don't forget, you don't know where Charlie's boat is,' I added, and immediately felt a sting of regret for making such a biliously jaundiced remark.

'You not help me?' She gave me her pitiable waif look.

I put my arms around her waist and she looked at me, responding with her doe eyes and a tender kiss. I melted. 'Of course I will.'

A farmer went past mushing his buffalo and smiling at the scene. It was still early and must have looked odd; a girl dressed for the disco being clasped lovingly by a man with a sandal in his hand.

I smiled back at the farmer and he said, 'Sexy Rose.' Then he laughed, going 'Yek yek yek', and whipping the animal's bony buttocks. Suddenly I could picture him doing the exact same thing to her.

I curled my lip in mock disgust. 'You haven't slept with him!'

She looked offended, folding her arms and fabricating a chaste expression.

The bullock driver laughed even louder. I couldn't blame him, and if I'd have been anyone else at that point I would have guffawed. How she could stand there dressed like that, having just screwed my brains out, and dare to put on that lavish mask of affronted innocence was a mark of her professionalism, I suppose. I fell for it.

'Wanker!' I shouted at the farmer.

Rose put her arms around my waist. 'You have girlfriend?'

I didn't want to lie to her, so I said, 'Um.'

Technically speaking Annie wasn't my girlfriend. OK, we'd kissed and spent a lot of time together, and if we were both prepubescent kids that may well have constituted a girlfriend/boyfriend relationship, but we were adults.

In my book – *The Technical Book of Love Affairs, Romance and Attracting the Opposite Sex, Not to Mention Getting Laid* (aka *The Selfish Bastard Bible*) – that does not make her my girlfriend. We hadn't slept together. And anyway, what's wrong with having a reserve? Girls do it.

'No, not a girlfriend as such. Not technically speaking.'

'I love you,' she said, making me feel like butter. 'Now we go to Max. My other boyfriend have boat. Him fisherman.'

'Other boyfriend? How many have you got, for God's sake?'

She led me by the hand and I stumbled along down the dirt road through town, led on like a buffalo on a rope. Dope on a rope. She didn't have me tethered via a ring through the nose but the allusion was there.

Jesus, I thought, picking up speed, my face burning, a discreet night spent in A Better Place would soon be front-page news in El Refugio. It began to dawn on me how easily I was being played. I just prayed that Annie wouldn't find out. How humiliating it would be for her.

We wound our way around the eastern headland and past the graveyard that sits on the shore at the beginning of a rocky beach. Rose stopped briefly to ask permission from the dead spirits to pass before carrying on, the fallen-in tombs and broken headstones too tired to acknowledge our passing.

And then I felt it, just as I passed the burst-open graves. I stopped and turned. The barest shadow or movement behind a palm tree. Someone was following us. I scanned the tiny cemetery. Old fallen coconuts lay strewn everywhere like baked skulls. Sun-dried palm fronds, their thick central spine with long curving leaves like the rib cages of dead grazers. A shiver ran down my back and I moved on quickly.

Rose's fisherman friend lived about a quarter of the way down the second beach. He was standing in the sea dragging nets from his outrigger. Rose shouted, 'Rommel!'

Rommel shouted, 'Sexy Rose!'

I shouted, 'Blow me.'

He dumped the nets and waded ashore. Rose pointed to the boat then the island where Max and Charlie were hiding.

'We go,' she said to me.

'How much?'

'Free!'

Yeah, I bet, I thought bitterly. A ride for a ride. I suppose I should have been thankful.

I procrastinated for a moment, flip-flops in one hand, spitefulness in the other. My secret, my island, my Maximo the fugitive. And now I was going to give it all away. For what? A shag.

I looked back at the trees one last time, and then up the beach the way we'd come. No one seemed to be there so I waded into the sea, tiptoeing around the urchins, and climbed into the boat behind Rose. Rommel wound the cord around the flywheel, yanked it skywards and aimed us at the island.

Nobody uttered a word until we were about halfway across, and Rose said, 'Look, there's Annie!'

I looked back at the shoreline, expecting to see a tiny speck hanging out washing on the line at Gladys's.

'No, there,' she said, pointing midway between us and the island.

Coming towards us after a night on one of the lagoons was the Swiss Cafe's boat, and inside were the bedraggled-looking threesome.

Shit. I pretended to suddenly be interested in Rommel's catch and began lifting lids off boxes, sticking my head in and trying to crouch as low as possible. I felt about as elevated as a snake. 'How many squid in here?' I said. 'Looks like a lot.'

'Yoo-hoo! Annie! Jiz! Brenda!' shouted Rose, blissfully ignorant of my dilemma.

I delved deeper in one of his big polystyrene coolers. If I could have climbed inside I would have, and shut the lid after me.

The approaching engine grew louder and I wondered if it was worth jumping over the side. Please keep going. Please don't stop. I slid off the seat so my back was lower than the gunwale, when a familiar voice asked Rose where she was going.

'There,' she replied, pointing at the island.

Annie's voice was distant, then right beside us, then fading. 'Ciao. Have a good day. Who is that with you? Why are they are wearing the shirt of John?'

Rommel tapped me on the head. 'I stop?'

'Don't you touch that bloody engine!'

Rommel just said 'Bolero' (playboy) and smiled, revving the motor harder.

My spirit lifted as we chugged seawards and the steamy inlet came into view. The water changed from a crafty crystal jig to a slow brown waltz. Rommel cut the engine and plumbed with a bamboo pole, once, twice, before sitting down and driving us forward again.

Rose was silently looking ahead the whole time, unreadable I thought, the only clue to her feelings a slight look of forestalled beration in her eyes. As though she'd wanted this meeting for days but now it was upon her, sucking her upstream, she was beginning to worry about what might happen. She looked like a kid who was going to meet her dad for the first time in years.

There's only one bend in the estuary on the island, and as soon as we drove around it Charlie's black box came into view, leaning sideways like a stranded black whale. A moment later a person appeared on deck. Maximo.

Rose stood up and leaned forward over the prow like a busty figurehead. She squeezed my leg and I felt abandoned, as if my job was done.

Maximo suddenly turned and quickly went below. A moment later he was back holding binoculars up to his face with both hands.

I stood and waved. Rose stood and waved. Maximo waved both arms vigorously in the air. He was shouting something but it was impossible to hear over the noise of the motor.

He looked through the lenses again and waved like mad, and I thought: OK, OK, we can see you, no need to go berserk. Shit, he must really be excited to see this woman.

Then he began pointing at us and shouting, and I thought he was saying 'You! You, John. You the man!' And then he did something very strange indeed, he leapt over the side.

Rose gasped.

Rommel aimed us so that we could offer an outrigger to the old man. The strange thing was when he cut the engine I could still hear an engine noise, only quieter.

We came alongside Maximo, his thin arms thrashing at the water, and I stood, tilting my head to make out the sound. Flexing my jaw didn't make it go away and I wondered if being deafened by the engine's din had left temporary hearing loss.

'Maximo!' Rose pleaded, holding out her hand to him. But still he thrashed, trying, it seemed, to get away from us. He'd jumped from such a height that he was stuck in the mud like a mangrove pod.

'Can you hear that?' I said, forgetting the old man. 'Sounds like… I dunno. Like a giant bee.'

And it did, except it came in and out, as if stuck on a yo-yo: Ying Ying Ying Ying.

Maximo eventually clung to the side of our boat, exhausted. He was furious. 'You led them here! You led them here! You fool!'

'But she…' I wasn't quite sure how to put it. I hadn't planned for this. Somehow I imagined he'd be pleased to see her. 'She said you were friends. I haven't told–'

'Not her, you idiot! Them!' He pointed out to sea and all three of us swung round to look.

There, racing towards us on Ziegwalt's commandeered jet ski, arcs of white spray fanning out each side, was Thomas the chief of police. Riding pillion was Ten, loudhailer in hand. She put it to her lips and an electrified voice said, 'Stay where you are, Bonga, and put your hands where we can see them. We have you covered!'

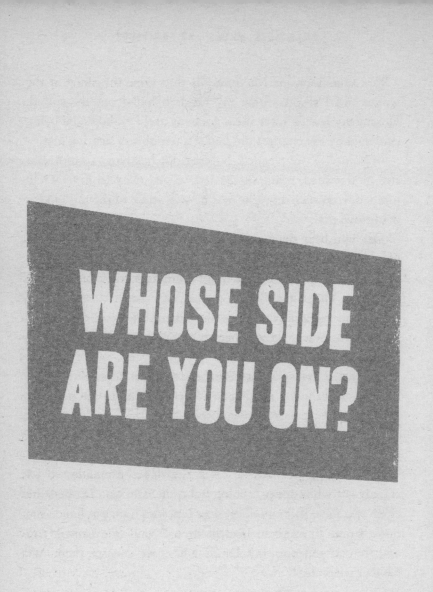

1

I was in a deep depression for days after that, blaming myself for allowing Maximo to get caught. Not just get caught, I told myself, but worse; effectively handing the man his death sentence. Given the things he'd told me about corruption and the non-existent legal system, it seemed likely he'd disappear without a trace. Either that or they'd just use the knife as evidence, convict him and throw away the key. I really had handed it to those idiots on a plate.

And their idiocy just made the whole thing worse. If that asinine pair had been clever enough to find him themselves, or even if they'd tricked me with some entrapment plan, it wouldn't have been so bad. However, this pathetic following me across on Ziegwalt's commandeered jet ski made me sick. Ziggy blamed himself for allowing them to take it. I blamed him too, to deflect the blame from me.

It would have been so easy for me to blame Rose for the whole cock-up, to lift the burden of guilt from my shoulders. And I tried, but however I dodged, it still came back to me. I should have known better, taken it more seriously than I did, listened to Maximo and Charlie when they told me under no circumstances to tell anyone.

It was all Annie's fault. No, it was Jiz's fault. If she'd have let me alone with the Italian Goddess for 5 minutes instead of trying to convert her into a lesbian this would never have happened. Annie and I would have had time alone, nature would have taken its course and I would never have ended up in A Better Place with my heart in a sling. A Better Place; the irony of that name was not lost on me.

And to add insult to injury Annie had now left town. She'd packed her bags the next day and left with Arnold Schwarzenegger and Woody Allen on the bus to the main port – a day's ride away. If I could have got to her the same day and explained the whole thing she might have changed her mind, but I'd been held in the police station all night for questioning. We all had, including Rose and Charlie. Annie had simply heard about the day's events, about Rose and me, and done what any self-respecting person would do. Keeping a secret in a place this small was impossible.

The next day when I ambled sheepishly round to Gladys's all I found were three open rooms all neatly cleaned and ready for the next customers. The plumber informed me that they had gone. I ran around to the Swiss Cafe and Janet told me the three girls had come in for breakfast before catching the eight-thirty bus south.

I pelted through town and got to the bus just as it was leaving. Annie's face lit up with pleasure but she quickly checked herself and looked away. I stood beside the open window, pleading with her to stay. No one was more surprised at my behaviour than I was.

Annie wavered, I could tell, constantly glancing at Jiz for guidance, then at Brenda. She asked me if I'd slept with Rose and I said no. She asked me where I'd been all night and why, and I told her the truth about the police station. It made me forget the lie.

I said I was sorry but it wasn't my fault and she crumbled, looking at Jiz. Jiz told me to piss off and slid the window shut in my hopeful face, almost trapping my fingers. The bus began to move off and something I'd never have reckoned on came out of my mouth. 'I love you!'

Pride, the need to move on, fear of losing the girls' friendship, Jiz's avarice disguised as altruistic counsel, whatever the reason – and I'd thought about it long and hard over the next week – Annie stayed put on that clapped-out bus as it trundled up the potholed road out of Dodge. I was left standing in a cloud of diesel smoke and dust, laughed at by kids. I deserved nothing less.

And why was I questioning Annie's reasons for staying on the bus? Why didn't I, if I was indeed sincere, get on the bus with her? Or chase after her in a tricycle? The reason, I told myself, was that I could not, having got him into this mess, leave the old man to rot. Telling myself that avoided the niggling doubts I've always had about my ability to stay in a long-term relationship.

I couldn't avoid those thoughts for long, I never can. I know my faults but can never prevent myself from faltering. I always bottle out of relationships, making one ridiculous excuse after another why I can't (can't, not won't) settle down.

And I didn't get on the bus because deep down inside I was afraid to; afraid to fall so deeply in love that I wouldn't be able to recognise or control myself. I always say 'I love you' and 'please don't go' just when the bus is leaving. Well, perhaps that's a little unfair on me, because I do say the 'L' word at other times. Nevertheless, I never know what I've got until it's gone. And if it comes back I find some other excuse why I can't settle down, or get hitched, just yet. There's always a departing bus in my relationships.

The unbelievable ways in which I've justified (to myself) my need for independence over the years are as preposterous as they are self-defrauding. I've spent years looking for Miss

Perfect and, however much I tell myself that she doesn't exist, I still insist on looking again as a way of not getting married to the one I'm with.

Not clever enough, not beautiful enough, too clever (might twist me), too beautiful (might leave me), the wrong hair, wrong nationality, and even once a mole on her finger! And so with Annie, the same old story. London, Hong Kong, Dubai, you name it, I've walked away from it there. Only this time my excuse was doing it out of a sense of justice, to help others. The fact is I wanted to eat my cake and have it. And when I got it I wouldn't want it any more because it might stifle my precious independence. An independence so irreplaceable, so nourishing and succulent that I was now left alone with it in my room, all to myself, to be with and to hold and cuddle.

And to add further insult to an already festering injury, as if all this self-inflicted loneliness wasn't enough of a penance for my mistakes, Rose was no longer interested in me either.

The girls at A Better Place told me she wasn't there but I knew she was just hiding; I could hear her singing her favourite karaoke song. Not one to dwell on lost love, I gave up trying. I didn't want to be a nuisance.

It wasn't until Elsie's funeral had finally been arranged a few days later, when all the Better Place girls, including Rose, turned out to pay their respects, that I finally got to talk to her. I felt lifted. It's amazing how cheering funerals can be when you're down.

It's all relative I suppose. I was only grieving for myself really, and when they brought that body out and stuck it in the ground my subconscious said, 'You see? There's always someone worse off than you.'

It's a bit like going on holiday to third-world countries. It's always been my theory that the reason people go on holiday to poor places is simply because it makes them feel good about their own crappy lives. It makes them feel better to see folks worse off. Go to India, feel rich, feel better, go home and lie to everyone about how wonderful it was. 'A cheap holiday in other people's misery,' as John Lydon put it.

And that's how I felt at Elsie's entombment – better. Partly I suppose that came from the mordant comedy of the whole episode. From the argument over whether or not she should be dignified with burial in the cemetery, to the moment when the coffin-bearers tripped over a dog on the beach and dropped her again. Not to mention Ziegwalt's bright idea of a stately trip by sea to the cemetery instead of down the street as was the convention in town. But then Ziggy could hardly be considered conventional.

The first obstacle the foreigners had had to overcome was what to do with Elsie. Now that Maximo, that huge menace to society, was locked away, French Bernard had been released. In fact they'd simply opened up the door to the makeshift cell, let one out and shoved the other one in; no questions, no answers, no forms, nothing. Bernard was now a free man and he wanted Elsie put in a hole immediately. The pugnacious puritans (namely Gladys and her cohorts) were having none of it.

'Bury that harlot and defile consecrated ground!' I imagined her barking. I hadn't seen her since the chase from the church but Bernard had told me that someone was against the burial and was lobbying the vicar and mayor very hard, using all their influence to stop it. And being El Refugio, it wasn't long before we all knew who that someone was. It was Bernard and the foreigners against the old dragon in a battle of wits that went on for a week.

Being stuck in my bedroom reflecting, all this information came to me second hand, usually from Frank, Ziegwalt or

Janet. This was The Refuge and the bush telegraph was as good as tuning into a live, minute-by-minute broadcast of events.

The argument over where Elsie should be laid to rest had been the only thing that kept her out of the ground. As soon as the Frenchman was out, he did the right thing and went straight round to the hospital/morgue to get her. Five days later he was still trying. 'Insensible Philippines bureaucracy! *Merde*, damn, shit!' he said, storming out the doors.

The problem was, as he pointed out once he'd calmed down, she had no known relatives anywhere, only friends at the brothel, and their word counted for zilch. She was no more an outsider that most of the residents. They were all immigrants. Bernard was furious, and if he hadn't been talked out of it by Jim the ever placid Englishman, I think he would have carried out his threat to blow up the hospital.

He appeared on the steps one morning, screaming at the top of his lungs for everyone to get out. Behind him he pulled a little trolley piled high with the whole town's supply of fireworks. The police were called, Jim arrived, and then Elvis Lam, and the whole thing was settled there and then with a sweep of the mayor's limp wrist.

'Let us not sin against this poor woman any longer,' Elvis said. 'Welease Elsie!'

In fact all Gladys did by delaying the burial was cause problems for the hospital. There is no real morgue in El Refugio and no electricity after midnight. The best they had been able to do for her was buy in blocks of ice every evening to keep her cold, and mop up the puddles every morning. She was beginning to smell.

Jim, the posh Englishman, a kind of amateur inventor as it turned out, had built a giant polystyrene cooler for her out of smaller ones, all tied up with bits of string. It held and drained off effectively but the body was perpetually sodden and was beginning to fall apart.

'She's rather like wet tissue paper,' he informed me a little too graphically one day over fried fish. 'Every time we move her to drain the box a bit falls orf.' Not only that, he said, but the weight of the huge blocks of ice, typically over a metre long and half a metre deep, had flattened her. She was still her old height but a metre wide and only a fist thick. 'Perhaps we could post her home,' he said.

So Bernard got his way and she would be buried out at the cemetery on the rocky beach. Jim came round to inform me that I should be there at twelve noon and that everything else was taken care of. No need to help carry the coffin, Ziegwalt and he had 'rigged something up'. By which I assumed he meant buffalo and cart. Very noble an exit.

The next day, a Saturday as I recall, found me standing beside Rose and the Better Place girls at the beachside cemetery, baking under the midday sun. Even under the trees the heat was incredible, reflecting off the sand and forcing us to squint.

I knew something characteristically unconventional was going to take place when I asked Jim why we had to do it in the noon heat and he replied simply, 'Tide.' Just as I was checking out the water, wondering whether the sea could really rise to engulf the grave, there was a very odd but strangely familiar sound in the distance. Exactly like an incoming goose honking.

Honk Honk! I squinted harder, scanning the clear sky for a sign of winged migration.

Jim said, 'Jolly good. They're coming,' and pointed out to sea.

It was Ziegwalt on his jet ski, towing a Jim-made raft. On the raft stood Bernard, saluting with one hand and holding on with the other. Behind him lay the coffin, beautifully carved by

Charlie, the whole lot flanked by two flags; one tricolour and one Philippines. Emotion welled up inside me.

Janet began to cry, Rose and the girls broke down in tears and big Frank, trying his best to maintain his composure, had to walk off for a moment 'to get some air'. He cried behind a palm tree.

Ziegwalt honked his horn again as they drew gently across the flat sea and did a one-eighty, reversing in as close as could be. The flags drooped and finally hung dead in the limp tropical heat.

Jim and I waded into the water and lifted the casket off the raft. A hole had already been dug, the depth dictated by the water table and only just shy of the standard 2 metres. The floor and walls of the pit were dotted with white shells.

The headstone, again carved by the Russian, read simply: 'Elsie Rodriguez. Gone to a better place.'

I started crying when I saw that. It said it all. She'd been held in contempt by the self-righteous people here and could never have been very happy. It saddened me so much, those words, because some people have to die to get to a better place.

The coffin was lowered in, and from nowhere one of the youngest prostitutes produced an old trumpet. She began to play like a virgin. I don't mean she played like a virgin, that would be impossible, I mean she played the Madonna song 'Like a Virgin'. Everyone bowed.

Rose suddenly went berserk, screaming and punching and flinging herself around on the ground. The girls held her down but she went wild, possessed, cursing and spitting acid. And then she tore off her blouse.

Everyone knew not to go close as she tore at everything; from the bark of trees, her fingernails bleeding, to her own matted hair. Eventually, nostrils flared, panting like a lion, she smashed a bottle, mimed cutting her throat and stormed off.

I was about to go after her but the trumpet player said, 'No. It is her way.' Both flags were chucked in with the coffin and the hole refilled by me, Jim and Bernard in turns.

We spent the rest of the day at the wake, eating barbecued fish that had been set up by Bernard just down the beach, and drowning our sorrows.

When the sun had set Ziegwalt put down his beer and drove out into the dark sea on his jet ski towing a raft packed with fireworks. He disappeared completely. All of a sudden the sky exploded into one enormous multicoloured pallet. Rockets, balls of sparks and whizzing genies shot in every direction. The raft caught fire with a little help from a jerrycan of fuel and we mourned Elsie's passing as the flames flared then slowly died.

2

Frank was in his usual position when I woke the next morning. I thought he hadn't noticed me as I slunk around the corner towards the shower. I'd become sort of invisible in my depression, as though the cloud that hovered above me cast a shadow that hid me from the world.

'The water ain't been switched on,' he said without looking up.

I stopped, put the towel around my shoulders then carried on without replying. I didn't mind a bucket and handpump wash. In fact I'd become used to it over the past week and enjoyed the physical work. It made me feel a bit like I was doing penance.

It didn't amount to much really, but it was something. At least I wasn't using the electricity. I was still paying to stay in Bonga's, along with Frank, but with no other customers now that the low season was upon us, it was the least I could do.

Frank was running the place in Maximo's absence, or rather his wife Mary was, cleaning and organising and doing whatever else needed doing. She even cooked for the pair of us, converting the old man's filthy, rundown kitchen into a neat and tidy workspace that I was happy to eat out of.

She'd cleaned up all the other areas too. Boxes of ammo were now in straight rows, the bullet belts for once in their boxes. Gas masks, puttees, grenades, gun parts and assorted odds and sods were in shipshape little groups. Uniforms, hats, helmets and boots were folded and paired in uncluttered, out-of-the-way corners. Tables, chairs, hung pictures and assorted weaponry that had always been skew-whiff were now squared up and hanging straight.

It all looked horrible.

It was so... un-Max like. Why do women always have to move things? It annoyed Frank as well. Every time he came in he'd stop at the top of the steps and frown. 'Somin's up,' he'd say and scratch his tiny head.

'She's moved the sandbags,' I'd reply without looking up from *Seven Pillars of Wisdom*. He'd sigh, I'd go to my room and it would pass without further comment. It was just being clean, hygienic, we told ourselves. Even the fresh vase of flowers that materialised every day could be forgiven.

Breaking point came, though. I was woken one morning by the sound of Frank going, 'No way. That's too much. Oh my Gaad. He'll never forgive us for this.' I dressed and went into the restaurant. Frank was standing there staring, mouth open, at Sergeant Chipstick. 'He's been dressed!' Frank said. 'Mair-ree!'

More than that, the manikin had been spruced up and now looked like a psychotic tourist. Gone were the ragged, moth-eaten, army-issue combat fatigues, gone was the helmet with the cobwebs dangling from it, and gone was the one remaining boot he wore (the other leg ended in a stump, the plastic foot missing).

Casual Mr Chipstick now looked like a London gent on holiday. He wore one of Frank's elephantine Hawaiian shirts, a pair of his lurid, hulking shorts, from which two chipped matchstick plastic legs poked out, and a pair of Maximo's patent leather ballroom-dancing shoes.

But worst of all, the most eye-catching, most gruesome aberration of the lot, was the face. He had two eyes.

'He...' Frank was lost for words, standing there in his underpants quivering all over like jelly. I wasn't sure if he was mad because she'd altered what didn't belong to her or because she'd used his clothes. 'He...' He took a step closer to the manikin, cautious, as though it might bite him, and squinted at the new eyeball. 'He's got two eyes.' He put his fingers in the socket and pulled it out. 'It's a ping-pong ball! It's a goddamn ping-pong ball! Mair-ree!'

Mary slowed down after that, and now limited her house-proud excesses to cooking and cleaning. To be fair to her it was a much better place to sleep now that she'd cleaned my room and changed the sheets. But without the old geezer it just wasn't the same. No traps, no labile grumpiness, no insults when I came in at night; all the things that should have made me glad made me sad.

I showered and shaved and reflected on the previous week's events, watching a column of ants work their way up the concrete block wall. Ants going up and coming down. Each time they passed a fellow soldier ant they touched antennae and moved on.

I wonder if Maximo's got light in his room, I thought. Or a shower or toilet for that matter. I'd wanted to visit him but was afraid of the rejection. What if he just spat in my face? I don't think I could take that.

It seemed everyone had visited except me, in fact. Even Frank and Mary had gone down to ask him about the guest house, and he'd instructed them to take care of it for the time being.

I watched a gecko twist its way across the rafter towards the ants, carefully eyeing its prey, taking little bursting runs then stopping to size things up again.

I had to decide one way or the other. Either I stay here and go to him, see if we can patch things up, or I leave town. If I didn't go to see him then I must leave this place. I could not hang around and watch him waste away. How could anyone be a tourist in this place knowing that it was founded on lies and inequity? A place where the big fish swallowed the little ones; where the sharks chewed up the minnows.

But how, I kept asking myself, would we be able to win against the might of a corrupt system? Half a dozen people, and foreigners to boot, at variance with everyone of power. Power: we had none, the mayor and his cronies had it all. Just look at Elsie's body; one word from Lam and the hospital let her out in a second.

And let's be honest about it, we would be alone. Janet had been to many community meetings and had told me how the Lams always buttered the people up with flashy images of a modern, idyllic retreat. Unrealistic visions of a resort town where large groups of Japanese tourists paid in the hundreds of dollars to stay, as they did on the five-star islands. 'Once we get the road built', of course. Never mind a few hundred thousand hectares of primary rainforest, you can have cable TV!

The crowd bought it. They always do when it comes to money. The tiddlers always get swallowed by the whales.

The gecko leapt into action, its tongue flicking in and out as it lapped up whole battalions of ants in front of my face.

I sighed and pulled on my shorts, wondering if the universe worked like this at every level, from cosmic to microscopic to atomic. From black holes swallowing up planets, to blue whales feasting on krill, to geckos munching on ants.

I watched intently as the ants scattered all over the wall and retreated down the lines to warn others of the giant monster that was gulping everything in its path. Then they started to regroup and attack. At first they were just one or two, running in sorties and nipping at the lizard's soft underbelly. Then they all started.

The gecko stopped what it was doing. 'What the hell's going on here?' Suddenly it was surrounded, and in a moment smothered with the little bastards. 'Shit!' It began to do a sort of square dance, trying to get them off its back, but ended up making a run for it. 'Sod this for a game of soldiers!'

Teamwork.

The gecko bolted through a crack in the roof.

I came out of the shower and walked across the yard, chewing everything over.

'Someone to see ya,' Frank said. 'Over yonder.'

Sitting there in the morning sunshine were Rose and Bernard. Bernard smiled. 'Maximo wants to see you.'

3

I stood in the entrance to the municipal building looking back at Rose and Bernard. 'Why don't you come with me?'

'He say he wants to see you alone, my friend. That is what he say,' said Bernard. 'Go straight to le shief. He will escort you. We are not allowed anyway,' he huffed. 'He does not like me. Asshole.'

Yeah, I can imagine, I thought, turning and entering the building. Thomas the chief had made a big show of Bernard's 'capture' that day and had no doubt trumpeted to the powers that be of his skill in law enforcement. Now he was the laughing stock of the town.

Bernard had reopened the bistro in memory of Elsie. It was now called Elsie's Bistro. He renamed the menu too. He now served 'Carte Blanche Quiche', 'Justice Juice', 'Liberty Lemon Chicken', and 'Maximo's Delight', a healthy vegetarian sausage that promised a pork substitute. 'No pigs in zhis one!'

The point of all this, of course, was to get the attention of any tourists who'd passed through in the couple of days since he'd reopened. Eventually they had asked about the names and Bernard had used their curiosity as a way to highlight Maximo's plight. Word had spread and the chief had got wind. He'd been made to look a monkey once and now Bernard had really got his goat.

I entered the municipal building and walked down the long, stiflingly hot corridor towards the chief's office wondering what mood he'd be in. If I were him, I'd lock Bernard away again. He may be a smart-arse but there could only be one outcome if Bernard insisted on getting his back up; sooner or later they would find a way of forcing the bistro to close.

After all, every business establishment in the village, from the smallest corner store to the largest enterprise, needed a permit to operate. That licence was renewed yearly by the mayor. And the mayor took advice from none other than the chief.

I don't think it mattered too much to Bernard. I'd had the feeling since the funeral that he wanted to go out in a blaze of glory. He seemed liked a man with a death wish.

Ten came out of the office just as I was nearing, stopped, hid outside for 5 seconds until I was by the door, then turned back and said, 'I have found him, sir.'

'Snake.' I brushed past her horrible face and entered. I was stunned. Maximo was sitting there with the chief drinking coffee.

'Ahh,' said Thomas, 'talk of the devil.'

Maximo looked around at me, his face full of emotion. He looked tired and drawn, his chin covered in silver stubble, making him look mouldy. I could instantly tell that something was wrong, that the chief's show of informality was a sham, laid on for my benefit. The old boy was scared. I wanted to weep.

'Maximo... Mr Bonga... and I were just talking about you,' Thomas crowed, instantly trying to take charge of the gathering by lighting a cigarette and putting on his couldn't-care-less cap. 'He's free to see anyone he wants and he asked to see you. For some reason.'

And there it was, the fear the chief had of my supposed detective skills, in those three words: 'for some reason.'

'Well,' said Thomas, taking his feet off the desk, 'my deputy and I will leave you alone to talk. Five minutes?' He came to the door, walking around the prisoner. He patted him on the shoulder as he passed and the old man flinched.

Ten asked if she should stay behind, sir, then followed him out when he said no, giving me a belligerent flick of the hair. She closed the door looking sickeningly coquettish. I wanted to sleep with her in spite of myself.

The door rattled in its frame and we were alone.

I ran across and locked the deadbolt latch, turned and said, 'Sorry.'

'I'm sorry,' Maximo said. 'Rose has told me everything.'

I felt as if a great weight was suddenly lifted off my head. 'I'm gonna do anything and everything I can to help you.' I pulled up a chair so eagerly it knocked a file off the table. 'I'll find out who did it and we'll–'

'Shh!' He put a finger to his lips. 'Not so loud. They only want us to talk here so they can listen. They're frightened of you. Everyone else who's visited has come to my room, but with you it's different.' He sat back and, for the first time in a week, I wouldn't mind betting, his crusty old face broke into a massive grin. 'Hee hee hee.'

'They think I'm a–'

'Shh! For God's sake, man! We're under interrogation from the enemy,' he hissed, shuffling closer to me and glancing at the door.

I glanced too, then whispered, 'They think I'm a detective! Hee hee.'

'We're so lucky we have a real detective on our side. Those monkeys don't know what they're doing, I can tell you that.'

I hesitated, wondering if I really was a detective or not, and decided I was. 'I told you, I'm with you on this. Have they got the brains to put you away?'

'They don't have brains, these Japs. They only have cruelty. Now then, this is what we'll do…'

'Japs?'

'What?'

'You said Japs,' I whispered.

He looked over his shoulder at the door as a shadow passed the frosted glass. 'That's right. Can't trust 'em. You in or out, soldier? I need to know.'

'I'm in.' I hesitated. 'It's Thomas the chief we need to concern ourselves with, isn't it? Not the Japanese.'

'When I saw the… um, the…'

'Chief?'

'No, the…'

'Deputy?'

'No no no. The, um…'

I thought of something, checked my sanity, then ventured, 'Japs?'

'Japs? Good God, no. The evidence, man. The evidence.'

I wondered if he'd lost the plot, being locked away in a room for so long. He'd always been eccentric but now there seemed to be an unbalanced element to him, as though a wire had worked its way loose in his head.

'You OK?'

He sat back, offended. 'Of course I'm OK. What, do you think being locked in a room six by ten bothers me? You think they've cracked me?'

'Well…'

'Huh! You don't know Maximo Bonga. Look,' he rolled up his sleeve and showed me a small cavalry tattoo on the side of his bicep. 'If I think of them as the enemy, as the Japs, I can fight them. I'm a Second World War veteran. I need to know who's the enemy.'

I breathed a sigh of relief. He hadn't gone mad just yet. 'What evidence?'

'What?'

'You said "evidence".'

'Oh yes. The knife. That's all they've got.' He sat back again, clearly fired up on nervous energy. 'If I could only get a glimpse at that file the chief has. Suppose we were to sneak a look at it. Then we'd know what you're up against at the trial.'

I blinked. 'What trial?'

'It's nothing.' He sat back rubbing his palms together like a man making a fire with a stick.

'You said trial.'

'That's right, private.'

'What trial?' There were footsteps approaching from down the corridor; they stopped as another door was opened and closed. 'What trial?'

'They have ten days to get me to court and charge or release me,' he whispered. 'Or they can bring a judge here to do it. I know because my brother went through it once. My only chance is to get to the state capital and be charged there. If it happens here it's over, I'll never get out.'

'Your brother was a murderer?'

'Course not. He stole a buffalo. Dead now. But that's beside the point.'

'The buffalo or your brother?'

'My brother. The buffalo's still in the field behind the school.'

'There's someone coming,' I said, looking at the door. 'Quick. What do you want me to do?'

'Steal the file.'

'What!' I said, doing a double take between Max and the doorknob.

'And the knife. I think it's locked in that cabinet.'

I looked behind me at the filing cabinet then jumped as a key was pushed into the door. The unmistakable rotund silhouette of the chief appeared in the glass.

'I can't do that!'

'I heard them saying that they might get someone to come here and formally charge me. They're going to try to keep it in El Refugio to cover it up. You must get that evidence before they charge me!'

The door handle turned. The chief cursed and called out to Ten, 'Why did you lock this door? We never lock it. Which key is it?'

I faltered as the chief jangled the keys on a ring. Ten shouted from next door that it was the one with a SWAT logo on it, and I distinctly heard the sound of a glass scraping the partition wall. They'd been listening.

I turned to Maximo. 'How many days left? You said they had ten days to charge you.'

The door flew open and Thomas burst in.

'One,' said Maximo.

'One what?' said the chief, all agitated and sweaty from the exertion.

Maximo smiled mischievously at me. 'Just one.'

When I got back to the guest house everyone was sitting there in the open area waiting for me. Silence descended on the place as soon as I went through the gate and into the front garden. The only sound was far-off music – a power ballad from Bonnie Tyler – and the snik, snik, snik of pruning shears as Mary trimmed the roses. She smiled at me in a kind of pitying way.

'Wow,' I said, going up onto the veranda, 'like group therapy. What's everyone doing here?' As if I didn't know.

Janet elbowed Gentleman Jim in the ribs and he spoke up. 'As you may or may not be aware, and it's my assumption that you are, seeing as how you're now part of our community, har-har-har. Though of course it's possible that you're not aware, given the fact that one can easily find oneself in an altogether different time zone once one has been, how shall we asseverate, caught up in the—'

'What he's tryna say,' big Frank interrupted, 'is that we want you to help the ol' fella.'

'Indubitably, indubitably.'

'More to the point,' Frank continued, 'represent him in court.'

'Represent who in court?' I swallowed but the spit wouldn't go down.

'Maximo,' they all chirped in chorus.

I scanned the faces in front of me, all seated around the manikin, then I looked out at Mary in the garden. Then I looked back again at them. Then, to make my point (i.e. that I thought they were all nuts and therefore to be ignored), I went down the corridor into my room to collect my soap and came back past them without saying a word. I took a towel from the line and went into the shower hut. I needed to wash off the prickly feeling I'd had since sitting next to the chief. I heard Ziegwalt whisper, 'Do you sink he miss zhe Eye-talian girl?'

The only other thing I could hear while I washed in the dark was someone in the distance still duetting with Bonnie Tyler on their karaoke: '... I don't know what to do, I'm always in the dar-ark...'

When I'd finished they were still there waiting. I walked straight past and went to my room to dress. Janet was sitting on the bed.

'My husband saw Annie today,' she said.

I tried to carry on dressing as though I hadn't heard. When she said her name my stomach fluttered. In my eagerness to look unflushed I quickly picked up a T-shirt.

'You just took that one off,' she said, and handed me a clean one. 'He saw her in the city centre buying ferry tickets.'

Don't let anyone know you miss her. Pretend she's just a casual fling. I went to my bag pretending to look for something, frowning.

'She misses you.'

'What was your husband doing in the city?' Change the subject and feign interest in something unrelated, thereby acquiring the relevant bits of emotional information without hinting at my own sentimental state.

'He goes down once a month for supplies for the cafe.'

'Huh.'

'Taddi had a beer with her. She is even thinking of coming back.'

I swelled with confidence now that I knew she was the one chasing me. I chucked the bag down with cocky abandon and shrugged. 'Up to her.'

'You like her, don't you John. I can tell.'

'She's all right.'

The room suddenly went dark. Big Frank was standing in the doorway.

'Taddi could ask her to come back,' Janet continued. 'He's usually down there a day or two on business. He calls me every day.'

I felt good. All the loneliness, all the sadness and pain, the regret and guilt all suddenly evaporated in the knowledge that Annie was thinking of me.

'She likes you, John, but she is waiting for you to say the same. She wants you to ask her back. A girl needs to be chased.'

'I don't mind. Ask her.' That was it. The best I could stretch to in front of other people for fear that my image of independence might be exposed for the sham that it was. Some playboy; in the whole time I'd been here all I'd managed was one night with a prostitute.

'Not many tourists stay as long as you. I know you like it here, so why not stay here with her? That is good, no?'

'She's got a business in Italy to run.'

Janet looked at the doorway where Ziegwalt's handlebar moustache peered out beside Frank's tree-trunk leg, then back to me. 'I think she would stay if you ask her. I am a woman. I know this thing.'

'And then we could stay and help the ol' man,' Frank added, coming into the room and sitting on the bed. It groaned so he got off. 'With you we can help him. Together.'

'I'm not a lawyer,' I said. 'Yeah I've done some detective work and I've given evidence in court, but representing Maximo…'

'I say, they don't have a lawyer either, only a simple case against him that, if it isn't contested, will be an open and shut case.' It was Lord Jim who'd now entered the room, followed by Mary and Bernard. He went on. 'The very least we must do is contest the rotten thing.'

It was like a Guinness World Record attempt for the most people in the smallest room. Frank had taken up three-quarters of the space so everyone else had to stand shoulder to shoulder beside the bed.

Janet kissed my cheek. 'Please?'

'His best bet is for him to be charged in the city,' I said. 'Maximo told me himself. That way he'll be taken away from here.'

'Und you sink zhey vill allow zhis? Very funny, haar haar haar.' Now it was Ziegwalt's turn. 'No. Zhey must keep it here,' he said airily, banging a fist into his palm. 'Zhey have too much to lose, I tell you.'

'No.'

We all looked at Jim.

'That, in my considerably humble opinion, and with my even humbler knowledge of the law of the Republic of the Philippines, is incorrect.' When he said the name of the country Ziegwalt huffed.

Jim held up a cautioning finger. 'Uh, uh, uh. Tarry a moment, my Lilliputian friend. We must not cogitate in terms of rational thinking, in terms of right and wrong and how a normal case in law would work. Remember, we are in El Refusio.' He allowed himself a moment to let the joke sink in. He often used the term to refer to what he called the world's most contradictory place, where the answer was always no but where no one ever did anything to stop you. 'In this town, as we all know, and I'm sure John here is rapidly learning by trial and error, if you'll pardon the pun, one must stand on one's head to see things straight.'

'Everything,' Jim went on, pulling at his frayed collar as if summing up, 'is upside down and back to front here. We could be the best educated, most skilled advocates on the face of our fair planet, yet with all the will in the world we'll not be able to help without adjusting ourselves to the law of the jungle.'

We all stood motionless, gawping at this funny man with his BBC English, dressed in stinking rags. He sounded like a lawyer but looked like Humphrey Bogart in *The African Queen*. A week's worth of stubble and a broken front tooth that he constantly tongued completed the appearance of genteel eccentricity.

'Your point?' I asked, wondering what his sudden interest was in helping Maximo.

'My point, and I promise you I do have one, is that this idea that his best bet lies in a trip to the state capital is fundamentally flawed. What do we have? Ask yourself that. And what do we not have?'

We all looked at our toes. Frank looked at his gut.

'What we do have is local knowledge.'

'Oh, come on.'

He cut me off with an 'Ah–buh-buh-buh-buh!' and a raised forefinger. 'Relatively speaking. Commensurate with and proportional to what we would not have in the city. We may not be local by any means, but at least here we would not need to know the legal system inside out. At least here they'd be playing by our rules. At least we'd be on home territory.'

Bistro Bernard nodded and said, 'Bon. Correct.'

'And just imagine if he was taken south. Most likely he'd disappear, or else get bumped off or locked away out of sight somewhere. It's my considered opinion that we should try our best to keep him here.' Jim stood and patted his shorts pockets. 'Now then, I don't know about anyone else but I'm a bit thirsty. Anyone care for an early evening sherbet?'

By eight o'clock Jim was blotto. More accurately, he was comatose on the floor of Bernard's bistro, ruining any semblance of ethical authority he appeared to possess earlier. He still had a burning cigarette in one hand and a glass of Bernard's best brandy in the other. The breeze made his eyelids flutter.

Ziegwalt was lying in the massive wicker hammock, snoring evenly. Frank was out cold by the barbecue pit, his forehead resting on the meat table, one hand still holding a skewered pork kebab upright like the Statue of Liberty torch.

Next to Frank, sitting upright in a chair and also out cold was Janet's husband Taddi, his guitar still across his lap. One hand was frozen, still fingering a chord as though he was playing. His mouth was open in silent song, his eyes shut with the emotion of the lyrics.

Janet was lying on top of the bar face down, one arm dangling each side. God knows how she ended up there, or who had persuaded her to dance, but once up she wouldn't come down.

And the most sozzled of the lot, completely pie-eyed and pickled before everyone else, and by far the most raucous drunk of the day, was lying on the floor beside me with no shoes on. Thomas Bacudo, the chief of police.

I poked his corpulent, meat-filled paunch with a toe. He snorted like a sow, rubbed his nose and rattled his tonsils.

He was still wearing his socks but we'd pulled his shoes off as a precaution. We didn't want him waking halfway through and disturbing us. Better safe than sorry.

Getting the chief here had been easy, getting him drunk easier still. Bernard had simply gone round to his office and invited him, promising reconciliation, and, more enticingly, as much grub and booze as he could quaff. Once here the rest was easy; every beer after the first few laced with a tot of rum, every rum after that a quadruple.

By five he was loud-mouthed and boasting of his own high-ranking pre-eminence, by six he was in a beer-drinking competition with me (my opaque San Miguel bottles were filled with water), by seven he was dancing with Janet, and by half past he was on the deck.

Bernard's head came through the kitchen serving hatch. 'He is compos?'

'I think he's dead,' I whispered back.

'Good.' His head went back in and a moment later he came through the door rubbing his hands. 'I hide his shoes in the free-zaire. You got the keys?'

196

I took a deep breath, gave the chief a swift kick in the ribs to make sure he was asleep and delved into his trouser pockets. An asthma inhaler, a tiny pocket address book... I dug deeper, feeling the flab of his leg but steering clear of his sweaty scrotum.

'You get it?'

'Hang on. No, that's not it,' I said, pulling out the last item, his wallet. 'Let me try the other pocket.' We had to roll him over on one side to get to the other leg but as soon as I put my hand in I felt them; a big bunch of keys with an 8-ball key ring. 'OK.'

'Good,' said Bernard. 'Now we make the ee-vi-donce disappear. Puff!'

The streets from the bistro to the municipal building were still fairly busy. It was only just eight o'clock. Eateries were just shutting up shop, kids were using up the last of their playtime energy before turning in for the night, women were having their evening gossip on every corner, and the men were lining up their booze and balut.

'You don't think it's too early. There might be someone about,' I whispered as we turned the corner. A young girl at a barbecue pork stall smiled at me and I smiled back.

'No. It is perfect.' He noticed my gaze and said, 'You are seeing how many people sell the barbecue now, no?'

I was. When I'd arrived this girl and her mother were the only ones hawking the little skewers of pork. Now there were about twenty all doing the exact same thing.

'Huh. It is the Philippines mentality,' he said. 'Like the parrot, they copy. They see one and they all copy, exactly. The Xerox Nation. In one month there is no more. Puff! They all stop. One month later one start, then all start. They have no, 'ow you say, *originalité*.'

I looked at the row of people all selling satays, or, more to the point, all waiting for someone to buy their satays, and said, 'They're nice people, Filipinos, don't you think? Very laid back. I like them. Wish the Chinese were like that.'

'Filipinos are the blacks of Asia.'

That's a new one on me, I thought. I'd heard all the usual observations that you hear regarding ex Spanish colonies (and which I usually countered); they were lazy (laid back), corrupt (poorly paid), had inflated opinions of themselves and couldn't take criticism (optimistic), prefer sleeping to working (not greedy), dancing to housekeeping (like to enjoy life), sex to study (and the problem is?), and had the worst food in Asia. That last one was my contribution. I would say the worst in the world, but that award goes to my own country. As a Filipino colleague of mine once said when I asked him if there was a Tagalog translation for the Spanish term '*mañana mañana*': 'We don't have anything that urgent,' he replied. He used to refer to his own country as 'the home of the seven deadly sins'.

I asked Bernard what he meant.

'They can resist everything but temptation.'

'Why do you stay here?'

'I know nussing else for thirty years. 'Ow I can go back to France, with their rules? Me with my crazy ways. Why have you been away from England for so many years?' he asked rhetorically. 'Because it is too, 'ow you say, regular.'

'Regulated.'

'Yes. Everybody in Europe is not free. That is why we are all 'ere, no? We can be free.' He patted my back. 'We were born a hundred years too late, my rosbif friend.'

I thought about it for a moment, about how that one little speech summed up every foreigner's reason for staying in retrograde countries, when suddenly everything went black. A blackout from God.

'Talk about luck,' I said, blinking.

'That is no luck,' he said, looking at his watch. 'Eight o'clock. Sank you, my friend.' He smiled. 'I pay the electricity man to close it for ten minwits. You cannot do this in France.'

We crept past the Hard Rocks. The videoke machine had gone off but the merry fishermen were still singing.

I looked up at the sky. The stars had gone behind a cloud and the night was getting humid. 'I think there's a storm coming,' I said.

Bernard looked up. 'Maybe first rain of the seasoning. It should have been last week. Maybe a typhoon. Turn here.'

And we were standing across the street from the building I'd been in that morning. We stood under a shop awning until a tricycle had passed, then crossed quietly. My flip-flops seemed to make a hell of a racket so I took them off and stuck them down the back of my shorts.

'You remember the window?' Bernard asked.

'It's the last office along the corridor, so it should be the last one in the building,' I whispered. It was so dark without a moon that I tripped up the podium step and stubbed my toe. We stopped and I rubbed it, feeling the sticky blood on my fingers.

'Bon?'

'Yeah,' I replied, trying to locate his face. 'Bon. I can't see a bloody thing. How can we find the window?'

'A-ha! Squid,' he said.

'Ay?'

I heard a rustling sound and a moment later Bernard was glowing under a low green light. He shook the clear plastic bag, held it up to his face and turned luminous lime green.

I was stunned. 'What is it?'

'I tell you, squid.'

I touched the bag, squeezing the cold incandescent fire. 'It's squid! A bag full of squid! They're glowing!'

'Of course. You have not seen bio… somesing in the sea?'

'Bioluminescence? Yeah. I thought it was algae. It's in the animals?'

His illuminated, ghoulish face nodded. 'Na-tu-ral luminosité. Good, no?' he grinned.

'It's amazing!' I fondled the bag.

'Shh. Now we go, English.' He turned and crept along holding the bag up like a lantern, the radiance barely enough to light the wall.

'Won't someone see us?'

'No. You must be close to see.'

Isn't the world strange and beautiful, I thought. Why hadn't anyone told me about this before?

'Feurck.' He stopped. 'The window is clo-sed.'

'The top. Above your head, the fanlight is open.'

'You think you can get in?'

'No problem.' I barged past him. 'You don't need to go in. Stay here and keep dog.'

'Dog? Where is this dog?'

'Lookout. You stay here and be lookout.'

'What about the dog,' he said, holding out the bag and peering into the darkness with alarm.

'There's no dog. It's just an expression.'

'Ahh. You mean like the guard dog. Bon. Bon.'

I looked up at the window. The fanlight at the top was a metre wide by a torso high. It was only just above my head but the whole window unit was flush with the masonry, with no sill to get a foothold on. Bloody architects.

'I'll get in and you pass me the squid,' I said, sizing up the problem in front of me and running my hands around the frame like an expert.

'Ok.'

'When I'm in you pass me the bag of squid.'

'Yes. I am ready.'

'OK.' I dithered, pointlessly inspecting the joints between frame and blockwork, even drawing a fingertip down the putty on all four sides.

'You go now?'

'All right, all right, don't rush me!'

'Sorry.'

I took a deep breath. 'Right. You give me a foot up.'

Bernard looked left and right, put the bag between his teeth and cupped his hands. 'OK. Ngeddy?'

I put my bare foot in, said 'One, two, three', and stood on his hands. Holding the top-hinged window open with the back of my head until I got my torso through, nearly impaling myself on the stay, I put a leg in so that I was sideways, resting on my belly and crotch on the sharp frame. The problem was width.

'I'm stuck!' I started to panic, trapped front and rear. 'Bernard. I'm–'

'Shh! Someone is coming!' He shoved the bag back up his shirt.

I lay there, barely able to breathe and being cut in two by the steel frame. 'Where?'

'There. In the field.'

I gazed into the pitch black. There was a low, throaty growl. 'The dog!'

'There is no dog, Bernard! You're the dog!'

'Hello?' he said quietly.

A cloud parted and the gentle face of a curious buffalo came out of the night.

'It's just a bloody buffalo, Bern. Maximo's brother's probably.' I yanked my leg and slipped in, dropping to the floor. There was a crash as the swivel chair shot across the room and hit the wall. I waited and listened for footsteps. Nothing. It was impossible to tell whether or not I was even in the right office.

'Psst! You are OK, kalbo?'

'Yeah. And don't call me baldy. I hear it every day from the locals.'

A phantasmal hand appeared through the fanlight shaking the glowing bag. I reached up and pulled it from him but it snagged on the metal nipple and tore, spilling its soupy luminous contents. They ran down the window like alien blood. 'Shit!'

A second later the hand reappeared holding a Bic lighter.

'What shall I do about the squid?'

'Forget it. Only five minwits the lights will come on.'

I'd forgotten about that. Flicking the lighter on I sighed with relief when I saw the nautilus shell ashtray. I went quickly to the filing cabinet and, after trying half a dozen keys, unlocked it. There it was, Maximo's knife in a plastic bag, still stained with dark-brown blood.

'Do not forget my file also,' Bernard said.

I heard him but wasn't listening, my senses absolutely focused on that sight. Suddenly the gravity of what I was about to do, what someone had done with that very weapon, hit me and my knees buckled. What if Max had killed her?

'English! Come on! Two minwits!'

What if all this was just El Refugio village fever taking hold of me? What on earth was I doing skulking around at night with a grave robber, stealing police evidence? Wake up before it's too late! I closed the drawer.

'John!'

I opened it again. It was still there staring at me. I could see Bonga's pitiful old face right there in that office as if it was only a minute ago, a defiant mask covering a frightened old man's loneliness and fear.

'John! Now! One minwit!'

I grabbed the knife, shoved it in my pocket, then took two files; Bernard's and Maximo's, before closing and locking the drawer and going back to the window. There was a sill on the inside. I stepped up, passing Bernard the files, before hurriedly climbing out into the night.

Just as we ran back and crossed the street to the shop awning again, the electricity came back on. The building was flooded in light.

'What shall we do with it?' I panted, mopping the sweat from my head with a shirtsleeve. 'Chuck it in the sea?'

'Yes.' He patted me on the shoulder. 'First we will go back and put the keys in le shief's pocket. Then we dispose the evidonce. Puff! But first you wear your shoes, my Pink Panther friend.'

I looked down. The toes of my right foot were covered in blood and a big piece of skin was flapping where I'd stubbed it earlier. I inspected it then reached behind me for the rubber flip-flops I'd stuffed down the back of my shorts.

I pulled it out. There was only one! 'I've dropped one of my bloody flip-flops!'

'Flop flop? What is this?'

'Flip… My shoes, Bernard, my bloody shoes! I've left one behind!'

'*Merde*.'

1

There was a cockroach on the table next to me. Every time Frank opened another can of tuna its antennae rose up and waved about. My one remaining flip-flop was on the table ready to splat it but I didn't have the heart. He'd become a friend.

'You gonna sit there all day, boy?'

'You've asked me that ten times, Frank.'

'Look, they ain't coming today. Maybe it's raining down south, and you know what that road's like. When that sucker gits wet ain't no one a-passin' through.'

'They have to come and collect him. Ten days, the law says. Ten days for an official to charge him or he's out. By my reckoning those ten days are up in...' I looked at my watch, 'fifteen minutes.'

'Huh.' He scooped out the oily fish and daintily spread it on a cracker. 'Who sez?'

'Everyone.'

'This is the Philippines, boy, not the land of hope and glory.' He looked about in a panic. 'Mary! Where's that hot sauce? Anyway, they don't know everything.'

'We know transport's on it's way. Janet told us.'

'Janet. Huh.'

'Janet heard it from one of her waitresses, she got it from her cousin who works in the municipal building who heard it from the janitor who was told by her friend the tea lady who serves the governor. So it must be true. She said that because the village didn't have the means to transport him the seven hours by road from here to the provicial capital, the state was being forced to come here and collect him.'

Frank huffed again and put the cracker in its rightful slot. 'Ng.'

I believed the story. The road south was only a dirt track, and short of transporting the prisoner by public bus there seemed little else they could do. They could hardly go in the chief's clapped-out jeep.

'They'll pay the attorney enough of a bribe to come here and keep it under wraps,' I stated. 'Create a fake trial and the old man'll disappear afterwards.'

'Huh.'

I picked up my flip-flop and turned it in my hands. 'By my reckoning someone will come here today and they'll take him, with or without evidence.'

'Huh.'

'It doesn't matter either way, really,' I said. 'If there's no evidence they'll conjure it up. If there's no witness they'll buy one. Anything to get this off their plate.'

'But they have evidence. The knife.'

I whacked the cockroach and missed. Frank, like everyone else except Bernard, had been kept in the dark about the knife. 'Yeah, there's that of course,' I said, watching the cockroach settle on a new crumb. 'But apart from the knife what have they got?' I looked out the corner of my eye at him. He wasn't suspicious, too concerned with lining up another cracker full of fish flakes.

I'd been on tenterhooks the whole day, first waiting for the chief to come round, handcuffs held out. 'You were seen disposing of this knife,' and he'd produce the weapon covered in seaweed. And when that didn't happen all I could think about was my lost flip-flop. They'd have a door-to-door search, just like in Cinderella, and would offer it up to each foot in turn. Who else in town had size-12 feet?

After we'd dropped the knife out at sea tied to a stone we'd gone back to the bistro and re-shod the blotto chief. He was in the exact same position we'd left him, only now covered in ants, all keen to feast on the scraps of food stuck to his face. No one else had budged either, and with the keys safely back in his pocket I was free to go to bed and lie awake worrying. And I hadn't stopped since.

'You sure they gonna tell ya? Maybe they've forgot.'

'This is El Ref, Frank. If that van arrives, someone'll be here to tell us.' I toyed with the rubber sandal once more, then put it down and inspected my bandaged big toe. Mary had cleaned me up. I thought again about how powerful the rumour mill was in this village, how one little conversation could spread village-wide in less than an hour. Sometimes I'd say something in Bernard's bistro over a beer and it'd beat me back to the guest house.

'Say, boy, why you only got one flipperty-flop there?'

'Lost it somewhere,' I said, and added as a precaution, 'around here. Days ago. Probably turn up sooner or later.' I thought I could trust Frank with what Bernard and I had done but better safe than sorry. He might quite innocently tell Mary during some drunken pillow talk and then the whole town would be in on it.

The flip-flop was the only potential complication in what otherwise had been a well-planned, brilliantly executed operation. Bernard had been around to see me this morning and informed me that the chief had woken at around six, none the wiser. They'd shaken hands, he said, and Bernard had cooked him breakfast. The only minor scare came when he went to his jeep and pulled out his keys. He sniffed them and frowned. 'Mm, smells like fish.'

Other than that nothing much had happened. Jim, in his poshest legal-eagle vocabulary, had been to the police station trying to scare them into thinking he was some kind of expert in law. The knowledge Jim held was in fact gleaned from a school textbook from the local library called *I Want to Know More About the Law*.

But when it came to performance art Jim was Laurence Olivier. I even believed he was a lawyer when he started waffling. Just give him a shirt and tie, shove a briefcase under his arm and he'd fool anyone with that accent.

I pulled my foot off the table and stood up, walking to the edge of the veranda and looking up at the heavy sky. There was electricity in the air. The garden plants were dead still, and there was not a mangy dog to be seen anywhere.

'Storm's a-brewin',' Frank said. 'Surprised she ain't here yet. Whole day just-a hanging there like that. Gonna be a big one, boy.' He lurched over and stood beside me. 'Yep, she's a-cooking.'

A growing rumble of thunder which sounded like ten-pin bowling rolled around the hills.

'Summin's up. Looka yonder.' He pointed down the path to the bend in the street. Running towards us, fearfully looking up at the sky as though it was about to fall in was a breathless Janet.

'They're here!' she said, stopping at the gate and looking skywards again. 'And guess what? They've brought a judge with them! And they're not taking him south! And they're not allowing us to speak to him! And guess what his name is? The judge?'

At that split second between Janet asking the question and answering it there was a huge flash of lightning over the silver-grey sea and everything was translucent for one blinding moment.

'Theodore!' she added. 'That's the judge's name. Theodore Lam!'

An ear-splitting crack of thunder and we all covered our ears.

In the few minutes it took to get to the police station I stared up at the sky and wondered if the changing weather was a good or bad omen. I decided it was good, and quickened my pace in anticipation of meeting this new Lam.

The family resemblance was unmistakable: broad flat face and wide forehead, sharp pinhole eyes, small ears, tight cheese-paring mouth and parsimonious nose. A real sneaky beak. He was a Lam all right.

Jim introduced us as I entered the chief's office, saying, 'Ah, my investigator. Please come in, John, and take a seat. Mr Lam, I'd like you to meet Mr Harris, my investigator, formerly of London and Hong Kong. John, Mr Lam, our worthy magistrate.'

I couldn't believe it; five o'clock in the evening and Jim was still sober. It had to be a record. And to my utter astonishment he was wearing not only a pressed shirt and trousers, but a bow tie. And, wonder of wonders, had combed his hair! He looked pink and shiny, like a schoolboy on his first day.

Janet came in behind me but was asked to leave by the deputy, Ten. She asked Ten who the hell she thought she was, and reminded her not to forget who was sponsoring her basketball team's new jerseys for this year's Christmas tournament. The chief put his foot down. Janet ground her teeth and stepped out. The door was shut.

'Investigators?' said Lam, and looked at Thomas the chief as if to say, 'What the hell is this all about? You never told me we were going to have to fight this!'

'He's a tourist,' the chief said. 'They both are, sir.'

Suddenly the mean look in Lam's eyes seemed to desert him. He still looked angry but now he appeared weary as well.

'So you're not a lawyer then,' he said hopefully, daring to smile a little.

'Indeed I'm not,' said Jim. 'But I think you'll find–'

'Then I'm sorry, but under the rules of this country you cannot practise law.'

'That is right,' Ten said, and we all looked at her. She blushed and asked if we'd all like a soda. We all said yes. Jim licked his lips.

'Quite right, quite right,' Jim said. 'However, under the legal code Mr Bonga may represent himself if he so wishes. And there's absolutely nothing to stop him appointing us as, how shall I put it, ciceroni?'

Lam flicked his eyes at me and I'm sure he was thinking the same thing: What the bloody hell is a cicerone when it's at home?

'For instance,' Jim went on, bending down to retrieve something from between his legs. It was a briefcase. Ziegwalt's. I recognised it instantly by the sticker of a half-naked woman holding four jugs of beer, with the word 'Oktoberfest' in suitably medieval Bavarian text.

Jim placed it on his lap and popped it open. 'Under section two of rule one hundred and ten, and section one of rule one hundred and twelve you cannot start legal proceedings against our friend without conducting a preliminary investigation. And that means not moving him until you have reason to believe he has committed a crime, which I assure you he has not.'

I glanced inside the briefcase. It was empty. I looked at Lam. He looked at the chief as though he wanted to strangle him.

'A preliminary investigation is required for all offences punishable by at least four years, two months and one day,' Jim added. 'And as this is a case of homicide, I'd say it more than qualified.'

'Ahem, ahem, quite right, and that's why I'm here, to conduct a preliminary investigation,' Lam said, obviously ad-libbing. 'To um… determine whether or not a crime has been committed.'

'And to see what is patently obvious to all and sundry; that Mr Bonga is not guilty of the crime thereof. Oh, a crime has been committed all right; we have the dead body to prove it. Unfortunately she's now six feet underground. Gone to A Better Place, you might say.' Jim permitted himself a congratulatory laugh.

My gaze was now glued to the rear window and the lumpy, egg-like stain that had congealed down it. The squid had dried hard and flies were still buzzing around, some of them bothering the two men sitting beneath it.

'God Almighty,' Lam said, swiping the air and beginning to lose his composure. 'Thomas, are you telling me we don't even have a body?'

'Sir, we had to bury her, sir. We do not have the facility to keep a body, and the road out is blocked. We have the photos, sir, and the evidence: Mr Bonga's knife.'

My heart stopped and my head filled with blood.

At that moment Ten came back in with the drinks and the chief asked her to bring the evidence.

I didn't know where to look or what to do. My whole body started prickling with nervous sweat and it felt as though I was going to pass out. The room blurred under the perspiration that flooded down into my eyes and my mouth dried up. I wanted out.

Thomas chucked her the keys and I heard the rattle of the tin filing cabinet behind me.

I looked down at Jim's feet, for the first time in shoes, and then at my own, for the first time in someone else's; Frank's. Two sizes too small. Then at the chief's, in boots. Then I saw it.

The drawer behind me slid open and I heard rummaging.

Beneath the chief's desk were his black-clad feet, a tiny cowry shell stuck in the tread of one. Right beside them was my lost flip-flop. I nearly did a flip-flop myself.

'It's... not here, sir,' Ten said.

'Of course it is. And bring his file while you're there.'

My stomach heaved.

'It's...' I heard the drawer close and another one open. Then that closed and the third one opened.

'The top! The top!' The boots were drawn in and the chief stomped angrily across the room, the shell going 'Tic, Tic, Tic' on the tiled floor.

Without hesitating I put my foot under his desk, put it on the flip-flop and pulled it towards me.

'Let me get it,' he huffed and opened the drawer again.

I bent down, picked up my flip-flop and shoved it in my pocket.

'Where did you put it?'

'I... I didn't put it anywhere, sir.' Ten's voice warbled under stress.

'What? You lost it! Is that what you're trying to say? You stupid woman. You're useless, do you know that? A useless piece of whale blubber.' He slammed the filing-cabinet drawer shut with such force that an ornament fell off and shattered on the floor. 'Well you'd better find it, my girl, or you'll be back to selling cakes in your grandmother's store.'

Ten started to cry. She crept out, mumbling that he had no right to speak to her that way, and that she would tell Uncle Bong Bong.

The chief was almost blue with rage. He sat down and said, 'Anyway, we have photos of the body with the knife, I can assure you, sir. And the knife itself. Though it seems to have been mislaid.'

Poor old Lam, he looked like he wanted the ground to swallow him up.

I wiped my forehead on a shirtsleeve, took a deep breath and our eyes met. For one small moment there seemed to be absolute recognition of what I'd done.

'So, where do we go from here?' Jim said. 'As I understand the law, you have ten days for the preliminary investigation from the time when the complaint was filed with you. And as the complaint regarding the alleged offence took place here ten days ago today, and I'm assuming Mr Thomas Bacudo filed the complaint with your office, you must, under the law, write a resolution today.'

Lam opened his mouth to speak but Jim cut him off.

'Either there are sufficient grounds to issue a subpoena or you dismiss it altogether. In which case,' Jim said, shutting his briefcase with a click-click, 'our man goes free.'

Jim, I thought, you're my hero. I smiled and went to stand.

'*In flagrante delicto*,' said Lam, and I checked myself.

Jim froze, both thumbs on the catches of the case. 'Oh, surely you're not serious.'

Lam looked down his nose and rolled his shoulders, gaining a little composure. Perhaps he'd suddenly remembered who his relatives were and how much was at stake if he let us walk all over him. No doubt he'd be staying with family and no doubt the chief and he would be grilled by them very soon.

'Yes. No need for the prelims, I'm afraid. *In flagrante delicto*.'

'What does that mean?' I said.

'Caught in the act.'

'In certain cases,' Lam went on, 'a person may be arrested by a police officer if caught in the act of committing an offence.'

'He wasn't caught in the act!' I protested. 'We found her on the bloody beach. He wasn't even there!'

'Mr Bacudo?' Lam looked at the chief and his eyes said, 'You'd better back me up right now or you'll be found on the bloody beach with a knife in your back.'

'Correct, sir. One of the villagers witnessed the whole thing and came to me. We have their statement.'

'What! Who?' I was out of my seat.

There was a scintillating burst of lightning that lit the room like a camera flash, followed by an enormous crack of thunder that made the windows rattle. The heavens opened and the rain began to fall, drumming on the roof.

'Whose statement?' asked Jim.

'We will inform you of the person or persons at the arraignment and plea in five days, should Mr Bonga wish you to know.' Lam stood. 'In the meantime he will be offered, as the law dictates, the services of a public attorney should he not have the necessary funds to appoint private counsel.' He stood, picking up his briefcase. 'You see, Mr Jim, I can also command the Queen's English. Now if you'll excuse me, gentlemen, I have some family matters to attend to.'

We all watched dumbstruck as he floated out of the room on a cushion of air.

When Jim and I got outside and stood under the eaves sheltering from the downpour, I said to him, 'Five days until the arraignment, whatever that is. What do you think we should do first? We need to prepare.'

Jim flicked a sideways glance at me as though he wished I hadn't asked, and then, avoiding eye contact, said, 'Um… I'll let you know,' and disappeared into a wall of rain.

2

Two things poured that week: water from the heavens onto the little village of El Refugio, and booze down Jim's throat.

The rain was like nothing I'd ever seen. It came down in huge thunderous droplets all day and all night without respite. Our world turned from sparkling turquoise to brown. Every street went from clouds of dust to knee-deep torrents of mud.

Trees came down under the battering, bamboo houses caved in. The beach was no longer flat, the sand now scoured and gouged by the enormous amount of water trying to drain off the land. And for the first time in five years, I was told, the Hard Rocks Videoke closed for one night. The roof had fallen in. The next evening, debris swept in the corner, they were singing in the rain.

Nothing came in or out of the village by land, sea or air. The sea, now rust-coloured with the earth being carried into it from the bowl-like shape of the surrounding hills, was chaos. Up until then it had been a millpond, mirror calm. Now even the bay was a choppy soup of brown and green. Mud, seaweed, palm fronds, driftwood, polystyrene, and even a wardrobe washed up on the beach.

The few boats that were not lashed properly ended up as driftwood, battered against Bernard's restaurant wall, and anyone who was reckless enough to venture out to sea came back very quickly with a look of utter panic on their face.

The road south was no longer a road but a fast-moving river of clay in which everything set upon it was carried out of the village. No buses or jeepneys or vehicles of any kind came in or out through those wet limestone cliffs, and according to Janet weren't likely to for weeks. Even when the rain stopped and the water drained, she said the earth road wouldn't be there any more. It would take weeks to get out.

The only other place that opened every night was Bernard's re-re-named The Refuge Bistro. And his only customer was Jim. He poured and poured and poured in heated competition with God. Neck and neck they were, in determined defiance of each other. The Almighty chucked it on us from the sky, and drunken Jim kept up measure for measure in a hateful display of self-destruction.

He'd gone from what looked like someone who could pull a rabbit out of a hat that day in the police station to someone who was too inebriated to keep a hat on his own head. Like all drunks he'd always had an element of tragic charm, but equally typically he was unable to face even the smallest loss head-on.

He'd entered that police station a lion, head held high, adrenalin (and alcohol) pumping through his veins, and put on the performance of a lifetime. The man who'd exited the same building half an hour later was a beaten-up old dingo.

I know because I'd seen it in his eyes, in his complexion; the smell of defeat oozed from the pores in his skin. One moment as rigid and whippy as bamboo, hard to uproot and only felled with a machete, the next a battered palm, its meagre root bowl so easily undermined by a swift tide.

And all because of a few remarks that hadn't gone his way. Anyone else would have come away from that hearing with a feeling of the challenge ahead. I had. We'd shown the judge that Maximo had friends, not necessarily in high places, but helpful ones none the less. Friends who were not going to allow a whitewash.

And that was all we'd set out to achieve; merely to let everyone know the old man was no fall guy. To be honest none of us, with the exception of Bernard, could have cared less about finding the culprit, we just would not stand by and watch some poor innocent get framed. And I for one thought we'd started off pretty well.

But then I'm not an alcoholic, at least not on Jim's level. And unlike Jim I didn't hide from the tiniest hiccups in life by diving into a drink. The big hiccups, yes, but not the small ones. At first we tried to coax Jim out of the bar and into a shower, using everything from Maximo's innocence to the promise of more booze. He wouldn't budge. His forehead was stuck to the bar top. He slept right there.

Ziegwalt knew him best and told us to forget it. In a few days he'd disappear as he always did, he said, and eventually turn up either in A Better Place or back at the shack he lived in.

In a way the loss of our most learned team member brought the rest of us together during that week. That and the rain. 'Ve are like Bayern Munich having zhe man sending off. Ve play harder ten man.' I couldn't have put it better myself. We pulled together and pooled our resources, such as they were.

Janet, as well as providing a meeting place, also kept us fed and watered during our daily and nightly discussions. She reminded us of the need to keep track of time by constantly pointing at the numerous clocks in her cafe. 'Time. Very important. Tea or coffee?'

She'd also, very astutely, asked her husband to go to the university bookstore in the city and pick up anything on the law. He'd returned the day after the Lam meeting, on the last bus that made it in, armed with half the shop. But without a beautiful Italian woman.

I tried to hide my disappointment but Janet picked up the scent of male heartache in an instant. Taddi said that Annie, Jiz and Brenda had decided to go south and climb a mountain Bernard had told them about. After that they were not sure.

Outwardly I tried to appear as though I couldn't care less, but inside, my stomach felt funny. I knew that I'd had my window of opportunity and blown it.

And so helping Maximo became a sort of therapy for me. I spent every day alone with the law books. Among other things I learned that (assuming the chief did in fact have a witness who'd confess to seeing the murder of Elsie) Maximo had no right to bail, as the crime he was on trial for was an offence punishable by a life sentence. He had the right to defend himself. He had the right to be visited by anyone. He had the right to be present at all stages, the right to testify as a witness, the right to cross-examine, and the right to a speedy and impartial trial. But above all, I learned, there was no jury in a Philippines court.

And as far as this thing called an arraignment and plea was concerned, it should be a simple hearing with the objective of fixing the identity of the accused, informing him of the charges, and a chance for him to enter his plea of not guilty. After that we would be given a minimum of fifteen days to prepare for trial. And that was all we wanted; enough time for us to find a way of getting him to the regional capital.

And that's where Ziegwalt's plan came into effect. Simply put, we would turn up at the station with so many townspeople wanting to see the proceedings that they'd be scared into taking it somewhere much larger. The sheer weight of numbers would scare them.

Lam buckled under mine and Jim's gaze, so, regardless of the weight of family pressure on his shoulders, the pressure exerted by public exposure would be greater. And apart from anything else, there was nowhere big enough in town to hold a large gathering. We could hardly cram into the chief's office.

I went around town trying to drum up support but it wasn't easy. Most had viewed Maximo as a crank. Although they agreed that he didn't seem capable of murder, they were not willing to voice his innocence in a public display. I badgered them, insisting that they were on the edge of a slippery slope. If they let this one go, I said, the Lams' stranglehold on the town would just get tighter. All they said was 'maybe'. And maybe, in this country, I'd learned, meant no.

Mentioning Lam was a huge mistake. As soon as I added the name to a sentence, however tactfully the name was disguised, they took a sharp intake of breath, their eyes widening. It was as if I'd mentioned God.

And the weather was dead against me. Most places were closed, and in a country where families gather around their little grocery store or eatery, that meant a ghost town. I had to knock on doors and it scared people. I scare people anyway, so no change there.

In the end I had about fifty maybes (nos) and only six yeses, all of those from A Better Place, all Elsie's friends, her 'bum chums' as Bernard called them. Such a gentleman. Janet did a little better simply because she was well known. She had 20 concrete yeses: the two basketball teams she sponsored plus Taddi's family and the cafe staff.

Frank managed two banner-wavers: Francis the Hard Rocks ladyboy, who, for some bizarre reason, asked if he could burn a pair of men's Y-fronts; and Maximo's part-time gardener.

Ziegwalt hadn't been able to get anyone, not even Jim, who was still missing (but we heard was drinking with some local men at a far-off fisherman's shack).

So all in all, including us but subtracting a few foul-weather no-shows, we would have about thirty bodies at the police station tomorrow.

As far as I saw it we had two lines of attack. First of all we would be waiting outside the police station in large numbers at nine o'clock in the morning, come rain or shine. They would be expecting a pushover but instead would be confronted by a wall of people that refused to budge.

Failing that, if Lam was unphased by the locals and insisted on hearing the plea, I'd go to plan B and quote the law. I'd quote everything I'd read, from a layman's guide to a thousand pages of text on the rights of the Filipino. A kind of bullshit baffles brains approach. Case dismissed; let's all go for a San Mig!

And if those two well thought out formulas added up to nothing, well, we'd have to fight the trial, and none of us wanted to talk about that. That would mean finding out who did kill Elsie. Though not a needle in a haystack, it was at the very least like trying to find one off-key singer in a congregation of 500. No mean feat when the person looking for them is tone-deaf. Despite everyone's faith in me, I was no bloodhound.

All that remained for me to do now, before tomorrow's circus, was to visit Maximo one last time to make sure he knew the drill and didn't say something weird. I knew he wasn't an idiot but he was eccentric, and all that time spent in that cell hadn't helped matters.

3

The rain was still heavy, though it had eased slightly since the first day. I looked at Frank. He'd finished his tuna and was eyeing the can he'd given me.

'D'you want that, boy?'

'Sure you don't want to come?' I said, standing and pushing it across to him.

'Seen him earlier.'

'Six o'clock, my visiting time, right?'

'Yup.' He opened the can and swigged the oil first. 'Looks like you got transport,' he said, pointing with the spoon.

Out of the sheets of rain the chief's jeep appeared, its one working headlight pointing skywards and making a beam of falling droplets. He pulled up at the gate but stayed inside, the rain bouncing off the makeshift blue and white striped tarpaulin canopy. It looked like a deckchair on wheels. Ten came running through the gate down the muddy path, one hand held over her head.

'Six o'clock,' she said, stopping under the eaves. 'We will take you.'

I looked at Frank, bewildered by this sudden show of police compassion. He looked at me, incredulous.

'I'll just get my sandals,' I said.

'And Mr Frank. Maybe you also would like to make a visit.'

'Went this mornin', doll.'

'The chief want you come.'

We looked at each other again and shrugged. Frank rose up like a buffalo from a paddy field.

The chief honked his horn impatiently. Now that Ten wasn't in the car he had to hold up the plastic sheet himself to stop the rain pooling and collapsing in.

'And Mrs Frank,' Ten added, 'she is home tonight?'

'No, she's... I don't know where she is.'

'We are friends,' said Ten. 'I like her. I stay here and talk with her. But, oh well, no mind.' She turned with unforgivable histrionics, said 'That is life', and ran back to the car.

Very suspicious. There's a feeling I get sometimes, quite a lot of the time in fact, a feeling of distrust that starts somewhere on the surface of my body, like sweat, and seeps inside.

I started having the feeling again as we approached the municipal building. Gladys was just leaving, hidden, she no doubt thought, under her floral umbrella. And it wasn't just her being there at this hour in this rain, but the way she skulked under the porch and tried to lower herself into the shadows when she saw us.

'What's she doin' here?' Frank said.

'Who?' asked the chief, comically looking left and right.

I leaned out into the rain and shouted at Gladys, 'You forgot your broomstick!'

Frank and I ran under the porch along with Ten, but the chief turned the car around and drove off.

Frank said, 'I thought he wanted to talk to me.'

'He come back,' said Ten, and smiled.

The moment we got into the corridor out of the noise of the rain I could hear shouting, a woman, screaming in frustration. It grew louder as we approached the little outbuilding where

Maximo was. As we neared, Rose came storming past us in a blind rage. Ten tried to stop her, raising a hand like a traffic cop. 'Stupida bitch,' Rose hissed, sweeping past in a boiling hot temper. She looked like Medusa.

'Tell Ten you want to sit in her office to wait for Thomas,' I whispered to Frank. 'I want to see Max without her earwigging.'

We went out the back and Frank did his part. Ten opened the ex-storeroom door, let me in and locked it. Twice. A padlock had been added.

Maximo was pacing up and down under a single bulb that hung from the low corrugated-iron roof. As soon as we were alone a grin crept across his wily old face. 'They gone?'

I looked through the small, square, barred window. Ten and Frank disappeared though the door to the main building. 'Yeah.' I turned. 'What was Rose doing here?'

'Never mind that,' he said. 'Take a look at this.' He pulled the iron-framed bed away from the corner. 'I started a tunnel.'

'What!'

'Move those chairs. Come on, soldier, look lively.' I hesitated. 'Move yourself, move yourself! You should be there already!'

I glanced through the window again and despite myself began shifting chairs. They hadn't completely cleared out the storeroom, only enough to install a single iron-framed bed. There was no toilet, so he was escorted to the one in the main building whenever he needed to go.

'What do you think of that, then?' he said, pointing to a puddle in the corner.

I tilted the bulb towards it and leaned in. 'It's full of water.'

'It's been raining.'

I let the light swing free, our shadows dancing back and forth on the wall, and went across, putting an arm down the 'tunnel'. It went up to my elbow.

'What did you do with the soil?'

'Flushed it down the latrine. Every time my pockets are full I tell them I want to go for a wotsit. Hee hee. They think I've got the runs.'

I looked at his trousers. They were covered in filth. 'Looks like you have.'

'That's mud. Only thing is the toilet keeps getting blocked.'

'So that's the reason for the stench around the offices. Ten told me the chief has been walking all the way across to the hospital building to have a poo.'

'You're 'avin' a giraffe,' he said, using one of my slang terms he'd picked up. I loved it when he did that because they were always slightly out of context and all the more charming for it.

'Not bad, eh?' He rolled his narrow shoulders. 'Got the idea from a film I once saw about British prisoners of war. They used a flowerbed to dispose of the earth. Got to keep the weeds down, old bean.'

'*The Great Escape*.' I saluted. Suddenly everything I'd come here to say about tomorrow's hearing seemed superfluous. Obviously he'd made up his mind about the whole thing. He'd told me that if he didn't get to the city he'd have no chance, but I never imagined he'd try to break out. I felt like forgetting about tomorrow myself and kicking the door down.

'Let's see what happens tomorrow, though,' I said, pushing the bed back.

'You been feeding MacArthur?'

Here we go. MacArthur, that mangy old chicken. It was his prize cock. Or rather, his has-been, moth-eaten prize cock. Now it was a sorry-looking, half-bald bird with foot rot. One of the few tasks he insisted we didn't neglect was the feeding of his bandy old rooster. It didn't eat normal food but a special mix that contained tablets called V-22, 'with 22 essential vitamins!'

'Yeah, but his sinusitis medicine is finished.'

'Hope he doesn't get that bird flu.'

I sat on the bed. 'About tomorrow. You're going to plead not guilty and insist that you represent yourself. I know we've already told them but just in case they ask again.'

'Did you bring my drink?'

I pulled the small bottle of Tanduay rum from my pocket. 'We're going to turn up in numbers and try to scare them into taking it south, OK? I've been reading up and we have a minimum of fifteen days from tomorrow until pre-trial, and that should give us plenty of time.'

He unscrewed the top and swigged, going 'Ahh,' then offered it to me.

'Are you listening?'

'Yeah.' He swigged again. 'You seen Charlie anywhere?'

'No. Now if we can scare them tomorrow and delay it, what with the road being down, I think we'll have enough time to cause them some problems. Don't get too drunk, you don't want to give a bad impression tomorrow.'

Swig. Belch. 'Yes, Sah!'

'So, you come in and say you want to represent yourself, and when–'

'All right, all right, I'm not senile. I heard you before.'

I studied the floor for a moment, wondering whether or not to ask the dreaded question again. 'Just in case it does go to trial, they're gonna want to know where you were that night.'

'I told you before, it doesn't matter where I was or who I was with.' He was losing his temper. He always did when I asked that question.

'It will matter if we have to defend you. We'll need to know your alibi and have a good witness to back it up or we're sunk.'

'Or we could find the bastardo who really killed that poor girl.'

I sighed. Why wouldn't he tell me? I'd been through this a hundred times with him but he either avoided the subject altogether, asking instead about his geriatric bird, or else got angry and told me to find the culprit. It was getting on my nerves.

'I told you, I am not a real detective. If there's no other way out, then we'll do our best to find out who killed her. But why not tell them where you were and get them off your back?'

He put the bottle on a chair and peered through the window. 'They want a whipping boy and I'm it. I told you on the boat, it doesn't matter how many excuses, witnesses, alibis or what-nots we come up with. They're going to win unless we come up with a substitute dope.'

'Dupe.'

'No. I mean dope. That's how things work here.' He held out both hands, left first then right. 'I have this, you want it, so give me this in exchange. They want me or a replacement me.'

I could hear voices coming down the corridor.

'The Lams have everything to lose if this gets out,' he said. 'And nothing to lose if I get out, as long as they have someone else to pin it all on.'

'But…'

'If this gets out, the rich Koreans and Japs will stop coming to the resorts. It'll ruin them. D'you think they care who gets put away? If I escape all they'll do is frame some poor bovine fisherman and he'll be here instead. That's how justice works here; you just need someone to blame, right or wrong doesn't come into it.'

'They don't have the knife,' I said triumphantly. 'Remember? It got mislaid.'

We both giggled and he sat beside me, putting his thin arm around my shoulder. I hugged him back. It was the first time we'd shown our affection for each other and it felt right somehow. I'm not sure where it came from but it felt right.

The door to the outer building opened and Maximo let go.

'D'you need anything?' I said, standing.

He shook his head. I saw something in his old eyes as he looked at me. Love, I think. Like a father's love for a son. I think he saw someone else through me also, in me perhaps.

The door opened. 'Tomorrow, soldier,' he said. *'Mi último adiós.'*

4

'No, Frank. You're too… conspicuous.'

'You sayin' I'm fat?'

'Yes. And too white. Far too white.' Ziegwalt went to speak but I cut him off. 'And you're too loud. Look, let the two girls do it. They'll blend in to the background. You'll stand out like… well, like a giant and a dwarf. Besides, we need both of you at the police station.'

'See,' said Ziegwalt, 'I tell you he is ein detektiv.'

'Yes I am. And that's how we should do it.' I tucked into the grub Mary had cooked, observing their faces. They shrugged at each other and kissed their partners, who turned to leave. 'Remember; one at the front entrance, just across the street, the other at the rear, on the beach. If Gladys leaves, only one of you follows.'

The two women nodded and left arm in arm.

The rain had stopped but the morning was still overcast, the garden flooded. MacArthur the rooster tiptoed behind the girls, his head pecking the air as he strutted along like a guard dog, seeing them through the front gate then turning back.

During the night I had a mini revelation in my sleep. I didn't know who'd killed Elsie but for some reason I had a feeling Gladys was involved. I didn't know why, but every time something happened she seemed to be around. And last night was the final straw. Or rather this morning was.

Maximo's two-legged alarm cock had woken me as usual at about five, but strangely, refused to let me get back to sleep this time. Just like man's best friend he stayed outside my bedroom window, refusing to shut up. I wondered if he was about to expire, emitting a kind of swansong.

Everything went silent for a minute and then something started scratching at the door. I opened it. MacArthur was there yowling like a banshee. And then he did the strangest thing; he started jumping in the air and flapping as if to say, 'I can fly! I can fly!' He took a short run down the corridor, head low, stopped, looked at me, then went further, stopped, looked at me. I followed obediently.

He had done a similar thing the previous night, trying to get me to follow in the other direction, but I'd ignored it. This time he went into the restaurant, turned and faced the wall and let off the most ear-splitting screech I've ever heard, his whole body shaking, before ending in a sort of pathetic cough. He was still gazing at the wall.

The wall with the salvaged P-47 Thunderbolt airplane propeller, the wall with the US flag hanging on it. And the same wall where there used to be a pair of crossed samurai swords. Now there was only one.

'We're lucky with the weather,' I said. 'Better turnout.'

'Typhoon Ana,' said Ziegwalt, leaning over the veranda and looking at the sky. 'She is gone.'

Janet came down the track jumping over puddles, stopped at the end of the garden and held out both wristwatches.

Five minutes later I was standing outside the station with wet feet, trying not to laugh. Twenty or so people had turned up, mostly basketball boys, and were milling about the entrance wondering what they were supposed to do. Janet shouted in Tagalog and they raised their banners. 'Free Bonga!' It sounded like they were demanding marijuana, *gratis*.

'Well, it's better than nothing,' I said to Bernard.

When I got into the office where the chief, Judge Lam and Maximo were waiting, the judge was shouting at the chief. They went silent as soon as I entered.

'What is this?' Lam said. 'Who are these people outside? Why are they here? This is not good. I cannot be here.' He tapped the desk nervously, picking up a pen and putting it down again. 'What is going on?'

'Just locals,' I said. 'They have a right to be here, in this room in fact, to listen to the plea.'

'Right? They have a right, all right. Ugh.' He sat back in his chair and puffed.

'They have no rights,' said the chief calmly. 'And they're not coming into my office, that is for sure.'

'I don't think you understand,' said Lam. 'They have the right to come in here and hear this. They have the right to watch any trial. They have the right to be present at every stage, however minor. And,' he added, pointing at Maximo, 'he has the right to insist on it.'

'Well, they're not coming in here, I have the right to insist on that.'

At that moment the crowd of voices suddenly broke into their 'Free Bonga!' chant, only this time it seemed like it was right outside the door.

'Monika, get back out there and do something,' the chief barked at Ten.

She went back out but stopped at the door. 'They are inside, sir! They coming!'

The chief withdrew the gun from his holster and stood. Lam grabbed him. 'What on earth do you think you're doing, man! Put that away.'

'Wait,' I said, and went into the corridor. Janet was marching towards me followed by the mob. I put a finger to my lips and Janet held up her hand. The crowd hushed.

'Look,' I said to Lam, 'I've done my homework. If you insist on doing this here you've got to find a bigger place. There are fifty people outside on a wet Monday morning. How many will there be next week, and the week after? Think about it. Everyone knows Maximo. He's a local. They help each other in the provinces.'

Lam seemed to weigh up the situation, sighed and sat down, arms folded. For a moment I felt sorry for him.

The chief, on the other hand, was incredulous. 'You're not going to listen to him? He's a tourist!'

'I don't think you understand,' said Lam. 'That man has the right to be heard in public.'

Thomas holstered his gun and paced. 'Arrgh… If you think I've been through all this bullshit just so you can give him his rights, you're wrong. I run this show. Me! Or you can tell your father to get someone else to do his dirty work.'

'Really?' said Lam. 'Shall we go to him now? How about that, hm? How about we tell him…' Lam checked himself and finished the sentence in Tagalog before turning in his chair, head forward. He sat back, cooling off. The chief folded his arms, sulking. For a moment there was silence. Maximo looked at me.

'And this needs to be heard by a judge,' I said meekly, forgetting he was one.

'I am a judge!' bellowed Lam, his face almost purple with rage.

I thought I'd got his goat enough for one morning and let it drop.

Lam looked at the door, at all the faces peering in, sighed, and said, 'We will go to trial. The question is where? Where in this town is big enough to hold a hundred people?' He put his face in his hands, trying to block out the nightmare.

'You haven't heard his plea yet,' I said.

He looked up at Maximo. 'How do you plead?'

'Not guilty.'

Lam turned to the chief. 'Give him and his friend… I assume you are going to defend yourself… a copy of the complaint and everything else we have. Why not?' he said erratically, suddenly smiling a little to himself. 'Let's go to trial. I like a challenge. We'll win hands down.'

Thomas the chief looked at him as if he'd lost his marbles.

'How about the *sabungan*?' a voice in the corridor shouted.

'What?'

'Yes,' said Janet. 'The cockpit. Why not? We could hold the trial there. It is covered up.'

'That's right, I chimed in. It seats, what, a hundred and fifty, two hundred people easily. It's perfect.'

'This is ridiculous,' said the chief. He huffed but seemed at a loss for words.

Lam rubbed his chin. 'Covered, you say?'

Ten minutes later, after Max had been politely put back in his cell, we were all marching through the village; myself, Lam, the chief and Ten at the head, followed by Janet, Ziegwalt and Bernard. Then a strung-out line of banner-wielding boys in basketball shirts, with Frank struggling at the rear.

'Nice to get out into the fresh air,' said Lam, walking with his hands behind his back. 'Away from the smell in that office. What is that stench?'

'Toilets,' I explained. 'Think they might be blocked with mud. Lot of rain lately.'

We walked out of town, all the store-owners wondering what on earth the commotion was before following us to find out, and turned left across the field towards the cockfighting arena. By now we'd also picked up most of the town's kids and all of its dog population.

Lam stopped and the whole crowd fell silent. He stood at the gate looking over the arena, hummed and hawed for a second, bouncing on his toes, then went in. We all followed, whispering.

As the judge climbed up the terraces to the top tier I watched his expression. In fact I'd been watching it all morning. The change was remarkable. At first afraid, then angry, he'd gone from appearing like a man who wanted to run away to one completely in charge. It was as though he was experiencing a feeling he hadn't enjoyed in a very long time. He looked like a judge.

He stood at the top and gazed down over the crowd, nodding approval. 'Mr Harris,' he said, 'I believe we have ourselves a courtroom.'

ICH BIN EIN DETEKTIV

1

It wasn't quite clear to me whether I'd taken a step in the right direction or scored a spectacular own goal by changing Lam's mind. If indeed it was a change and not some elaborate counterplot.

But what had we achieved? Not a great deal when I looked at our goals. We'd gone to the police station hoping that the crowd would scare him into taking the old man out of town. That hadn't happened. I wished with all my heart that it had, and then I could have washed my hands of it all and told myself that victory was ours. That I'd redeemed myself by saving a man's life.

Out of sight, out of mind? Maybe, but that's the way selfish people think. And I would have claimed it as a life saved. I'd have told myself that he was now in the capital undergoing cross-examination in a fast and fair trial. I would leave The Refuge quickly, and a week later be lying on a beautiful Boracay beach sipping mojitos with Annie. I'd picture Maximo back where he belonged running his guest house, a free man.

How long that self-deception would have lasted before my conscience kept me awake at night is anyone's guess. Sooner or later I'd start to think about him, and either go back to check or try to contact Janet.

The other route, of getting the whole thing quashed on the grounds that there should be a judge present had also been tipped flat on its face. Under the legal system a judge was allowed to hear the plea without prosecution and without prejudice when 'Acts of God' prevented it. Some obscure Article of Law said so, according to Lam. And why did we believe anything the enemy told us? Because we had no choice.

We needed Jim. I needed Jim. Without him, I said, we'd be way out of our depth in this whole fiasco. Surprisingly, I thought, given their previous record for blind faith in me as ein detektiv, they agreed. Or at least didn't disagree.

They didn't say anything, in fact, just allowing a sort of dull realisation that we were indeed up El Ref creek without a paddle sweep across their faces. Not only were we without a paddle but, to make matters worse, our opponents were riding a jet ski, waving at us as they streaked past.

The trouble is Jim was no longer of this planet. I don't mean that in the metaphorical sense, but literally; we could not find him anywhere. And believe me we searched. The bar, the karaoke bar, eateries, the beach, door-to-door, A Better Place and every fisherman's hut along the near coast. We even checked with all the jeepney drivers who plied the route south. Not a sausage.

We went to the shed he'd been seen drinking at. He was no longer there. When we inquired with the neighbour and it turned out that it belonged to one of Thomas's mistresses my heart sank.

Although angry, I wasn't altogether contemptuous. As a matter of fact I had to commend the chief, or Lam, or whoever's idea it was to strike at our Achilles heel. They'd really hit the nail on the head with the first blow.

All of us, especially Ziegwalt, had been wondering where Jim was getting the cash to drink 24/7, and now we knew. Clearly they saw him as their greatest threat and had sunk him with one well-aimed bottle of rum. He'd fallen for it hook, line and sinker. Glug glug glug.

All any of us could hope was that he hadn't fallen off the rocks and drowned. Bernard said that was implausible because when Jim was legless, he really was legless. When Bernard suggested he might have committed suicide, however, we all looked back at Jim's best friend. Ziegwalt just looked at his belly and fumbled with his thong.

The most likely scenario, Janet ventured, was that he'd simply gone off to one of the nearby settlements to dry out. He'd done it before. Anything was better than the thought of him being found face down in the bay. I was going to raise the possibility that the chief had paid someone to assassinate him but thought, better of it. Even I couldn't believe the Lams would go that far.

Whatever, he was gone and I was terrified at the prospect of watching a second human being fall to oblivion because I hadn't done enough to prevent it. So, with no other option we went to the dreaded plan B: try to find out who had killed Elsie.

No one, I think, knew what was going through my head, but when I allocated tasks to each person that night, they seemed to trust me completely. I doubted myself completely, but entered nonetheless into fully fledged detective mode. If it came up trumps and we found out who'd done it, all well and good. If we drew blanks, well, then I'd go to plan C: run away!

I was beginning to wonder, though, if I possessed hidden resources. Perhaps, after all, I wasn't the shallow, avaricious narcissist I'd taken myself for. Maybe I'd just needed a higher purpose all along, something other than the endless pursuit of women as a means of satisfaction, and this whole episode had taken me to that lofty platform few of us ever reach. A sort of enlightenment. Maximo Saves!

2

'Kokonut leader, zhis is kokonut ein. Do you zhere?'

'What?'

'Kokonut leader, zhis is…'

'I know it's you, Zig, but what's all this coconut stuff?' I pulled the phone from my ear and frowned at the luminous display as if that would clarify things. It was early evening and the glow lit my chest in an easy green light. I wondered if it was made from squid. 'Anything happening?' I whispered back.

'Zhe swift leaves zhe nest. Zhe swift leaves zhe nest.'

'Ay?'

'Zhe swift. She is flyink.'

And then he made a ridiculous chirping noise and I thought, Jesus, why had I chosen Ziegwalt to spy on Gladys with me instead of Bernard or Janet? He was like an undergrown boy scout.

We'd all decided on different people that we felt needed to be under surveillance for at least a few hours a day over the coming week. The trial had been set for 15 days after our last meeting with the judge and, with nothing else to do, it seemed prudent to investigate things.

Frank's wife and Ziegwalt's girlfriend had followed Gladys the first day, sticking to her like glue, and had returned only when she'd gone to bed at midnight. Their findings were less than thrilling: the market, the store, El Ref's vet with her pooch to have its usual pink rinse, and to the hairdresser for own matching pink rinse. It was the same little barber shop where I had my head shaved, so the next day I went back and steered the conversation towards Gladys while the barber scalped me. Nothing.

Frank and Mary were covering the cop shop, Bernard the church (the only other place Gladys had visited) and Janet and Taddi A Better Place and the Lams' house respectively.

I had suggested it the other way round but Janet nearly killed me. 'They can hang Maximo Bonga,' she said, 'but my husband is not going near that place.'

'Koko vun to koko leader. Zhe svift es flappink. Repeat; zhe svift es flappink.'

I sighed. 'OK, Zig. See if she's got her phone.'

The plan was simple enough. Gladys had a mobile phone and it seemed likely that she'd stored all her personal numbers on it, perhaps even maintaining a record of all recent texts and calls. We had to get hold of it somehow, and that somehow was a simple switch.

I would wait in the street, she'd come out, and I would pretend she'd dropped it. I knew she hated me but that didn't matter. I would hold out Janet's phone (the same model, we made sure) and ask her if it belonged to her. She would do one of two things: either she'd say it wasn't hers, without even thinking, in which case she'd have left it indoors. I would stay behind and break in to get it. Otherwise, she'd check in her handbag and find it. If that happened, plan B, 'The Swipe', would come into effect. Waiting along the street in a dark alley was Bernard. Upon a signal he would jump out and swipe the bag. Simple.

Except now, for reasons known only to Gladys, she had decided to exit at the rear, on the beach. Ziegwalt was hiding in a beached outrigger.

'I'm coming round,' I said, pocketing the phone and making a dash for the path that joined beach to street. As soon as I got there I could see that Ziegwalt had taken things into his own hands. The moon picked out the two figures in magnificent monochrome. I ran onto the beach and dived behind a boat, peering over the reeking nets.

'I vould like to use your phone, please,' Ziegwalt said as if reading from a script.

Gladys looked up and down his body as if she'd never seen a dwarf before. I couldn't say I blamed her. After the typhoon the heat and humidity had come on with a vengeance, and Ziegwalt was now dressed day and night only in his thong, white socks and sandals. He looked wonderful in the moonlight.

'I haff ein emergency and zhere is no phone on zhe beach. Sank you.'

'Are you mad?' Gladys said. 'Get out of my way. Go and use your friend's phone. If you have any friends. And what on earth were you doing hiding in that boat?'

'I vas shleepink.' He yawned melodramatically.

Gladys had heard some porkers in her time but this was a lie too far. She swung her handbag at him. Ziegwalt ducked a second too late and it hit him over the head. The strap broke and the handbag flew through the air, hitting the boat and spilling its contents only a metre from me. No phone. I dived under the nets and held my breath.

'You pervert!' she screamed. A moment later she was scrambling in the sand beside me, shouting out curse after curse in English, Spanish and Tagalog. 'You should be in a psychiatric hospital, you disgusting hobbit!'

'I only vant to use your phone,' Ziegwalt said apologetically. 'Let me helping you.'

'Get away from me! Go back to the madhouse you came from, you evil midget!'

There was the unmistakable clicking sound of lipsticks and compacts being dropped into her bag, some pig-like snorting, and then the fading sound of Gladys's nylon tights swishing as she stormed off along the beach.

Silence.

My phone rang. Still lying in darkness beneath the nets, I reached into my pocket and opened it.

'Koko ein to koko leader,' Ziegwalt said in stereo, 'do you zhere?'

I put the phone away.

'Zhe svift haff flown zhe nest. Repeat; zhe svift haff fly. Cheep cheep cheep.'

I lifted the net. Ziegwalt was rotating, trying to get a better signal.

'Hello-o? Koko lea-der? Do you zhere?'

'I'm here, Ziggy.'

He jumped. '*Mein Gott!*'

I climbed out. 'She hasn't got it; it must be in the house. Let's go.' Ziegwalt stood there, looking into the distance, then at me, then at the boat. 'Ziggy, I saw into her handbag. It wasn't there,' I explained. 'She must have left it in the house. Let's take a look.'

We walked up the beach and through the gate to the veranda of the house. I knew there were no guests, and the other maid had also left for the rainy season. Our research over the course of the day told us that the only person who had gone there was the plumber, and he'd only been gone an hour. Other than that, she had been alone.

I slid up the sash window. 'Right, you stay here,' I whispered to Ziegwalt, one foot through the opening. 'Keep dog. Woof

woof. Call Bernard and tell him to guard the front. Any sign of Gladys, call me, OK?' I ducked under and entered.

His massive head looked in. 'Oh. Very nice inside. Like zhe church.'

I pushed his head out and closed the window.

It was indeed like a church inside. I was in the living room. It was like a shrine to the Lord: wall-to-wall religious regalia, from posters and prints of Jesus to an array of crucifixes, Bibles, little model cathedrals, Virgin Marys, Josephs of every shape and size, and a scene from the nativity played out in miniature with little plastic donkeys and sheep.

The sofa and two armchairs had lace covers woven with angels on clouds. The cushions had patterns depicting the halo-wearing disciples, and the rug that covered the centre of the floor was printed with *The Last Supper*. And all made visible by fake flickering candles with little glass flames and dancing elements inside.

I pulled out my phone and dialled Gladys's number. From somewhere in the house a high-pitched synthesized rendition of 'O Come, All Ye Faithful' rang out. I suddenly wondered how close we were to Christmas. It was getting really hard for me to keep track of time in the Philippines, mainly because no one else bothered. Virtually every public clock, where there is one, is broken, and time is measured more in moons and festive seasons than days and weeks. My mind wandered to the speed of life I'd led in Hong Kong and London when Ziegwalt rapped on the window.

'What?'

'I should go mit Burn-hard?'

'No. Stay here.'

The sound of the phone was coming from the first floor so I quickly headed up. The first door I opened was the toilet, then the hall cupboard. The third was the master bedroom. On the bedside table, glowing like kryptonite in the darkness, was Gladys's phone.

I was distracted for a moment by a framed black and white photo of a couple. It was a wedding scene: a very beautiful bride standing beside a tall white man in a naval uniform.

'Psst!'

I hung up my phone and looked through the window down at Ziegwalt, who was still looking in the ground-floor window. Just as I turned and picked up Gladys's phone it rang. I dropped it as if electrocuted.

On the screen there was one word only: PADRE.

I could see by the look on Janet's face she was not pleased.

'You did what!'

'Appropriated her phone,' I said, holding up Gladys's jewel-encrusted handpiece in the hope it would calm her. Janet had volunteered Gladys's phone number but hadn't questioned my reasons.

'I thought you were just going to ask her some questions,' she said, then slumped in the chair, calling out to her husband to bring her a beer.

'I'll have one,' I said.

'Und me,' said Ziegwalt.

Bernard said, 'Bon. I will not say no.'

I was still buzzing from the adrenalin but Ziegwalt was like a cat on hot bricks, pacing up and down with his hands behind his back. Janet told him to sit down or go home to bed. He looked like MacArthur strutting around.

'Why did you steal the phone?' She looked at her watch and told Taddi it was nearly midnight, and to bring the candles before the electricity went off. 'Surely you do not think that old lady had anything to do with all this.'

I pulled off my T-shirt and hung it over the chair to dry the sweat. 'Firstly, I was regularly at Gladys's guest house with Annie and heard her cursing every time Elsie went past. She even said she would put a knife in her back.'

'That's just talk. She hates prostitutes coming to El Ref, we all do.'

'Then how come she's now the main witness to the murder? Bit strange, don't you think? When the knife went missing and their case against Maximo fell apart they miraculously found a witness. Gladys of all people.'

At the pre-trial hearing the judge had issued us with a file containing the necessary paperwork, including stipulations, admissions of facts and evidence. It also listed two material witnesses: Mr Geronimo B. Ondangan and Mrs Genevieve G. Velasquez.

Ondangan turned out to be a simple fisherman, more or less as Maximo had predicted; an illiterate who'd say what he was told to say. No one knew who this other witness, Mrs Velasquez, was at first. Theodore Lam, every time we asked, would simply shrug his shoulders and say how should he know, he was only the judge. And the chief, being the accomplished arsehole he was, said he wasn't at liberty to say. 'She's Mrs Genevieve G. Velasquez,' he'd repeat with a smile.

We dug deeper, eventually going through Father Hilario's church records to look up the name. And there it was; Mrs Genevieve Gladys Velasquez (formerly Smith).

'Why didn't you question the fisherman first?' asked Janet.

'We did. Or tried to.'

'And guess what?' said Bernard, 'he has "gone to sea for a week".'

'And what's the bet he appears only on the day of the trial?' I said. We all snorted with appropriate irony. Except Janet.

'So she hates Maximo. So what? That does not make her a killer.'

'So what? She's a liar. I was there in her place that morning. When they found the body, Gladys was still at home in bloody curlers. If she saw what happened why didn't she tell the chief the night before? Come on, Jan, you wouldn't wait until morning.'

'So she's lying. People do that all the time in this country.'

'That's why I took her phone,' I said, taking a beer. The lights flickered, Janet had a second to glance at her watch and everything went black. I squeezed the phone tighter. A moment later Frank and Mary came in, Frank holding his Zippo out then falling over the dog.

'Candles, Taddi!' shouted Janet. 'It's midnight!'

'She's a liar and she has something to hide,' I continued. 'Nobody would go to the police this long after the event if they weren't trying to cover something up.' I took a candle from Taddi and put it on the table, all the faces now flickering around it. 'And why was her married name Smith?'

Taddi nodded. 'Janet, do you remember the committee meeting when she went mad?' Janet sighed at the memory.

'What happened?' I asked.

'Do you know that old surfboard you've been using? Well, no one knows how it got here, except that a foreigner brought it in about thirty years ago.'

I nodded. When I first arrived here I'd walked out of town along the beaches towards the mangrove inlet. There wasn't much of a swell but a perfect little right-hand break was rolling off the reef. I'd spent the rest of the day sitting there, dreaming of riding it. When I got back to town that afternoon there were two kids playing in the flat bay on an old Lightning Bolt surfboard. It was like manna from heaven. I felt like the luckiest person on earth.

Taddi continued. 'When you said there was good surfing here, we–'

'Well, it's not good, but it's rideable. Perfect shape, but small. You see, the South China Sea is–'

'OK, rideable waves,' Janet interrupted. 'We decided to bring it up at the next meeting. Why not use it to promote El Refugio? As soon as we mentioned surfing Gladys went crazy.'

'And did you know there's the remains of a Second World War landing craft on the beach near the mangroves?' Frank said fatuously.

'So that's what that old wreck is. I thought that was the ferry to Manila.'

'It's better than the ferry to Manila!'

We all chuckled and supped our beers.

Except Janet. 'But stealing her phone...' she said, 'What is that going to achieve?'

'What else are we supposed to do? They're going to lock the old man away based on this flimsy-arse case, so why not do everything to derail it? Look,' I leaned in and quoted Jim, 'what have we got and what have they got?' Everyone stared at me. 'That wasn't rhetorical.' They stared at each other and I wished Jim was here.

'Ve know zhat Gladys is ein lion,' said Ziegwalt.

'Liar,' I corrected. 'Yeah, we've got that, but we've got to prove it. That's what this hinges on. They're going to put her up there and she's going to lie and say she saw him do it.'

'Why is she going to say that?'

'Who cares?' I stretched. 'She hates prostitutes, she hates Maximo, she hates me, she hates the world. It doesn't matter. What matters is we blow her out the water.' Ziegwalt frowned. 'Figure of speech, Zig. We've got to find out where she was that night. And this,' I said, placing the phone on the table, 'will help us.'

'How?'

I turned it on, went through the menu to the call register and pressed select. 'Missed calls, received calls, dialled numbers; they're all still on there. And every single one, bar none, is to or from the same person: Father Hilario Resurreccion.'

'The padre?' exclaimed Mary, shocked into speech.

Bernard looked at her. 'I never hear you speak before.'

She looked back at the floor.

Bernard rubbed his face and shook his head.

'What is it, Bern? Is there anything about Elsie and the priest we need to know?'

'No. You know everything about my Elsie. She was a prostitute. I am not ashamed to say it. She did not know Gladeese.' He hesitated. 'But one time she have a photo of the priest in her purse. I ask her why and she say for good luck. Only this.'

'Bernard, if there's anything else…'

'I tell you all. You think I do not want to know who does this to my Elsie?'

A tear welled in his eyes, twinkling under the dim light, and I wondered for a split second if he was being sincere. I decided he was, and that if either of them had been lying it would have been Elsie.

'Hilario,' I said. 'He must have something to do with this. Why would Gladys go there at that time of night?'

Bernard pulled out a piece of paper with his notes on it. 'She comes to the church at eleven-twenty. She leave at eleven forty-five. Only this.'

'Frank? What happened at the police station today?'

'Nothing. Damn boring day, boy. Just the chief playing checkers with some ol' farts.'

I'd already questioned Janet and Taddi and the answer had also been negative. The Lams had a barbecue in their front garden, and A Better Place had been relatively quiet for once. Rose hadn't gone out all day now that she'd finished working for Gladys.

'So,' I said, putting the phone into my pocket, 'same places tomorrow everyone?'

'I can't make it tomorrow,' said Frank. 'We need to visit Mary's folks out of town.'

'Me alzo,' said Ziegwalt. 'I need to go back to zhe beach to check mit zhe haus.'

'You've got a jet ski. Can't you just do half a day? You can swap with Janet and do the whorehouse.'

'Oh.' He grinned. 'What will you do?'

I took my shirt off the chair and put it on. 'I'll be in the confessional.'

3

There was one girl ahead of me outside the ornate wooden confession box the next afternoon in church. She couldn't have been older than twelve. I wondered what on earth had gone on in her life that warranted a confession. Her face was an open heart, an unmasked expression of pure fear.

I wasn't sure I really cared. The morning, in fact the whole night, had been a bad one for me, and I'd woken in a foul mood. MacArthur had started flapping and squawking right outside my window at five o'clock as usual. Even he didn't know why, but that primeval instinct got those useless wing muscles itching at least once every day.

I knew exactly what he felt like. My feet had been the same since I was a teenager; that feeling deep inside somewhere that made me get up and go. MacArthur had once been a flying, soaring bird in his species' bygone days, and I had once been a roaming hunter-gatherer. What use was that rooster today? A 'bird' in name only.

And what was a man nowadays if he no longer had purpose? What was left for my generation of men? No wars to fight – not legitimate ones anyway – no longer the breadwinner. Women had the careers and the know-how. We didn't even need to light fires any more.

All this went through my mind as I lay awake that morning suffering that damn bird's squawks. Every time I opened the window to chuck a stone at it he ran off, and every time I tried to get back to sleep he started again. And when it was daylight and he'd finally had enough, I had all this reason-for-being nonsense going round in my head.

Now, at four in the afternoon in the queue for confession, I was just plain pissed off at everything. Especially the moron who'd been behind that stupid little velvet curtain for the past half-hour.

'Come on! I haven't got all day!' I finally shouted out.

The whispering stopped. There was the rustle of a bag inside the booth, the curtain slid back, a woman exited and I barged in front of the girl to enter. I yanked the velvet curtain so hard behind me that the rings broke and went tinkling onto the stone floor. I didn't even apologise, just letting the drape hang off the rod.

'I'm not getting on my knees,' I said, looking at the mesh divider, 'so you can forget it.'

Father Hilario's dark image moved closer to the screen, then moved away slightly. 'You do not have to kneel,' his deep voice said.

'I'm not a Catholic.'

'Anyone can confess.'

Him, the darkness, the smell of damp dusty wood; it all seeped into me very quickly, calming me. I took a deep breath and said, 'I'm helping Maximo Bonga.'

'I know.'

'I need to ask you some questions. About the murder of Elsie.'

'This is a confessional. You should have let the girl go first.'

'This is more important than someone confessing to having a naughty thought, don't you think? Don't you think that sticking a knife in some poor girl deserves a little more attention than a teenager's crush on teacher?' The anger quickly came back. 'I mean, what is it when a religion teaches people that it's OK to sin as long as you confess afterwards? Why don't people just not murder each other in the first place?'

'We do not teach people that. They have evil in them already. We are here to help them see what they have done wrong by confessing. This confessional is really just a mirror.'

'Why don't you take a look in it then?' I couldn't help it, it just came out. Hardly a subtle, detective-like approach, but, as I said, it was all MacArthur's fault.

And I thought I'd done my research well. Gladys's phone was full of calls to and from the Father, including two on the fourth, the night Elsie was killed.

'What do you mean?' He seemed to shift slightly.

'What's your relationship to Gladys?'

There was a pause before he said, 'Nothing. I do not have a relationship with anyone. I am a celibate. Can we do this in my study?'

'I didn't ask if you'd had a sexual relationship with her, did I? I asked you what your relationship with her was. There are many kinds of relationship and sexual is only one of them.'

'I do not have to answer these questions, you know.'

'Yes you do. How long have you and Gladys been sexually attached?'

'You are talking nonsense. I just told you that–'

'You just told me you've been having sex with Gladys. Where were you the night Elsie was killed? And I warn you, I know you spoke to Gladys that night because I have a record of all the phone calls she received, and your name is on it.'

I pulled out the phone and went through the call register. 'The third,' I barked, 'the day before, ten-thirty in the morning you called her and spoke for two minutes and twenty-seven seconds.

Five-thirty, same day, she called you, seven minutes. Ten-thirty, eleven minutes. On the fourth, the night Elsie died; five minutes and twelve seconds. And one o'clock in the morning, possibly minutes before the girl was killed, a call lasting eight minutes and forty-three seconds.'

'But what has that got to do with Elsie?'

'Because,' I lied, 'around the time of each one of those calls made or received, Gladys also called a six-two-nine-eight number, immediately before or after speaking to you. And that, my friendly padre, happens to be Elsie's number. Now, what do you say we cut the ol' crapola and talk straight.'

He was hyperventilating, I could hear it. I pushed an eye up to the net. He was wiping away the sweat with a hanky.

'I... I... I am a priest.'

'You're not above the law. And if you don't answer now I'll call you as a witness at the trial. I might anyway.'

'I... I do not have any idea what you are talking about,' he said, and he drew his curtain. He was so tall it was like watching a butterfly escape a cocoon.

I darted out and blocked his way as he went to go out the back. 'I think I've said enough for now. But you should be aware that we are watching you and Gladys round the clock. If you two want to get together I couldn't care less. I don't go to church so I'm not a hypocrite like some people. But I'll tell you one thing,' I said, trying not to blink, 'we know who killed that girl, so the sooner you come forward the better it'll be for you. Don't let others take you down with them. All we're doing now is trying to find out who else knows and who is genuinely ignorant.'

He was standing sideways, frozen mid-step as though about to run, exactly as I'd stopped him.

'It's a bit like an amnesty,' I said with total confidence. 'You have until the day of the trial to come clean. After that there's no mercy.' I patted him on the shoulder. 'Have a good day, Confessori.'

Without looking back I strutted down the aisle like MacAthur. What a performance. A real Sir John Gielgud, that one. I should get a BAFTA.

Even the sight of Rose waiting outside in the shade didn't phase me. It was going to be a beautiful evening. I'd go home for a celebratory wank, then have a beer at Bernard's and catch up on the latest gossip. Rose could eat my dust. And if she thought she was going to inveigle me with her cute smile and those urgent eyes, think again, love. I'd learned my lesson. And if Annie never comes back you will be the last woman on earth I'd go with. Huh!

As soon as I cleared the arched entrance into the setting sunlight Rose came across to me and held my arm.

I stopped and looked at her hand. 'What?'

'I have a baby,' she said.

Here we go, I thought, she's after money for some past love child.

'Really. Where is it? Let me guess. Manila?'

'No.' She pointed to her belly. 'In here.'

The boat wasn't due to arrive until midday, and allowing half an hour's break for Rommel the captain, that meant my departure should be around one o'clock to the next port down the coast, about four hours away. According to Rommel's wife, he'd gone there to pick up some tourists bound for El Refugio. According to her the road was still down and boat was the only way in or out now that the sea had calmed.

It didn't bother me either way, so long as I could make a quick exit without anyone seeing. I checked the time on Gladys's phone. It was only eleven o'clock in the morning. I was packed and ready. I had been since the previous night.

I'd palmed Rose off with my classic backpacker's excuse to escape the clutches of a clingy woman. I'd been using my Scott of the Antarctic paraphrase for years: 'I'm just going to renew my visa. I may be gone some time.' Those words have symbolic resonance for me. They're emblematic of my worldly cowardice, my inability to commit. My throwaway, collapsible charm that I carry around like a nifty backpack, ready to be donned at the slightest notice. She'd swallowed it. 'Two or three days max; to get to immigration and back.'

I knew the back way to the far beach, and within 10 minutes I was peeping out from the trees. My timing couldn't have been better. Just motoring through the channel between Charlie's island and El Ref was an outrigger. I asked Rommel's wife if it was Rommel and she said it was.

Looking left and right to see that the coast was clear, I dashed out of cover into the sunshine.

As the boat neared the shore I picked up my bag, went to the edge of the water and suddenly went weak at the knees. I could not believe my eyes. I should have realised from its lopsided, uneven keel who the passengers were.

Sat there grinning at the prow like a mad figurehead was Brenda. Behind her sat Annie.

Without thinking I turned around, ran left then right like MacArthur, before diving head first into an old wooden boat on the beach, bag and all.

It groaned. Not like wood groans or creaks, but like a person does. Then the nets moved! I rolled to one side, my heart pounding, and a hand came out from beneath the polystyrene fish boxes. There was a long wet fart and Jim's face appeared, squinting and smacking his lips.

'Where the hell have you been?' I asked, wondering if he'd died and come back from the pit of hell. He looked like death warmed up. He looked like Jim.

'Where the hell are you going?' he said, looking at my bag.

The sound of Rommel's boat drew nearer. I threw the nets back over the pair of us and clamped a hand over his mouth.

'Keep quiet, Jim,' I whispered. 'Please.'

'As you wish.'

There was a 'Shhoossh' as the boat ran onto the high tide shale, and then the sound of voices.

Brenda: 'I do not know. I sink I see him, but I cannot be sure.'

Annie: 'Where?'

Brenda: 'There, beside the boat.'

No. Please God, not like this. I'll change my ways, I promise. I'll go back, but don't let them find me in here hiding like some... cowardly tourist who can't face his mistakes. I promise to be a better person. I was heading in that direction helping Max, and I really have suffered. And, don't forget, Rose wasn't exactly honest with me either, Lord.

'John?'

I didn't open my eyes, just laying there praying for all I was worth. Suddenly the world went bright.

'John, why you are in the boat?'

'What?' I opened my eyes and looked from side to side as if the boat had sneaked up under me. Annie's face was framed by a warm halo as the sun hit the back of her head and outlined her cascading hair. I blinked, then frowned and glanced around me.

'She asks why you are in the fisher's boat,' said Brenda, peeping over Annie's shoulder and blocking out the light. She had a burnt nose. 'My cast it is coming off! See!' She lifted a bare two-tone leg and plonked it on the gunwale like a cannon.

The sudden added weight on the side of the boat, up on blocks for repair and without outriggers to stabilise it, was too much. I felt myself moving to one side as the whole lot – me, Jim, all the boxes and nets – began to topple over. The chocks underneath slipped and we were dumped unceremoniously onto the beach, Jim still clutching an empty bottle of rum.

As I pushed Jim off and untangled myself from the nets I noticed an odd look in Brenda's eyes; a far-off look as she stared at something beside me. There was only Jim next to me and no one ever looked at him that way. Except perhaps his mother when she gave birth to him, but even that look probably vanished once the morphine had worn off. It was a look of infatuation, as though all her get up and go had got up and gone.

I was just going to speak when Jim said, 'How do you do?' and held out his hand to Brenda. He had the same look.

Love at first sight was something that happened in movies, never in real life. It was a concept that lonely people clung to because of the very fact that they had precisely nobody. The bizarre thing is that they'd met before without really seeming to notice one another, like people in a crowd. I suppose there's such a thing as love at second sight.

'I...' said I.

'I...' said Annie.

We both watched as Brenda pulled Jim to his feet with characteristic aplomb. They were gazing into each other's eyes. 'I am Brenda.'

'Allow me to introduce myself. I'm Jim. Would you like a cup of tea?' He picked up her huge backpack, buckling under the weight, and they turned and strode off together.

'Such a gentleman,' said Annie. 'Is so nice.'

'It's horrible.'

She looked me square in the eye. 'I come back for you, John.'

'I can't believe Jim,' I said, clucking my tongue and avoiding eye contact with the one person I really wanted to look at. I wanted to kiss her but instead went on about Jim to avoid showing my feelings. If she really knew me she'd realise I was exposing my own sentiments. 'Jim and Brenda; who'd have thought it? Huh, love. He'll be back to his usual drunken stupour in two days so she better learn to carry him. People don't change.'

She grasped my chin in one hand and turned my head to face her. 'John. I come back for you.'

'I'm sorry. I was going to leave but now I've changed my mind.' I went to kiss her but she stopped me.

'Did you sleep with her?'

I looked down the beach at the departing figures of Jim and Brenda arm in arm and something very strange happened to me: I told the truth. I wasn't thinking about how it might affect my chances with Annie, just that I didn't want to lie to her.

'Yes. But only once.' Small lies are all right. It's all about the weighing scales of honesty, I decided in that millisecond. 'You didn't seem–'

She put a finger to my lips. 'New start?'

'Mmm,' I mumbled and she moved her finger. 'I can change.'

REFUGE MADNESS

1

The trouble with telling the truth is someone always gets hurt. However well intended, sincere and well chosen those words are, they're bound to feel like daggers to somebody's heart. And that's why I didn't tell Annie about the pregnancy.

First of all I wasn't, technically speaking (here I go again), lying. She'd asked me if I'd slept with Rose and I said yes. She also now knew when and where it had taken place.

She asked and I told her the truth. That seemed like a pretty virtuous thing to do, I reckoned. And if Annie had inquired as to Rose's maternal condition, I'm sure I would have told the truth about that as well. But she didn't. So I didn't. Sorted.

And even if she had, and even if I'd told the truth, I felt my back was covered anyway. Rose was a prostitute, albeit a part-time one, and as such slept with men, lots of them. That baby could belong to at least a dozen men in the village.

Why pick on me? Simple: why bother with a penniless fisherman when she could have a better life?

Perhaps I was just judging her by my self-serving standards, but with Janet's advice still ringing in my ears I'd convinced myself otherwise. Without letting on who exactly I was talking about, we had a heart-to-heart one night about Filipina women in general: European versus Filipina, to be precise, East versus West, poor versus rich. I had steered the conversation earnestly towards working girls, narrowing the field down to A Better Place: 'Say for example, just hypothetically speaking, Rose...'

I told her about my experiences in Asia and my view that not only did East and West not mix in the long term, but also couples from different parts of the same continent, perhaps even opposite parts of the same country. And, to further complicate affairs of the heart, it appeared that one also tripped up on intellectual compatibility, background and financial independence. The idea that opposites attract is like saying sirloin steak and chocolate go well together. It may be novel but it's hardly the basis of a satisfying long-term diet.

'OK,' I said, 'it's true that a weaker person is often attracted to a stronger one, but that's something else.' It was still love, we both agreed, but loving someone for what they can provide, or perhaps to fulfil an emotional need to care for someone. Every relationship is about loving someone for what they can provide, but more often than not that something is an equal tenderness.

Which had brought us very nicely to A Better Place and the girls who work there. They were not bad girls, she'd finally conceded, but she maintained that some were just too lazy to work, or had simply acquired expensive tastes. Somewhere along the line they had raised their sights but couldn't keep up with the payments. They all had expensive electronics and good clothes, smoked and drank a lot, all of which needed paying for. And no working-class local could afford these things.

All ammo for my arsenal. But would they lie to get what they wanted? And would they pretend to be pregnant, or (and this is where I really stuck my neck out) get pregnant and claim a different father just for financial gain?

Janet had looked at me, the question 'Have you made one of the Better Place whores pregnant?' on the tip of her tongue.

'The young ones?' she said. 'No. They are still kind-hearted. They haven't learnt the benefits of deception. Rose? Definitely. She is not a bad person but she is not dumb.'

I felt dumb.

She went on, 'Virginity is a valuable asset here in the Philippines.'

'It's overrated if you ask me. I'd rather have a woman who knows what she's doing.'

'You are not from here,' she said. 'They are poor. And girls here have one valuable thing that they hold on to. It is worth everything. They will not give it up unless they think the man is going to marry them.

Most Better Place girls were single mothers and fared badly in this country, she said. They were discarded like trash, and the best they could hope for once they'd given birth out of wedlock was to be another man's mistress. 'The land of single mothers,' Janet called the Philippines.

And that, she explained, was the reason these women had the potential to be devious. In a macho society where roosters ruled the roost and spread their seed far and wide, and where monogamy was a word that didn't translate well, the unmarried, unchaste ones had little choice. They had suffered under men and so were prepared to use their sexuality to their advantage. And why not?

And that made me feel a whole lot better, regardless of whether she was right or wrong about Rose. As far as I could tell I hadn't done too much wrong. And, although a little circuitous, I didn't feel at all bad about keeping a low profile over the few days before the trial. Sooner or later Rose would see me and everything would come to a head anyway.

Rose thought I was out of town so I stayed out of town. Not literally, but in my room, or in the restaurant sizing up our case with the others. Everything would clash around the day of the trial, I could see that. A sort of 'what will be, will be' attitude had come over me.

It was as though I wanted it, was looking forward to the comfort I thought veracity would offer. I would be on trial myself. And in my state of mind, the more people there to witness it the better. I'd been running away far too long and now had no fear of what could well turn out to my judgement day. A woman who was pregnant by me – a Catholic and a prostitute to boot – at the very moment I'd met and fallen in love with another woman in the same insane little village. Perfect. I'd come to this place to escape my nightmares and they'd followed me and multiplied tenfold. My very own public crucifixion.

2

Annie and I walked past the bistro towards the Swiss Cafe just as Bernard was coming through his gate.

'You are late,' he said, tapping a watch that wasn't there before looking up at the moon to confirm the time.

'And so are you. Janet will tap her watch at us both.' He looked drawn so I put an arm around his shoulder. 'How you feeling, mate?'

'I miss her. More than I ever think.' He kissed Annie on both cheeks, a little over-affectionately for my liking, and we walked on. 'You two are in love,' he said. 'Do not forget that.'

That's a bit of a weird thing to say, I thought.

'It is true that you do not know what you have until it has gone, my English friend. Every day Elsie and me we fight and argue, and now I wish we had kissed and made love more. You two must kiss and feurck more.' He stopped. 'Go on, kiss her now! Show everyone so they know what love is. Show these people who hide love from public eyes. Kiss. Show them!'

I gave Annie a kiss on the lips.

'Yes!' shouted Bernard, and for a moment I thought he was going to ask for one. Instead he let out a long, abandoned sigh, shoved both hands in his pockets and we walked on.

'Any news of Lord Jim?' he asked as we climbed the stairs to the cafe.

'Nothing. Saw him for five minutes in a canoe then he vanished with Brenda. Puff! as you would say.'

'Pity. He is a terrible drunk but his English is *très belle.*'

'We looked everywhere,' said Annie.

'Arnold Brendanegger has abducted him,' I said, and permitted myself a laugh at my pithy rap. Annie glared at me. 'Brenda, I mean.'

Everyone was in their usual chair in the cafe and I sat in my allotted space. I was a local now. Ziegwalt was the last to arrive. He now went about town on a unicycle he'd had shipped over from Germany, and parked it in the corner, patting the seat lovingly before sitting at the table and grabbing a beer. As predicted, Janet's head came through the serving hatch like a cuckoo clock and she tapped her right wristwatch.

I asked if anyone had seen Jim and Brenda.

'Brenda?' said Ziegwalt matter-of-factly, studying the label of his beer bottle. 'She is mit Jim. San Miguel is Spanish or Philippines company?'

'Yeah, we know that, Ziggy,' I said, 'but what we don't know is where.'

'Brenda unt Jim?'

'Yes, Ziggy, Brenda unt Jim.'

He raised his eyebrows. 'Brenda is mit Jim on zhe beach.'

'What beach?'

'Zhe beach vhere I am livink, of course.'

We all looked at one another with open mouths. 'Well, why the bloody hell didn't you say?'

He shrugged. 'You do not asking.'

I couldn't believe my ears. We'd been looking all over for the pair of them for three days – well, everyone else had; I'd been cowering in my room from Rose – and Ziegwalt had been with them all this time.

He smiled. 'Unt zhey are zo in luff. *Mein Gott*. Every day naked togezzer on zhe beach, in zhe vater, in zhe trees. Zo vunderbar.'

'Fantastico,' said Annie.

'Magnifique,' said Bernard.

'Never mind that bollocks,' said I, and tried to shake the unnerving image of the pair of them in a naked embrace, scrawny little chicken-legged Jim wrapped in Brenda's bountiful arms. 'I can't believe you didn't tell us.'

'I haff been busy mit zhe detektiv verk.'

'Jesus, Ziggy, you could have said.' I caught myself, remembering that I was the last person who should lecture people on opening up.

Annie took the beers from Janet and placed them in front of us. 'Tomorrow I go to her.'

'But the trial's in two days,' I fretted.

Ziegwalt shook his head. 'He vill not coming. I am already asking. He fears.'

Ziegwalt went to grab his beer and I put a hand on his. 'Fears what?'

He drew his hand in. 'People.'

'Ziegwalt, you're not making sense. Who?'

'Zhat is vhat he say; "People". Zhey give him zhe beer unt zhe rum for free.' He said 'rum' at the back of his throat: 'gggrum.' 'Unt vhen he say "no more", zhey get angry. Zo he hide. Unt now he hide viz me.'

'The chief,' I said. 'They know his weakness.'

Janet brought in the food and we all agreed that Annie was our best bet to persuade Jim to help us out via Brenda. Also, we would each take it in turns one last time to cajole an alibi out of the old man.

We'd all been to see Maximo every day and had used everything, from sweet talk and promises of help to expand his business, to threats of violence (that was my contribution). He wasn't budging. All he would say was that if he told me where he'd been that night he'd have to kill me. And if he told the court where he'd been his life in this village would be ruined anyway.

Someone outside shouted and Janet looked over the balcony. 'The posters are here.' She went to the door, unbolted it and let in a young boy carrying a log of rolled up paper. She cleared the plates and untied the bundle. We all grabbed a poster.

'The People of the Philippines in Support of Our Trusted Friend & Mentor Maximo Bonga', it read in large black text. And underneath: '(In accordance with R.A. No. 8493.)'

'What's R.A. Number 8493?' asked big Frank.

'Something in the law books about speedy trials,' I said. 'It looks good if we seem to know what we're doing. Bamboozle them with some technical stuff.'

Under that it read: 'Trial to take place at the *sabungan* starting this 19th, 9 a.m. Limited seats available!'

And under that was a picture of a very young-looking Maximo Bonga, with the words 'INNOCENT UNTIL PROVEN GUILT!' in huge red letters.

'Guilty,' corrected Janet. 'There is a y in guilty.'

The boy blushed. 'Printer no have this letter.'

'Who cares,' said Bernard, 'it will make them think about this *merde*.'

'Where did you get the picture from?' Janet asked me.

'It was in one of his old boxes. Him and a woman standing outside the guest house. I just cut her out the picture. Still looks like him, though.'

We all stared at it for a moment. It was as if the realisation of what we were up against suddenly hit us all at exactly the same time. Janet broke the silence.

'I'll put them all over town tomorrow,' she said, and rolled them up. 'Now, if everyone can leave when you finish your food, Taddi and I are feeling horny and we have not had sex for two days,' she said, smiling at me, 'so let us all go and make babies.' She slapped her thigh with rugged abandon, ruffling her husband's hair like a small boy. 'And do not forget; squid fishing in two days. It is a full moon!'

'But I no want to make-a the baby.'

'Just a figure of speech,' I said as Annie and I walked back through town. 'How about the rocky beach? It's a nice night. Just sit out under the stars until we fall asleep.'

Annie looked at the night sky for confirmation then said OK, so long as we could find a secluded spot. I told her I knew just the place. 'But first I want to buy a bottle of gin.'

She huffed. 'You English.'

'What?'

'Why you drink so much?'

I shrugged. 'To forget, I suppose.' I went into a grocery store, bought a bottle and proudly showed off my purchase to Annie. 'Look at that, only a hundred pesos for a quart of gin, tonic, ice and calamancies. That's two dollars. Superb.'

When the lady handed over the money she smiled and said, 'We will support you. Bonga is innocent.' On the door to her shop was one of the posters, and inside doing his homework the boy who'd delivered them earlier. Her thickset husband popped his head around and shook my hand, saying that he'd definitely be there on the day.

He was the first person to voice his hatred of the Lams to me in public. Others had in the relative safety of a boat or a moving tricycle, but never in such an exposed location and without any fear on his face. 'Screw the Chinese,' he said, and gave me extra calamansies.

'Power to the people,' I said, raising a fist.

'To forget what?' asked Annie as we walked away.

'The weather. Shite food. Don't Italians drink?'

'Of course, but not just to get drunk like the English. *Mio Dio*, you people never stop.'

I shrugged. 'You live in a beautiful country. It's sunny, you've got nice beaches, mountains for skiing, great food. What have we got? Meat pie and rain.'

We crossed the village and began to walk around the rocks at the far end and I said, 'What do Italians think of the British?'

'We think that you are a little dirty.'

'Dirty?'

'Yes. The way you dress.'

I looked down at my crud-covered feet and flip-flops, and at my frayed shorts with the torn pocket hanging down like a sow's ear. Then at this specimen beside me.

As ever, Annie was immaculately attired; Gucci black leather beach sandals – completely noiseless against the chronic 'flip' and 'flop' of my footwear – ankle-length, figure-hugging powder-blue skirt, and matching Versace boob tube. Her underwear, I'd learned over the past few days, was always D&G.

I looked back down at my own feet. She was right; I looked like something the cat dragged in.

'But that's just cheque-book fashion,' I scoffed. 'Anyone can dress like that if they have the money. Just go into a shop and buy the outfit. No imagination. The English, on the other hand, are individuals.' I held out the bottom of my shirt to indicate that she was looking at a perfect example of that idiosyncratic uniqueness.

'Dirty, you mean.'

'Yeah. Let's face it, you've got style and we haven't. We're still living in the past. Most people in Britain still live off processed food. The first time I saw a fish on a plate was in Asia. A fish that looked like a fish, I mean; one with a head and tail. Most kids in my country think a cod is a flat rectangular animal covered in breadcrumbs.'

'What is a cod?'

'It's a rectangular animal covered in breadcrumbs.'

We rounded the headland by the cemetery and crossed onto the shale of the rocky beach. The area was deserted as usual and the stretch of land in front of the graves was so nice in the moonlight that we sat right there. I took out two plastic cups, squeezed in half a dozen calamancies, put in the ice, gin and tonic, and toasted.

'That is why you no live in England?'

'Maybe,' I said, puckering at the sour taste. 'Just got used to it out here now. Asians seem to have something that we've lost. Even in Hong Kong. It's a faster pace of life than London but they still value a family dinner every night around the table. And proper food, none of that crap from packets.'

I lay down and stared at the black sky, resting the cold cup on my chest.

A few silent moments passed before Annie said, 'What about the dreams? They stop?'

Often over the past few months I'd woken in the middle of the night and found myself standing at the bedroom wall, scrambling with my hands as if trying to break free. For the first few terrifying minutes I never knew where I was. Another legacy of six years living in Hong Kong, in shoebox-sized apartments, I reckoned. I imagine prisoners are the same when they first leave jail. On top of that my dad had recently died while I was overseas and I was struggling to absolve the blame I felt for having put work over loved ones. I'd give up every penny saved just to be able to say goodbye to him. It wasn't much of a stretch of the imagination to see how I'd replaced him with Max. Their ages were pretty close, and like all people of the same generation, they seemed so similar.

'Yeah.' I hesitated. 'Since you've been back.'

I turned and we kissed, both our skins slippery with sweat, then gritty with sand.

'I take away the pain,' she said, and sat up, pulling off her top and bra, her glorious breasts lit by the moon. She pulled off my shorts and then her skirt, sat astride me and froze.

'What?'

She looked into the trees. 'Nothing. I think I hear someone. Is nothing.' She kissed me again and began her bending rhythm.

I think her head went back between her shoulder blades. It's hard to be sure because my head was turned to one side, trying to see into the darkened cemetery behind us. And in particular trying to focus on the phantom figure of Bernard as he pulled earth and roots indiscriminately from an old cracked tomb.

3

'Everything is bon?'

I pretended to rub sleep from my eyes to avoid direct eye contact with Bernard.

He slapped me on the back as though he wasn't a grave robber at all, but a common or garden Frenchman on his way to the office in the morning rush hour. We trotted down the street.

It was astonishing, as if the man I'd seen in the cemetery last night was someone else; a night whisp spookily flitting in and out of the palm trees and headstones. I'd said nothing to Annie, partly because I didn't want her to stop what she was doing but mainly because she was simply too normal to cope with such a vision. It was an indication of the advanced stage of my El Ref infection that I was able to deal with it so evenly. It takes about three months in this village.

In fact the only thing that had played on my mind the whole night was not why he had done it, but whose head he'd nicked. At first I told myself it was just a man gathering a fallen coconut, and that the sweat had blurred my vision. But as Annie stroked ripples of pleasure through me and my eyes cleared, I saw Bernard step out of the palm trees into the moonlight with a skull. He looked like a Shakespearian actor standing there, glancing left and right before creeping off with his booty. Old habits die hard.

I cleared my throat. 'Bernard. Did you see us last night?'

'The cemetery, you mean?'

'Yes.'

'I see you and your girlfriend but I do not watch. I am not the pee-pee Tom.'

Well, that's all right then, you must be normal. I waited for him to take the hint that what he had done was, how shall we say, a little out of the ordinary, and he read my silence accurately.

'You are thinking why I take from the graves, no?'

'Well, it was a little, how shall we say, out of the ordinary.'

He pinched his long nose in thought and ran his fingers through his balding grey hair. 'I cannot help it. Like the kleptomane.'

'But you know you're doing it.'

He looked at me. 'I am not insane, you know. I just...' he fished for the right explanation, looking up at the cliff, 'I like to be the treasure hunter. I always like archaelogy since I am small boy. I do not know, maybe the danger, maybe the unknown. And those skulls and bones are very beautiful to me, like the memory of a life in my hands. I know it is wrong but do I hurt anyone? The people are dead.'

'Their families aren't.'

He sighed.

I thought about the next question and said, 'It wasn't Elsie's head, was it?'

'*Mon Dieu*! What do you think of me?'

Suddenly a booming voice echoed off the cliff. 'Testing. Testing. *Ein, zwei, drei.*'

I looked up the road towards the trees. A startled buffalo trotted out of the bushes before going back to munch on some grass. Then it came again, only this time there was the sound of a mic being dropped, some muffled voices and then feedback.

We walked up the dirt track heading out of town, the morning sun peaking over the cliffs, then across the muddy area in front of the cockpit arena by the paddy field and entered through a gap in the terraces. Beside the cockpit stood Ziegwalt twiddling knobs on his 'portable' sound system, and next to him Judge Lam seated at a desk in the pit itself. Also placed in the enclosed fighting square were two opposing desks with chairs, at right angles to him, exactly like a courtroom.

'No, Ziegwalt. That's too loud.' Standing on the topmost tier of the terraces was Elvis Lam, hands on hips, ferocious pout on lips. 'We only want to make sure everyone in this arena hears, for goodness' sake.'

'Please, ein minwit.' Ziegwalt held up a hand at his critic, equalized his master amp, picked up his mic and whispered, 'Mary haff ein little lamp, vun two sree. Yar?'

'Lovely.'

Ziegwalt looked under his arm at us and, via half a dozen speakers that were rigged to the rafters, said, 'Guten morgan.'

Before I could reply we were barged out of the way. Two men came from behind carrying what looked like the pulpit Father Hilario stood at on Sundays.

'Ah,' said Judge Lam, acknowledging us with a nod. He removed his half-moon reading specs, closed the file he was looking at and pointed to the ground beside his desk. 'Mr Harris. Mr Jones. Good morning to you both. Have a seat.'

'Jones?' I said, looking at Bernard.

'My papa was Welsh. My mama is from France.'

'No relation to Tom Jones?'

'As a matter of fact, no.'

I watched the two men struggle through the chicken-wire gate into the ring with the oak lectern, holding each end like a coffin, and followed them in. As I passed Ziegwalt, still fiddling with knobs like a technician trying to receive a signal from outer space, I whispered, 'What are you doing?' He looked up, perplexed. 'Why are you helping them? It's like sleeping with the enemy.'

He flicked an infinitesimal glance at Lam and pulled me down to a squat, pointing at his gear. 'You see?'

I leaned closer, looking at the back of the amp to a thick black wire. 'No.'

'Now look under zhe desk.'

I looked across to make sure the judge wasn't watching, got on all fours and followed the wire. It ran into the earth floor, along and up the leg of the desk and terminated in a switch taped to the underside.

'Zhe svitch. You can see?'

'Yeah,' I said, reversing out.

'Zo. Vhen ve are shpeaking, alles ist gut. But,' up went the stunted finger, 'vhen zhey are doing zhe yakkety yakkety,' he mimed flicking the switch. 'Huh! No sound!'

I didn't know whether to laugh or cry. If our best hopes lay in Ziegwalt and his half-witted scheme to sabotage the opposition we may as well let Maximo rot.

'Well done,' I said, patting his shoulder. And then it dawned on me that I'd just witnessed a very rare daytime spectacle indeed for this place. 'Where's the electricity coming from?'

'Zhe village haff power every day from today. Ahh, Zhe Refuge…'

I looked at Bernard and he had the exact same look of comprehension on his face.

Tricky bastards. They were trying to curry favour. Give the villagers the one thing they've never had before. I looked up at the mayor, still on the top terrace, now talking on his phone.

These Lams had the power to provide power. They were God in this village. Let there be light!

'Never mind,' said Bernard, 'these people are not idiots. They know when this is finished they lose it again.'

'Good work,' I said to Ziegwalt, and could suddenly see his logic. If nothing else, the sound of the judge's voice going on and off would be a good laugh, and that would at least help undermine Lam's promise of 24-hour uninterrupted power.

'Could you sit at the desk and try the mic?' Lam's voice boomed out. Ziggy did as he was told. 'Very good, Ziegwalt,' he said. 'And Miss Montellano, if you'd be so kind as to try yours.'

Miss Montellano? I looked about, wondering who the hell he was speaking to. Then, from halfway up the terracing a young Filipina woman dressed in an open-collar, crisp white shirt and black trousers stood up, dusting off her bum. She came down the tiers, her shoulder-length black hair bouncing in harmony with her shirt. She went to the desk opposite me, smiling.

'This is Mr Harris,' said Lam. 'Mr Harris, Miss Maricel Montellano. She's the circuit prosecutor, or fiscal, as we like to call them, from Manila. Arrived this morning.' He was all business. 'Mr Harris is a detective. He's helping to defend Mr Bonga, who has decided, rather unwisely, to defend himself. Look forward to hearing your findings.'

Suddenly the arena seemed stiflingly hot. Sweat ran down my scalp, my waist itched and I wanted to be anywhere other than here. She was a real bloody lawyer! This was something I had not bargained for at all. Having the Lams against us was bad enough, but a real live lawyer! *Merde*, as Bernard would say.

I said hello, which turned into an awkward thumbs up, before fumbling for the mic.

'You must switch it on first,' she said, trying hers. 'Testing testing, *isa, dalawa, tatlo.*'

'Ahem.' I took a deep breath. 'Hello. How's that?' My tinny voice ran up the steps and hit the tinny roof.

'That's fine,' said Lam. 'Now, court procedure is very simple. Mr Bonga will sit there, and you, Mr Harris, will sit there, exactly where you are now.'

And for the next half an hour he went into detail while we stood, then sat, then slouched in the rising morning heat that had trapped itself in the space. The motions of both parties, if any, would be heard, he went on, and then Miss Montellano would present evidence against Bonga. We had all the paperwork, he reminded us, so there would be no surprises as far as witnesses were concerned. Once she'd finished, I would be given the floor.

I avoided fainting when he said this by telling myself that he was referring to Jim, not me. I still lived in hope. Then Jim and she would be allowed to rebut evidence before the filing of memoranda took place, and finally judgement. Proceedings would start tomorrow morning at nine on the dot.

When Lam asked us if we had any questions I waited to see what Miss Montellano had to say first. She asked how long he expected the trial to run for and Lam said as long as it takes. When I said I had no questions he asked me if I was sure. I wasn't sure about anything other than how far out of my depth I was.

He suggested that Maricel and I use the rest of the day to get acquainted with the case and each other. And just as we were about to leave he said that I might want to visit Maximo as well. 'Seems he tried to escape last night.' He dipped into his pocket, brought out a balut and began to tap it on his head, then delved into his other pocket, retrieving a tiny bag of salt. 'He didn't get very far.'

4

'You're joking.'

'No.'

'Oh, damn me.'

Annie turned and began to walk away. 'OK, OK, sorry, sorry.' She turned and looked at me, her eyes unblinking and cold.

I could see she'd had a rough morning; her hair was tangled and matted with leaves, her T-shirt was dirty and her shorts wet. On top of that she'd hurt her hand and wrung it continuously.

It was still quite early but she'd managed to get to Jim's beach and back. She looked thoroughly pissed off, her Italian nostrils flaring.

'Did he say why?'

She shrugged. 'Same reason. I ask Brenda and she say he is so scared.'

'Scared? I'll give him scared.' I threw the banana I was about to eat at a dog. 'Sod off.' It jumped up from its sleeping position, sniffed the yellow object and walked off. 'What the hell am I going to say to Maximo? I told him Jim's going to be there tomorrow.'

Annie put her arm around my shoulder. 'Brenda will try again but she think he no come, he must live here. You will leave. Is OK for you to upset the Mafiosi.'

'Lam, Mafia? Yeah, real Don Corleone that one.'

Despite our language difference she caught the caustic tone of my voice and looked at me with vacant non-interest. Sarcasm, it seems, is universal. My flip-flop pressed down on the banana and it discharged its sweet white meat.

'I'm going to see Max now,' I said. 'Want to come?'

'Yes. I explain to the old man myself. Is better from a woman.'

We went through the cruel village, the air opaque with heat, and entered the municipal building, its superabundant imbecilic human contents strewn about like tired dogs. Ten took us to Maximo and as she opened the door to his cell I noticed two men outside filling in the hole he'd dug.

There was a look of fear on the old man's face this time, as if blocking the escape route had broken him. I looked out the window as Ten left us. 'What happened? How did they find it?'

'MacArther tried to dig his way in from outside.' He saluted. 'But! I have not given up. A soldier never gives up.'

'MacArthur? Your chicken? You mean to say that bird knows where you are?'

He wasn't listening. He'd noticed Annie, his eyes widening. The expression on his face suddenly changed from a man in incredible mental anguish to one that could only be described as philanderous.

He stood to attention, saluted, then buttoned his shirt to the top and cleared his throat. Offering his hand he said, in an accent I'd never heard him use before, 'Señorita, it is an honour and a privilege to meet one so beautiful as you.' He bowed, kissed her hand and continued: 'How fitting, how tragic that my eyes should be covered from beauty until now, the day of *mi último adiós*.'

Annie seemed to be in a state of awestruck rapture. 'I have heard so much about you,' she said, with a look equally flirtatious.

'What?' I said.

Maximo hadn't finished. In fact he'd only just started.

'Should you find someday, somewhere on my grave mound, fluttering among tall grasses, a flower of simple frame: caress it with your lips and you kiss my soul. I shall feel on my face across the cold tombstone, of your tenderness: the breath – of your breath: the flame.' And he leaned in slightly.

Annie, to my utter astonishment, leaned in as well. They embraced.

'Can you leave us alone for a moment?' she said, wiping a tear from her eyes.

I looked behind me wondering if someone else had come in.

'John. Please. We talk.'

Had I just lost the woman I love to an 85-year-old younger man? She was behaving in a very unfitting way for a girlfriend of mine. And he was just... an old geezer.

'But I thought we...'

'Five minuti. Please,' she prayed. I wavered. She kissed me. I left.

As soon as I got outside my ear was glued to the wall. Nothing, just the hot dry blockwork and the crackling sound it made when my sweat soaked into it.

The two labourers were leaning on their shovels smoking cigarettes by the hole, concrete mixed and ready to scoop in.

'Do you mind?' I said, and pointed to the pit before going down on my knees and sticking my head in. No sound. Damn. I tried standing by the door but Annie told me to go away.

I gave up and spent the next half an hour sulking in Ten's office, ignoring her outrageous flirting. In the end I couldn't wait any longer and told Ten to fetch Annie. 'I don't think it's appropriate for the prisoner to collude with members of the public not involved in the trial.' She agreed.

When we went back in they were sitting on his bed talking.

'Ready,' said Annie.

They hugged and Maximo approached me. 'She is a very beautiful woman,' he said, and put his arm around me. 'Too good for you, compadre. Want me to take care of her?'

'Cheeky old twat.'

We separated and he looked down at my banana-coated feet. 'You need to get some proper footwear, soldier. You can't turn up like that.'

'I don't have any shoes,' I said. 'And nowhere in town has anything bigger than size eight. I'm a twelve.'

He thought, then said, 'Try Sergeant Chipstick's boots. He's got big feet.'

'The manikin? He's only got one foot.'

'The other one's somewhere. In the big ammo chest, I think. Tell you what, take off the boot and let MacArthur sniff it. Put some of his feed inside and let him eat out of it. Then let him sniff out the other boot. He sniffed me out.' He patted me on the shoulder and coughed. 'Do you know, I think I'm losing my voice.'

As soon as we were outside the building I asked Annie what Maximo had said to her.

'We talk,' she said.

'About what?'

'Things. Him, me, you.'

'And the alibi? Did you get it?' I said eagerly, holding out both hands to catch it.

'No. I ask but he refuse.'

'Shit. You told him to lose his voice by tomorrow, right?'

'Yes. Don't worry, he no kill her.'

'Are you sure?' I said, wondering at the far-off look in her eyes. 'How do you know he didn't do it?'

'Because I know.'

'How do you know?'

She looked me in the eyes. 'He tell me.'

'He gave you the alibi, didn't he? He did!'

She looked away.

'Yes! I knew it. Woo-hoo!' I danced. 'What is it?'

'No.'

'What do you mean, "no"?'

'I no tell.'

God, I thought, one hammy reading of a century-old poem from Philippines' leader José Rizal and she's anyone's. Pathetic. (Note to fellow travelling philanderers: look up last words of executed revolutionaries and recite as chat-up lines.)

I pleaded. 'Annie. Now come on, this is not a game. Tell me. Please.'

'No, I swear on our lady.' She crossed herself.

'Annie.'

'No.'

'Annie! This man's life is at stake! He could go to jail for life!'

'Is what he want.'

'I don't give a shit what he wants. It's what I want. I'm the one who has to stand there tomorrow and help him. Now if you have the key to all this let's have it.'

She wasn't budging.

'I don't believe this.' I went into a crouch, head in hands. 'You're insane, both of you. God Almighty.' I sighed.

At that moment there was the unmistakable sound of a brass car horn and Ziegwalt came peddling past on his unicycle wearing only his thong. *Honk, honk!*

'At least I have Ziggy, at least there's one person I can count on these days.'

He waved at us and nearly totalled himself on a blissfully unaware buffalo.

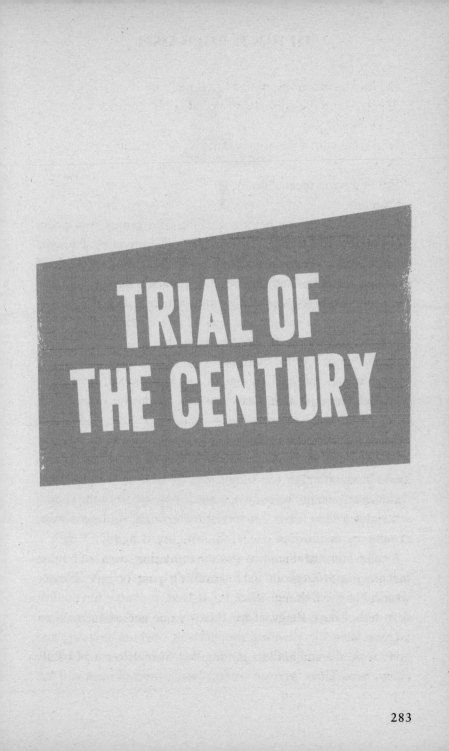

TRIAL OF THE CENTURY

1

'One small step for man…'

It felt weird, like I was walking on skis, each step a two-point landing. The boots had obviously never been worn before and the rubber soles were as stiff as iron. When I lifted one foot in stride, the one on the ground was on tiptoe, unbending. From flip-flops to cast-iron combat boots.

'… one giant leap for mankind.'

That wasn't the only change in my appearance. If my new outfit felt weird, it must have looked a damn site weirder: 12-hole hobnail boots (MacArthur, as predicted, had sniffed out the other one inside a broken-down spin dryer in the back yard like a bloodhound) and puttees; a pair of Bernard's seventies floral slacks that, although too small, were as near as I could get to decent trousers; my own shirt, a black bow-tie from the church store and a blue blazer borrowed from Frank – it went twice around my middle but at least the arms were the right length.

I walked through the silent town that morning with the bottom half of a glam rocker and the top half of a camp bouncer. No one stared. For the first time since I'd arrived, probably for the first time in the history of the village, there was no one around to stare.

Gone were the yawning shopkeepers opening shutters, and gone were the stallholders putting out their colourful Chinese plastic pots. There were no sisters placing trays of meat and fish in glass display cases at the *carinderia*, no kids playing on their way to school, and no tricycles bouncing along the potholed streets. Ghost town.

When I reached the cockpit, the reason became clear. The dirt road was lined each side by every imaginable mode of transport, from bicycles to three-wheelers to jeepneys and horses. Rows of buffalo were tethered up on the grass verges like parked vans, chewing the cud, mounds of shit piling up at their arses.

The entrance to the cockpit itself was bedlam as everyone tried to get a ringside seat. It was twice as crowded as the Cock Box Derby for one very simple reason: the female half of the population had turned out in droves. Girls as young as five, teenagers in groups of five, mothers of 25 with infants on the teat, and grandmothers of 55, all crawling along at a snail's pace. The whole river of people converged on that one entrance, kicking up clouds of dust in the morning light.

There were hawkers running up and down the terraces as people waved pesos in the hot air, demanding sustenance for the long day ahead. Women selling balloons to kids, barbecued fish to men and grilled pork to anyone who had enough cash. The lottery-ticket salesman from town had set up his table by the entrance. Even my barber was there with his scissors, snipping away in the space between rows of tricycles at 40 pesos a trim.

It was impossible to get in. It wasn't until Ten saw me, my shaved, sunburned head sticking out like a sore thumb among the sea of black hair, that I moved at all. She was standing on top of the police jeep with her megaphone.

'E-stop pushing! E-stop!' No one listened, so she said it in Tagalog. 'Tegil!' Still no one listened. I waved from the crowd, and when she saw me her electronically enhanced voice said, 'Mr John, go round the back.'

The boots came in useful in the paddy field quagmire. I reached the rear wall and stood gazing up at the underside of the terraces, a staircase in reverse. A kid was looking over the top.

'Oi!' I shouted. 'How do I get in?'

He disappeared. A moment later a small voice from somewhere in the wall said, 'Sir.' I crouched and peered into the wedge where the angled steps met the ground. The boy's head poked through a gap. 'Here.'

'I can't get in there!'

He smiled.

Shit. My clean clothes. My dignity. I lay on my belly and slithered under the gap, passing my borrowed briefcase to him.

The other side was another world; a boiling mass of a crowd all talking at once. The terraces were solid bodies, not a patch of seat in sight. Lam, already sitting at his desk on the earth-floor arena, was going over his paperwork and mopping sweat off his neck with a floral hanky. Maricel Montellano, the young prosecutor, was doing the same at her desk.

I felt like a fighting cock must feel before being torn to shreds in the ring, everyone's eyes falling on me. God knows how Maximo must have felt. He was sitting at our desk already, resplendent in the full ceremonial battledress he'd asked Annie to get ironed and bring him the day before. Next to him was Janet, and behind them, held upright by his freshly starched uniform, a very chagrined-looking chief of police.

I dusted myself off and entered the ring. Give them a show of my confidence, I thought, and dispensed with the gate, vaulting the low fence. The crowd lapped it up. I bowed. The chief remained sullen, lifting his chin and adjusting the belt that kept his belly up.

'Seems you are the last,' he snorted.

'Just collecting a last piece of evidence,' I retaliated with a cockiness that came from the crowd without, not the ferocious flutter within. I blew it by smiling and going to the wrong desk out of blind panic.

'Yes?' the prosecutor asked, looking up from her file.

'Um… just wanted to say good luck.' I blushed. The heat walled in and bounced off everything at once; a rancid mixture of sweat, wet rice fields, sour cow dung and cigarette smoke.

'You will need it.'

'That's not very nice.' I swallowed, just, and went to my rightful place beside Bonga.

He looked at me and smiled. 'OK?'

'Yeah. You've lost your voice, don't forget.'

'Forgot.'

I deflated. Was this going to be the fiasco I feared or just plain torture?

The only other person inside the ring was an old lady I recognised as the headmistress at the school. She was sitting directly in front of Judge Lam at a school desk like a sleepy old owl, pen poised over a book.

'Excuse me, chief, what's she doing here?' I said.

'Recorder,' he replied. Next to her was a man with skin as dark as ebony and as wrinkled as bark. No idea who he was but he looked like a farmer or a fisherman.

I scanned the crowd for familiar faces. Most of the people I knew well were in the front row. Francis the ladyboy (he winked), Ziegwalt and his girlfriend (he was wearing a shell suit and did his trademark double thumbs up), French Bernard, Big Frank and Taddi. And, wonder of wonders, Charlie the Russian, wearing only his loincloth and his enormous beard. He raised a clenched fist à la Che Guevara. Annie wasn't there because she'd gone back to speak to Brenda and Jim again.

Well at least I'm not alone, I thought, and put a hand beneath the desk to feel for the cut-out switch. The sweat dripping off my hand made an excellent conductor and I received a mild electric shock, jumping back with fright.

'What is wrong?' asked Janet, seated next to me.

'Mosquito.'

'Look,' she said, pointing up at the top tier. 'In the corner. Father Hilario.'

Silent and barely recognisable in a T-shirt, and belying his size, was a casual version of the man I'd bullied in church. He hadn't come to see me since our meeting, so I was surprised to see him here, right in the thick of it. I scanned the top tier for any other surprises and saw the girls from A Better Place, minus, thank heavens, Rose.

'What's he doing here?' I asked.

Before Janet could reply Judge Lam banged his gavel down on the desk with such ferocity, amplified so effectively by Ziegwalt's multiphonic PA system, that the whole place jumped as one. The silence was so sudden that everyone wiggled a finger in their ear to make sure they hadn't been struck deaf.

'Ahem,' said Lam, 'well done, Mr Neuhuber.' Ziegwalt bowed. 'We are here today,' Lam went on, his voice filling the rafters, 'to hear the case of the People of the Philippines versus Mr Maximo Angelino De-Bonga.'

His initials spelled M.A.D. Not a good omen.

Judge Lam waited to see if anyone dared say anything, and when only the buzz of flies filled the air he continued. 'Mr Bonga is accused of the murder of a Miss Elsie Azalea Rodriguez on the night of…'

E.A.R., I thought. That's pretty neutral. My mind was racing, the weirdest random thoughts just popping into my head.

The next half an hour was taken up by this one man's monotone voice filling the air while everyone else listened.

Nothing much happened. Lam went through the motions, literally, deliberately explaining to everyone present how we could have filed for postponement, or a motion to discharge the accused to become a state witness (we already had Gladys), and various other motions. All designed to baffle and dupe the general public, we thought.

His strategy was simple, I reckoned; to make the whole thing look like an open and fair trial, and to get everyone bored senseless on the first day. That way they'd go back to their normal lives by lunchtime and forget about it. Primed for a whitewash. A very common tactic in the Philippines, according to Maximo.

His plan didn't pay off. At ten o' clock, once all the formalities and procedures had been read out, and when he assumed everyone had had enough, we recessed, the judge no doubt thinking that everyone would go about their business. What he didn't realise was that no one in this place had any business to go about. This was village life, not the city. Nobody moved.

He looked around at the crowd, repeated into the mic that nothing else would happen for at least 2 hours so we might as well go. People simply bought more food from the hawkers and sat waiting, reclining on the terraces. Poor Lam. Obviously no one had told him that most people in El Ref had neither jobs nor anything else to do.

And when he returned an hour later hoping that the interest had died down he got the shock of his life to find everyone exactly where he'd left them. Not only that, but an arena further swelled to bursting with all of those people who hadn't been able to get in before.

So when 'Police Officer Thomas Bacudo the Fourth' was called to the stand that morning, sweating in his full uniform, he had not only the heat against him but a 300-strong crowd, restless and oozing a lust for action that was palpable.

'In your own time, officer,' said the prosecutor.

Thomas walked up to the lectern, cleared his throat, gripped the sheet of paper with the speech he'd prepared, and raised his chin, pulling the neck fat free of his tight collar. He leaned forward into the mic and said, 'On...' then looked sideways at the judge. 'In English or Tagalog, sir?'

'This is the Philippines, Mr Bacudo,' he said in that slightly affected way that epitomises the well-educated Filipino. He'd already picked up some of Jim's poshest English. 'Unless someone is unable to express themselves in English that's the medium of communication in the courts. And don't lean into the mic, please.'

Someone in the silent crowd sniggered. The chief gritted his teeth at the unholy humiliation of it all. He spoke as if reading from a teleprompter, without punctuation or pause:

'On the third I was busy as usual with the full workload that is comprised of an officer of my standing in such a community as El Refugio and its surrounding large environs of the province which comprises among other notable areas and districts such large difficult towns to control as–'

'Just tell us what you found on the beach on the fourth, please,' said Maricel the prosecutor. 'Thank you.'

A tiny ripple of laughter caught. Someone said 'police officer' and huffed.

Thomas seemed to be speaking in some strange accent that none of us had heard before. He sounded like a nervous kid in an oral English-language exam. 'Yes, Ma'am,' he said, and instantly regretted the show of subservience to a young woman. 'Well, I was called to the beach location, or in that vicinity, by Mrs Gladioli Velasquez to see what she said was a body on the beach.'

'And what time would that have been?'

Thomas looked at a notebook. 'Around precisely two-thirty in the a.m. on the morning of the fourth. That being of a Sunday nature, daytime. In the a.m. Ahem.'

'Go on.' The prosecutor sipped at a fresh young coconut through a straw.

My eyes, on their return journey from her to the chief ran over Ziegwalt in the background. He was glaring at me, frantically miming putting his hand beneath the desk and switching off the mic. It looked like he was feeling up an invisible woman.

'I proceeded to the beach in my commandeered police vehicular transportation system, and saw a large crowd standing there by the water'.

'Your jeep, you mean.'

'Yes.' Thomas blinked rapidly and went on. 'On the sand thereof I found Elsie, Ms Rodriguez, with a knife – I mean sword – beside her. Her throat had been cut.'

Sword? Hang on a minute. I paused, one finger under the table ready to flick the switch. 'Sword?' I said, standing.

Lam whacked his hammer and all heads swivelled back to that side of the ring. 'Mr Harris! First of all you'll get your chance to question this witness. Secondly, Mr Bonga is the one who'll do the questioning.'

'He can't, he's–'

Crack! 'Harris!'

Heads were going back and forth like the crowd at a tennis match.

I shut up and sat. 'The sneaky bastards. I bet they took your samurai sword,' I whispered in Maximo's ear.

He shrugged. 'We took their knife.'

Maricel spoke. 'When you say Elsie, do you mean this woman,' said the prosecutor, holding up a photograph, 'Miss

Elsie Azalea Rodriguez?' She showed the photo of Elsie to Thomas who nodded. 'Let the record show that Mr Bacudo the chief of police has identified the deceased in photo zero zero one.' She placed it on the desk by the old owl then went to a side table and, lo and behold, picked up Maximo's missing samurai sword.

I quickly looked through the paperwork at the exhibits in the case and found exhibit 001 marked as simply 'Weapon'. Shit. Why hadn't I checked it?

'Never mind,' I said to Maximo. 'I'll check my video. I've filmed in your place. There's bound to be a shot with that on the wall. All my videos are dated.'

'And is this the weapon you found by the body of Elsie Rodriguez on that day?' she asked the chief.

'Yes, it is,' he said without even looking.

To my utter astonishment no one in the crowd murmured except my supporters club in the first row. There'd been 50 witnesses on the beach that day. Cowards.

'Let the record show that Mr Bacudo has identified exhibit zero zero one as the murder weapon.'

'Objection!' I shouted, standing. 'Speculation.' It seemed like a lawyerly thing to shout.

'Bonga?' Lam said, and Maximo nodded. 'Sustained.'

'Sorry,' said the prosecutor. 'As the weapon found beside the victim.'

'Yes,' said Thomas.

'And can you describe her injuries to us?'

'She had a six-inch-long, one-inch-deep horizontal cut to her throat, bruises around her neck, like strangle marks, scratches on her face and hands, and her fingernails were broken and bleeding.'

Janet wrote it all down furiously as he spoke, wanting to see his expression but too busy with pen and paper. The soft sound of someone crying broke through the harshness of Thomas's voice. It was Bernard.

'Um... should I carry on?' asked the chief.

'Yes,' said Lam. 'Everyone must hear this.'

Thomas went back to his notebook. 'Fingernails broken and bleeding,' he repeated and looked up. 'Umm... her throat had been cut.'

'That's all?'

'Yes.'

'What did you do then?'

'Well, Monika and me – that's Miss Garcia, my assistant – we arranged a careful inspection of the site before organising the transportation of the body to the village morgue.'

Organised chaos, more like. I looked at Maximo. He had one finger on his bottom lip, watching the whole thing with a kind of detached interest. He'd shaved this morning and as usual had left a blob of cream beside his ear. I went to wipe it off and he flinched.

'Something on your ear,' I whispered.

He wiped it off and gave me a look.

'Anything else?' said the prosecutor.

'No ma'am.'

'I was just trying to wipe it off for you,' I said to Maximo. 'There's still some there.'

'Any questions, Mr Bonga?'

'It's caked on hard,' I said, leaning in to pick at it. 'The heat's made it like a meringue.'

'Mr Harris!' I jumped. 'Does he have any questions?'

'What?'

'Do you have any questions for Mr Bacudo the police chief?'

I stood. 'Um, Mr Bonga has some problems with his throat. He's lost his voice.'

I waited a moment, swallowing the humid silence. My voice sounded weak. Everyone stared. Was I saying something stupid or did I just look the village idiot in these clothes? A woman halfway up the terracing changed her baby from the left breast to right one.

'So he's asked me to speak on his behalf. If that's OK.'

'Objection!' The prosecutor stood. 'Mr Bonga represents himself. No one can speak on his behalf.'

'Do you consent, Mr Bonga?'

He nodded.

'Let the record show that Mr Bonga agrees. Now sit down, Maricel.'

The woman with the baby had really nice eyes, set off dusky against her open white blouse. Her collarbone showed on the side where the baby was suckling, one small hand gripping on for dear life. I was in a trance, the heatwave between us corrugating the air. She ran a hand through her hair.

'Well?'

She opened her mouth in a silent gasp to fill her lungs, the baby rising and falling on a cushion of soft beige flesh.

'Mr Harris!'

I flinched.

'We're waiting!'

'Oh, um,' I picked up some papers, put them down again, then picked them up again. 'Um... so... you say you found her on the fourth at...' I looked at the chief, then at the papers, then at Janet's notes. The writing was indecipherable, like a spider had run through a pot of ink and danced all over the page. I couldn't make out a single word. Was it Swiss?

'Two-thirty,' Janet whispered.

'Two-thirty.'

'Yes,' replied the chief.

'On the, um, fourth.'

'Yes.'

'In the morning?'

'Yes.'

'And there she was.'

'Yes.'

'So you found her... this, um... girl... on the beach?'

'Yes.'

'At two-thirty.'

The chief glanced at Lam.

'And this was on the fourth?' I said.

Lam sighed. 'I think we've established this already, Mr Harris, don't you? He's answered the question.'

I looked at Maximo then Janet and they looked back at me.

'Any more questions?'

I tried to breathe. I was frozen in 35-degree heat.

'Any more questions?'

Janet elbowed me in the ribs. 'Ask him about the sword.'

'Is that a no, Mr Harris?'

I had lockjaw. All the nerve-wracking days leading up to this had blocked my windpipe.

'Quick! Ask him where the knife is!'

'I'll take that as a no, then,' Lam said, and dismissed the witness.

A bead of sweat trickled down my forehead into an eye and my vision swam.

What a let-down I'd been. First the chief and then Ten; two witnesses who deserved a thorough roasting and who'd got off scot-free thanks to yours truly. And when Lam remarked rather pithily that Maximo's throat infection seemed to be contagious I didn't even hear the ripple of laughter that ran around the crowd, only feeling its vibration in my clogged ears.

After another hour or so, when not much had happened other than the crowd fidgeting and scoffing their way through bags of fried pork, Lam dismissed proceedings for the day, saying we would resume at the same time tomorrow.

I spent the rest of the day wandering along the shore and only stopped when I saw Annie coming back from her second Jim and Brenda expedition that evening. The news was not good. She'd climbed over to their secluded beach only to find a lone Brenda sitting in Jim's shack crying. Jim had scarpered again and she knew not where.

'Mr Heronimo Ondangan,' the old owl read. A leather-skinned man with a body belying his 50 years took the stand.

Heronimo? I looked down at the witness list. Geronimo Ondangan, it read. I'd been in El Refugio long enough to spot a fisherman when one passed. Their skin texture gave them away, and its colour of deep russet. Also the build, not large like a farmer or builder, but small and sinewy, bamboo-ey, with knots for elbows. Even hidden under a stiff shirt and trousers the form was unmistakable. But mainly you could tell them from the smell of cologne. Fishermen use buckets of it to disguise the smell of fish guts they can't scrub off.

He crossed nervously to the judge and awaited directions. Lam pointed at the pulpit and he stood in front of it, innocently wondering what to do next, a beautiful smile creeping over his tawny features. The crowd roared with laughter, and Lam was forced to employ his hammer. He stirred the air with the gavel's handle. 'Other side please, Mr Ondangan.'

The poor man rotated on the spot and the crowd roared, like kids watching a wind-up toy dance. '*Sa kabila*', Lam added in his native tongue.

The man blushed and bowed, said, 'I am afologise', walked round and stood at the lectern, ducking his head in a conscious effort to stay beneath Lam.

The judge allowed the assemblage banked up around us to get it out of their system, taking the opportunity to inspect the little mallet. Babies were shifted, bums changed cheeks and throats cleared.

I gazed around at the faces on this humid maritime morning, the second day of the trial.

If someone had produced a seating plan the allocation couldn't have been more accurate. Everyone, it seemed, had marked their place on the terrace the previous day by placing an object, and now occupied exactly the same spot. The only difference, as far as I could tell, was Father Hilario, who now hid himself in the opposite corner. And Ziegwalt, who'd been given the task of spying on Rose and so was absent.

All the girls from A Better Place were there again, all lined up in their best Sunday dresses, all holding a bag of sour mangos and shrimp paste, or spitting out melon seeds.

'I do,' said the fisherman, now sweating and wondering what he'd just sworn to. He looked desperate, like a man who was very keen indeed to change his mind. Gone was the sweet grin and sailing eyes, replaced by sheer panic. He was a rabbit frozen in headlights, his hand visibly shaking as it was withdrawn from the Bible. The power of the church to strike the fear of God into poor people never ceases to amaze.

Ten wiped his sweat off the cover, placed it back by the recorder, and took her place obediently by her chief.

Maricel watched through her dark eyelashes and black hair, her head cocked to one side, chin in hand as though watching her child in the school nativity. She had the silkiest hair I'd ever seen. Lam nodded for her to begin and she stood, looking at the silent man.

'How old are you, Mr Ondangan?' she said.

'I am pine, ma'am.'

The audience burst out laughing and Ondangan smiled, glad that he had done something to please them. Lam loomed up and they hushed.

Maricel took a deep, stoic breath. 'Do you speak English?'

'I e-sfeak English, ma'am. Tank you.' He glanced at the crowd for further encouragement, but when it didn't come he looked confused.

'How old are you? *Edad?*'

'English, Mr Ondangan,' said Lam. 'Don't be shy.'

'I am pipty pibe,' he replied. He had the habit, like so many Filipinos, of mixing up his Ps with his Fs and his Bs with his Vs when he spoke English.

'And please tell us, what is your job? *Trabaho?*'

'*Mangingisda.*'

'English.'

'I am pishingman,' he said, seeming ashamed of his noble profession, like so many brilliant tradesmen when confronted with lesser mortals who hide behind expensive clothes and language. People like me, I thought, and wished I had a proper job, ruing the day as a school leaver when I dismissed my natural bent for carpentry in favour of an office-bound profession.

'And can you please explain what you saw on the night in question.'

The fisherman looked at the police chief. The question was repeated in Tagalog. The chief nodded very slowly at the fisherman and it was like he'd switched on a recording.

Geronimo stood stiff to attention and said, suddenly in new, improved English, 'On the night in question I am pishing and then I come to the land and then I am see Mr Maximo Bonga and he is killing the Miss Elsie Azalea Rodriguez and she is dying, tank you ma'am.'

Maximo tapped my arm and whispered, 'He's not even a local, that's a southern accent.' Then he went back to stroking his cock.

I shouldn't have been at all surprised by this fisherman. Maximo had told me this would happen, that the whole thing would be a sham. But the reality of it, the ridiculous pantomime of this poor man standing there out of bribery or thuggery was breathtaking in its parody of justice. Even Judge Lam looked appalled.

I looked down at Max's lap. His one request from the previous day had been that MacArthur be allowed in the court with him. Lam had agreed and I'd had to carry the mangy bird here with me. Now he seemed more interested in that scrawny thing than the balance of his life.

MacArthur stared up at me with his beady little eye and I thought, there's more truth and honesty in that damn chicken than there is in this whole village.

'Where?' asked the prosecutor. '*Saan?*'

'El Refugio veach,' the fisherman said, pointing at the entrance.

'Your witness,' Maricel said, and sat down. Geronimo went to leave but Lam told him to stay put.

Three hundred heads turned to me. Even MacArthur snapped sharply in my direction, his glossy black eye hooded by a pink skin, egging me to do my best. Go get 'em, tiger!

I stood and Maximo whispered, 'Ask him to identify me.'

That's simple enough, I thought. A strategy that, if indeed he was from out of town and couldn't even recognise the accused, would make at least one witness fall by the wayside.

As I cleared my throat to speak there was a slight commotion to my right, and a man's voice going, 'Excuse me. Sank you. *Entschuldigen Sie*. Sank you. Sank you.' Ziegwalt slid sideways through the crowd, looked at me, shook his head slowly and went to sit.

'Judge,' I said. 'I mean, Your Honour. Can I just have a quick word with Ziegwalt, please?'

He nodded.

Ziegwalt stood there yawning, his mouth open in a silent roar. I beckoned him over. He looked at Lam for permission then marched around and through the gate. 'What are you doing here?' I hissed. 'You're supposed to be watching Rose! Do I have to do everything?'

My anger came not from a feeling that I was the only person with any sense, but from fear. A fear of Rose and our secret, which multiplied fifty-fold whenever she wasn't under my or someone else's watchful eye. I didn't care what she did or who she did it with, so long as she didn't do it near me. When she vanished I panicked.

'I am vatchink her,' he said.

'Then why are you here?'

'Because she is here.'

I followed his stunted finger and my stomach turned to the burning bowels of hell. There on the topmost terrace was Rose, looking flush with the hormones of early stage pregnancy charging around her body. I couldn't breathe.

'Mr Harris. Your witness,' said Lam, looking at his watch.

I had to go through with it. Just the one question and that'll be all. She won't say anything in here. You're safe here. She may be volatile, but the last thing she wants is the whole world to know about the baby.

I looked at the fisherman then at MacArthur, then said, in as simple English as I could make it, 'Who is Maximo Bonga?' He didn't appear to understand the question so I repeated it in Tagalog exactly as Max whispered it, '*Sino si* Maximo Bonga?' The fisherman frowned like it was the most stupid question he'd ever been asked.

My eyes were now fixed on his right arm. In slow motion his fingers loosened, the arm came up and he pointed at Maximo sitting beside me. I looked at MacArthur as though he'd murdered Elsie. He ruffled his feathers.

'Did you see this man kill Miss Elsie Azalea Rodriguez on the beach on the night of the fourth?' asked Lam, then again in Tagalog with wonderful bilingual dexterity.

'Yes, sir. I am see it.'

And then, like a banshee wailing from hell, if hell was up and heaven were down, came a screeching voice as sharp as a razor and just as terrifying.

'He's lying!'

Everyone, including MacArthur, swivelled on their seat and looked up.

'Maximo was with me that night!' Rose, her face on fire with thwarted disclosure, her hair standing up like whipcord, teeth gritted, stood and glared at anyone who dared challenge her. Only Lam had the guts.

'Silencio!' he shouted, banging the hammer.

'I will not!' she shouted back. 'He was with me and–'

'Quiet! This court will not be prejudiced by such an outburst!'

'And I am pregnant with his baby!'

The sharp intake of collective breath was audible as the hot air trapped within the space got sucked in. It was like an instant vacuum.

'Chief Bacudo!' Lam said. 'Stop her!'

Thomas the chief was already on his way up the terracing in giant strides towards Rose, his truncheon drawn, belly bouncing.

'You can do what you want but he is the padre of this child and–'

'Shut your mouth!' the chief screamed, whacking his stick against a wooden column as he raced up.

'And any test will show it!'

Thomas reached the top and dived on the poor girl. There was the briefest of scuffles, all the women in the place screaming, before she was dragged out. We could still hear her shouting as she was carried across the paddy field and down the road. Gossip caught hold like wildfire in a parched breeze.

'Silencio!' Lam shouted, but it was no good, the excitement was just too much for everyone. 'Monika,' he said to Ten over the din, 'please take the accused back into custody. This is over for the day. And Monika…'

Ten looked back.

'Please inform the doctor that we'll be needing his services in matters of a maternal nature.' Ten looked bemused. 'A pregnancy test.' He looked to Ziegwalt, made an upward motion with his finger and pointed to the mic. A moment later Lam's voice was on full volume. 'Court is adjourned until next Monday morning.' No one moved. 'Go home!'

2

'The dirty old bastard. I never thought he had it in him.' Frank rummaged through the cooler, shaking his head.

I opened the first stage on Bernard's air cylinder and tapped him on the shoulder. He put his regulator in, adjusted his mask and rolled backwards into the abyss.

Night diving, one of my favourite pastimes and easily the best way to relieve the day's stress. I'd already been down and now it was Bernard's turn. Janet had supplied the food, the local dive shop the boat and gear.

'Hey, where are the sandwiches?' Frank's white, moon-like face in the black night looked starved. 'You said they in here, boy.'

'They are,' I said, reaching behind me and unzipping my wetsuit. The boat rocked and I held onto a stay. 'You eat too much.'

'I'm eating for two: me and my worm.' He dug deeper in the cooler. 'Gotcha.'

'Mine is the one with hot sauce,' said Annie, pulling at my zip.

Talk about getting let off the hook, I thought, standing there looking at the top of Annie's head. Just when I thought my goose was well and truly cooked Rose tells everyone that Maximo is the father. I wasn't sure whether to laugh or cry or be pissed off with Rose for lying, if indeed she had already known she was pregnant when she slept with me. Or be annoyed with myself for believing her. More than anything I was afraid Max was getting himself into another mess with a woman that young and, let's face it, devious. Not for the first time I felt like an overprotective son trying to shield an ageing parent from the pitfalls of a dishonest modern world. I suppose in a place like this he knew best. I was the outsider here.

However I looked at it, though, I couldn't help feeling good. Annie hadn't said a word to me about it, never suggesting that the baby could be mine. To promote the idea of me as the victim in all this, I reminded her of the time span between Rose's supposed encounter with Maximo and the one with me, pointing out that she was already pregnant and knew it.

'Still can't believe it,' Frank said, sandwich in one hand, beer in the other. 'Old man Bonga. Hooee! Takes some beatin'.'

'Now you see the alibi,' Annie said as I stepped out of the wetsuit and took a beer from Taddi.

'No, not really,' I said. 'So he slept with one of the local whores. So what? He's a man like everyone else. Just because he's old doesn't mean he doesn't want sex.'

'You do not know El Refugio,' Janet said, checking both watches. 'Bernard has got twenty-two minutes at a max depth of nineteen metres.'

'I think I do,' I said, and opened the beer. 'I think I know that it's a place based on lies and deceit. A two-faced society where everyone shows one side in public but does something completely different at home.'

'And?'

'And Bonga does what he says. Unlike everyone else here who says: Do as I say and not do as I do. Everyone pretends to be good and then stabs you in the back. It's bullshit.'

'That is true,' Janet said, 'but it does not change one thing; that man will never get respect here again.' She picked up a dive wheel and glanced at her watch.

'Oh, come off it, Janet, half the men in this village go to A Better Place,' I said. Taddi suddenly needed to pump the gas lamp.

'So what? You are missing the point, John. Whether they go or not does not matter here. What matters is that you are not seen to go. Yes, it is two-faced, but that's the way it is in this country. If you are not seen you are not guilty. And when in Rome you do like the Romans; whether it is lies or throwing rubbish on the beach or sleeping with prostitutes. Your point is moral, mine is reality. You are right, but however right you are, it is wrong here. See?'

'What, you're saying it's OK to throw rubbish in the sea?'

'No, but here it is only wrong if you are seen.'

'Well, the point is he's off the hook,' I said, and sat beside Annie for warmth against the cool night.

'No,' Annie said.

'You heard Lam.' Frank squinted as the lamp flared. 'He say he gonna git the doc to give her the once over. Git the date of conception fixed an' all.'

'That will only tell us the date, not the time.'

Shit. I hadn't thought of that.

'But what about the other girls,' said Taddi. 'There were five other girls there when Maximo spent the night at A Better Place.'

Annie shook her head. She pointed to the cooler and Frank gave her a roll. 'He goes to her when she is working at the guest house. Sometimes no witnesses.'

And then I remembered the smell of his aftershave that night in the front yard when I'd stumbled in drunk. 'We're back at square one.' I guzzled the beer. 'Looks like Bernard's plan may come in useful after all.'

Bernard had reminded us that, even if we could prove Maximo had been with Rose that night, if we didn't have an alternative patsy they simply would not allow us to prove him innocent. They needed a scapegoat.

I looked over the side at the inky water.

Twenty minutes later, exactly as Janet had suggested, the faint beam of Bernard's torch cut swathes of green beneath the surface. I prepared myself to pull him up. The beam of light shortened and lengthened, going out just as he broke the surface. He inflated his BCD, took off his mask and blew out the mucus, holding up a massive lobster. 'Puff! We will have good luck, my English friend.'

I smiled. As I helped him into the boat I looked back at the shore half a mile off. All the town's lights were ablaze for the first time since I'd arrived. The carnival was back in town, music blared from a dozen karaoke machines, the sound drifting over the placid bay, and I wondered if all this was really happening. It was as though not being in the village made it unreal, the distance offshore making the place a fantasy, disconnected from reality. I'd had the same feeling when I went to see Charlie on his island before, a feeling that even the smallest distance might as well have been a thousand miles in this place.

A firework rocket was let off, its silent trail of sparks drawing a line in the dark sky. A flash, a phut and silence again.

Bernard shivered as he pulled off his wetsuit, grabbed a beer from the cooler and raised it to everyone in the boat. 'To my beautiful Elsie. And to our friend Max.'

3

'Zo, I am in Pattaya und zhe town is full because of zhe high seasoning. I am alone, you see, zo I find zhe room in zhe shmall hotel. Thailand ist gut.' Ziegwalt nudged me in the ribs and winked before going on. 'I am tired from zhe Lufthansa flight – First Class – but it is my first night zo I vill go for zhe beer und zhe sex. Zo I go...'

I turned back to Maricel the young prosecutor and smiled. 'Nice day.'

She looked up at the bright morning sky, crisp against the municipal building, and nodded. 'There must be something better to do on a weekend.' She glanced at her sports watch. 'It's quarter past nine. He's late.'

The trial had stopped for the weekend but Lam had instructed the prosecutor and me to meet him 'to go over a few delicate points' before Monday. I had jumped at the chance, seizing it as an opportunity to hit them with our trump card: The wrong weapon. But since I'd checked my video camera and found no footage inside the guest house showing the samurai sword, it all looked a bit bleak on that front.

After last night's dive we'd toyed with the idea of submitting the photos of dead Elsie from the stolen file. But when we looked closer the knife was two-thirds obscured in every picture by Ten's hand as she pointed at it. It didn't look like a samurai sword, but it didn't look much like a knife either.

'Und zhere are many sexy girls in zhe bar all looking at me. Zo, I go over...'

'What do you think he wants to talk about,' I said to Maricel, shifting slightly away from Ziegwalt's non-stop yapping in my left ear. The two of us had been sitting on the concrete step when Ziegwalt had come jogging past in his thong.

'That woman, I suppose,' Maricel said. 'Rose.'

'Seems like Maximo has an alibi after all. Course we knew it all along, he just didn't want us to use it,' I said, allowing myself a well-earned gloat.

'Not much of an alibi,' she said.

'She's a witness, she'll testify.'

She looked at me and her brow closed in. 'Prostitutes don't carry much weight in this country when it comes to the law. So she's carrying his child. So the test proves that it was conceived on the third. So what? He could still have done it.'

'Und zhe girl is a beauty, und she say to me, "Yes, I like boom boom," und ve...'

'Well, she's no worse a witness than your fisherman. I mean, come on, he's clearly a muppet. The chief tells him what to say and he says it.'

'Puppet. So because he doesn't speak very good English he's no good? Is that a crime where you come from?'

'You know as well as I do he wasn't there. And you know Maximo didn't kill that girl.'

She shifted to face me and I looked into her beautifully deep, black eyes. With those peepers and the slight lilt to her accent she had to be of mixed blood, probably Spanish. Like so many people in this country she most likely had the genes of the clergy from a few generations back. Catholic priests have been up to their old tricks for centuries.

'I work for the government,' she said with harsh purpose, 'and if they say I have to work on this case then I'll work on it. I serve the people.'

'You serve the Lams.'

'I do not work for the Lams!'

I snorted with as much derision as would come out of my nostrils without snot. 'If you believe that then you've been in Spain too long.'

'I'm a Filipina.'

'How long were you in Spain?'

A flush of hot discomfort ran through her delicate skin. She fished for a response that wouldn't let her down.

'Come on,' I smiled, sensing I'd guessed right. 'How many years?'

'I went to study there.' She shrugged dismissively and lifted her chin.

'University?' No reply, just an infinitesimal frown. 'Secondary school?' She coughed. 'Primary School! Oh my God. You've never even lived here! You're as much an outsider as I am!'

'I was born in the Philippines.'

'So if a dog's born in a stable, it's a horse, is it? I've never heard such bollocks.'

'So what? So that means I'm working for the Lams? You don't know what you're talking about. Their power doesn't stretch that far.'

'Yes it does. And you should open your eyes. Did it ever strike you as strange that someone as young as you should be asked to prosecute on a murder case? You told me that this is only your second case since qualifying. Doesn't that seem odd to you?'

I'd pieced it together very quickly. We were in Asia's only Catholic country and the word 'nepotism' originated from the cardinals of that church. It all made sense to me: a young Filipina from a privileged family, educated and trained abroad, comes back because she'll get to the top here much faster than she would in the west, and gets told to go to work with a relative on a case that requires appropriate family bias. Boom.

'Why didn't they get someone senior up here?' I went on. 'Why didn't they take it to Manila for trial? Why did old man Lam himself turn up in the capital and hand-pick you; the youngest, most inexperienced lawyer of all the circuit prosecutors?'

She looked at her feet, fumbling with her briefcase.

'Und zhen she take off mine clothe-ses. Oh, zo gut. Und zhen…'

'Maybe he– '

'Maybe what, Mari?' I said, shortening her name for effect.

'Maybe he wanted to help my career, give me a good case.' She looked at me with self-determination. 'And I'll do it. And I'll forget what you've just said because as far as I can see they're the rantings of another foreigner who's lost his way in this insane little village. This nest of cuckoos. They should have named it the Cuckoo Coast, and you should have flown over it.'

'Und she undresses, und she is ein mann! Zhe lady-man! Huh!' Ziegwalt slapped his thigh at the hilarity of his story. 'But I am zo horny zo I do it anyvay! Har har. Und vhen…'

'Shut up, Ziegwalt! For God's sake, man.' Anger born of hurt pride boiled up inside me. 'Why do you keep going on about sex all the time? Every one of your stories revolves around young girls or your perpetual erections. Give it a rest, man.'

A tear welled in his eye.

Now I'd hurt Ziegwalt's feelings. He stared at his thighs then stood, saying, 'Zo! I must go.' He looked up at the brooding sky. 'Auf Wiedersehen. Until ve meet tomorrow.'

'Ziggy. I didn't mean it like that.'

'Tomorrow.' And he hopped onto his unicycle and wobbled away from me.

Maricel stood and brushed her cotton-covered buttocks, shaking her head in disbelief at Ziegwalt's pink bum as it disappeared round a building, the church of all places.

The next moment I was standing with my jaw on the floor at the person coming the other way.

Not Judge Lam, looking extraordinarily relaxed and casual in jeans and polo shirt on this Sunday morning, but the man walking beside him. Laughing and joking together like buddies of old. Like a gift from God. The one person I wanted to see before Monday and here he was. Thank you, Lord.

Dressed, unmistakably by a woman, in clean shirt and pressed trousers, and looking like the world's best barrister on his day off, was Gentleman Jim. My man.

'Excuse us for a while, please, chief,' Judge Lam said as he followed us through the door into the chief's office, with a sweep of his hand presenting Thomas with the exit.

Thomas frowned slightly, unsure exactly what Lam was suggesting. That he should get out of his own office? He looked at the outstretched hand, then at the open door.

'We'll not be needing you for the moment.' He smiled.

Still the chief stood there, his face going from confusion to punch-drunk stupefaction. He rolled his shoulders, twitched nervously and stepped involuntarily outside his own empire, his throne room, the place from which he controlled this mad little world.

Lam shut the door. For a moment Thomas was still there, we could see him through the frosted glass, his bulbous silhouette rigid from the colossal snub to his authority. I couldn't help smiling.

'Now then,' said Lam, sitting – very comfortably it has to be said – in the chief's chair, 'where were we?' He opened a foolscap folder. 'Ah yes. Seems our Mr Bonga has been up to some shenanigans. The local doctor's done the test on our Miss Elarmo – Rose to those of you who know her well – and it appears she's telling the truth. At least regarding the date. She is pregnant, and conception would have been on the third or the fourth of April.' He looked up and removed his bifocals. 'Now Jim, let's get started.'

I couldn't believe my eyes. Was this even the same mean-spirited man who'd first arrived in a storm of clan-induced hatred? A man who I'd despised from the word go, based purely on his lineage? He didn't even look like a Lam now. Gone were the piercing black eyes ('piss holes in the snow', as Frank so accurately described them), and the sharp nose now seemed more like a letter opener than the hooked dagger it once had. Even the broad flat forehead, like a drive-in movie theatre (another Frank contribution), had vanished under a new fringe that could only be described as a Beatles hairdo. What had come over him?

'I have been discussing the new developments on this case and it seems we may well be able to wrap things up within the week,' Lam went on.

Maricel butted in. 'Hold on a minute. Who's Jim?' She looked at the judge, ignoring the freshly bathed and shaved Jim seated at her side.

'Sorry. Of course you haven't been introduced. Sir James Digby Pelican-Fishpatrick,' he said, gesturing at Jim. 'Jim, Maricel Montellano. The freshest of prosecutors working in our fair country.'

Sir James what-diddy-what-what? I did a double take. Had James been knighted? A real Lord Jim?

Jim noticed my perplexed look and whispered, 'Sounds stranger than it is. Actually double-double-barrelled. It's spelled Pelli-Caan Feisch-Patrick. Italian-Greek and German-English descent.'

'Not that, Jim,' I hissed, 'the bloody knighthood. Why didn't you say?'

He wafted a dismissive hand in the air. 'A trifle. Yours for the price of a seat in the House of Lords.'

'Jim will be taking over the case from Mr Harris,' Lam went on.

'Excuse me,' said Maricel, 'he can't take over the case. Bonga represents himself.'

'Correct,' said Lam, once again putting on the bifocals and pulling a sheet from the file. 'And he's agreed to allow James here to speak on his behalf.'

'What?'

'Yeah, what?' I echoed. 'When did you speak to Maximo?' I asked Jim. 'We've been looking all over for you.' I sounded annoyed even though inside I was more than happy that he'd turned up.

For the past few days I felt as though we were all about as stable as an unanchored boat, likely to be swept away by the slightest sea change. And though not exactly a Danforth, Jim represented an anchor of sorts, even if a poorly made one. It wasn't his fault the seabed was made of shifting sand around this coast.

'Saw him last night,' he said, 'when I heard about his connection with Rose.'

'Not forgetting the other new witness that has come to light,' said Lam.

'What new witness?'

'All in here,' Lam said, tap-tap-tapping the folder. 'This is your copy.' He slid it across the desk and Maricel engulfed it like a starved dog. 'You can go over it all in good time. Let's talk about Monday's proceedings and whether or not we should call this woman Rose and all of her 'colleagues' to the stand. What do you think, Jim?'

Incredible. One day with him and already the judge was asking his opinion instead of the qualified lawyer's. It's amazing what a posh accent can do for you.

'Rather volatile,' Jim said. 'Could cause something of a brouhaha, judging by the contretemps that took place at Friday's session. I would advocate not. Let's get this over and done with. Just put Rose and the doctor on the stand. Maricel?'

Her mouth was gaping in disbelief. 'Hold on,' she said, raising a hand. 'Let's go back a moment. I don't think anyone should be allowed to represent Bonga. He represents himself.'

'They're not representing him. They're merely helping him out.'

'If he needs help he appoints a qualified lawyer. If he cannot afford it the state will appoint one for him. If–'

'Oh come off it, Maricel, this is El Refugio, not Manila. If he wants to do it with friends that's his lookout.' Lam reached into his breast pocket, pulled out his customary balut and tapped the shell on his head as usual. 'What are you so worried about? Don't think you're going to lose, do you?'

'It's not a matter of winning or losing, it's a matter of law. And the law states–'

'The law states that a man – or woman – may defend him – or her – self. And that's exactly what he's doing. Only with the help of these two gentlemen. Now can we move on? Thank you.'

I allowed myself a smirk at Maricel's expense. She opened the file again.

'So,' Lam went on, 'the doctor stands and so does our young Rose. The five other girls – all witnesses nonetheless – do not. Agreed?'

'For the sake of repose, I think that's prudent,' said Jim, and we all looked at Maricel. She said nothing.

'Settled,' said Lam, and wrote something down. 'That makes… one, two, three, four witnesses to go. Not including the star himself.' He leaned back in the chair, peeled the top off the skull, and with two delicate fingers plucked off the chick's head and popped it in his gob.

4

'Never trust a man who eats unborn chicks,' I said, watching as Judge Lam settled into his seat for the day. Just his presence in the cockfighting arena on Monday morning was enough to reduce the boiling crowd to a gentle simmer.

'I like balut,' said Jim. 'Rather appetising. Increases one's libido. Have you tried it?'

I had tried it and hated it: the little foetal birds curled up, eyes closed, still awaiting their time to hatch. The taste, a mixture of boiled egg and fish, and the texture like putty, including the underdeveloped skull and beak, was rancid. 'I had the shits for a week.'

I looked around at the crowd. Everyone was there as usual, the main addition being umbrellas because of the rain clouds forming. Also sitting on a bench beside the chief was Rose, looking adamant. Unusually, her hair was tied at the back, adding to her resolute but still beautiful eyes. Her dress was a plain, home-made white sackcloth. Jim's doing, in an attempt to make her appear a little less scheming and a lot more sincere. We wanted her to seem hard done by, poor and honest.

Sitting on the bench opposite, and flanked rather timidly by Ten, was Gladys, her eyes burning into Rose like two well-aimed lasers. Rose gave as good as she got, staring right back. I was just thankful neither of them was staring at me.

'Where's our man?' I said.

'He'll be here,' Jim said, and addressed Maximo. 'Now Rose is going to tell it exactly how it was, so don't worry.'

Max leaned sideways, stroking MacArthur on his lap, and said, 'What about that old witch?'

'Don't worry about Gladys, when she—'

'Rosana Alibangbang Elarmo,' squawked the recorder, and Rose stood up.

'Shh,' said Jim. 'You'll see.'

Without taking her eyes off Gladys, Rose strode to the pulpit and said she'd tell the truth, the whole truth and nothing but the truth, so help her God.

It didn't take long for Gladys's mouth to open. '*Puta!*' (prostitute) she hissed.

Lam looked at her, twiddled his mallet and said, 'One more remark like that and you'll find yourself in a cell too, madam.'

Rose, unbending in her ways despite the veneer of placid congeniality, spat at Gladys. The projected globule couldn't reach across the space but it got close, hitting the side of Gladys's desk and forming a stalactite. '*Bruha!*' (Old witch.)

'Quiet!' Lam raised his gavel but didn't bring it down. Both ladies, having skimmed off their early-morning venom, hung back from the verge of physical violence. 'Both of you shut up unless you're spoken to. Now, Miss Montellano. Go ahead.'

'Umm, excuse me, Your Honour, but Mrs Velasquez is supposed to be next. My witness,' said Maricel, standing.

Lam looked through his half-moons at the sheet then over the top at the owl.

'Sorry,' she said. 'She's right.'

Lam sighed and asked Rose if she wouldn't mind stepping down again for a while, promising that she'd be next, only to be reminded by the recorder that she wasn't next but third in line.

'Of course,' said Lam. 'Our new witness; has he arrived yet?'

'No, sir,' said the chief. 'Should I go to fetch him?'

'Yes, if you would. Now, can we please get on?'

Gladys, without invitation, stalked over to the lectern as Rose dismounted, wiping it down dramatically with a frilly hanky before climbing up. When the Bible was offered, with great ceremony and for everyone to see, she placed the handkerchief over it, pulled a sour face and put one finger on top as though it had been infected by Rose.

'John, go and ask Rose not to flare up, would you,' Jim whispered in my ear. 'It's not going to help.'

'You go.'

He looked at me, then at Lam. 'If I may, Your Honour, I'd like to enter into a moment's discourse with Miss Elarmo.'

Someone in the crowd clucked their tongue and said 'goddamn Americans'.

'John.'

'Jim,' I hissed, 'she hates me.'

'Oh, poppycock. Get over there and don't be so feckless.'

'She's nervous,' said Maximo. We both turned to him. 'That's why she's angry. That's her way. Tell her I love her and I'll stand by her.' He stroked MacArthur.

I stared into the old man's eyes, the tiredness brought on by his drowning years drawing me in like an old book. A story that keeps its secret right up to the last page.

'Go.' Jim gave me a shove and I went and told her.

'Max loves you. He will stand by you. Shut up and don't annoy anyone again. Bye.' I didn't wait for her reply and came back. MacArthur looked up at me with a critical eye. 'What are you gawping at?'

Maximo giggled and tickled the bird playfully. 'D'you want to hold him?'

'No, I do not.'

'He likes you. You've got the touch. It's a bit like having green fingers. You need—'

'Can we save matters avian until later, chaps?' said Jim.

Maximo smiled sentimentally.

'And the emotion,' I said. 'Let's not start sucking each other's dicks just yet. We haven't won.'

Lam leaned into the mic and said, 'There will be absolutely no talking in this court today. Does everyone understand?' He swept his earnest eyes over the crowd. 'If anyone chooses to speak during this session they will be removed and not permitted to re-enter. Silencio. *Tahimik*. Understood? Miss Montellano, your witness.'

She stood wearily, glanced at me and said, 'Mrs Gladys Velasquez, in your own words could you describe what you saw on the night in question.'

'Please.'

'What?'

'Ask me nicely.'

'Please.'

'That's better, young lady.' Gladys looked so far down her nose at the prosecutor I thought she would fall backwards. She straightened in her corset, raised her eyebrows as if this whole show had ruined her daily schedule, and spoke in her haughtiest voice.

'Well now, it was at around two in the morning, I suppose.' She used a single finger to remove a hair that wasn't in front of her eyes. The stiff perm (blue today) was resolute in its clinging purchase to her scalp. 'I was in my yard and—'

'What were you doing in the yard at two in the morning?'

'I'd heard a noise.' She swivelled and glowered at Rose. 'No doubt my so-called helper was up to her old tricks with some man or other. Hmpf. You give someone a chance for a better life and they behave like dogs, mating in every alleyway.'

'Mrs Velasquez,' Lam said, 'please stick to the question.'

'Of course, Theo, forgive me, but it's hard to stay in control when you've been through so much. God tests us in strange ways.' She allowed her bottom lip to quiver. Up went the hanky.

'Water?'

'No. No. Ahem. I just need a moment, Theodore.'

And the Oscar goes to…

I reached under the table and started to flick Ziegwalt's power switch on and off.

'I went –ide in the fron –arden.' She frowned and tapped the mic. 'There was a sound. And when I got there I heard a –oise –ming –own the –each. Ahem. Down the beach.'

A few giggles rippled around the gathering. Lam looked them into silence. 'Ziegwalt.'

Ziegwalt blushed. 'Zhe electricity, not gut.'

'And what did you see?' asked Maricel, frowning in my direction. I sat back, having achieved nothing, but satisfied nonetheless.

Gladys blubbered theatrically, adjusting her huge square specs. 'I… Oh Lord, I saw that girl being attacked.' The back of her hand went up to her forehead and she swayed like a born-again Christian who'd just seen the light.

'Someone get her a seat,' said Lam. 'Please go on, madam.'

She sat and wiped her brow.

It was unbearably hot, I had to admit. I bent down to glimpse under the eaves and could see a mass of rolling black clouds building. The space tingled with electricity.

'I… I heard a scream and saw…'

'What did you see?'

She turned. 'Him. Mr Bonga, God save his soul.'

'What was he doing, Mrs Velasquez?'

'He was struggling with the girl, and…'

'You mean Miss Elsie Rodriguez?'

'Yes.'

'And then what did you see?'

'I saw him attack her from behind. He pulled out a long sword and then she… Oh!' Gladys stood and slipped sideways, doing a kind of stuntman tumble onto the floor, ensuring that only her hands and knees got dirty.

I'd like to thank the Academy…

Ten came to the rescue and helped her towards her seat.

'One moment, Mrs Velasquez, we haven't finished with you yet,' Lam said.

The prosecutor said she had no more questions. Lam looked at Jim. Jim rose and straightened his tie. He was about to say that he wanted to question the witness, but turned to the entrance instead.

'*Paraan! Paraan!*' (Excuse me.)

Everyone turned to see what was going on and who was so important that the chief himself had been sent to fetch them. The crowd parted and the chief entered the ring, arm out, the flat of his hand a human buffer.

'*Paraan!*'

And behind him, towering above every other person present, was the unmistakably gangly figure of Father Hilario Resurreccion, dressed splendidly in white.

There was a shriek and all heads snapped back to the other side of the arena where Ten and Gladys had been standing. Ten now stood alone looking down at the floor. This time Gladys really had fainted.

'Jerry,' said Lam, casting about.

'Doctor Jericho Neri,' hollered the owl, assuming that she was to call him as another witness.

A small man waddled over and disappeared behind the witness desk to administer to the fallen woman.

The priest halted briefly, then walked on towards the stand.

'Looks like my scare tactics worked,' I said, chuffed.

'On the contrary,' said Jim. 'He was on the bus heading out of town when I caught up with him.'

'What were you doing on the bus?'

'Executing the noble art of retreat.' He raised his chin.

'Running away, you mean.'

'Yup.'

'Coward.'

'Takes one to know one.'

'I always knew the priest had something to do with this,' said Maximo. 'Our army chaplain was the same: yellow.'

'Well, we were both heading south,' Jim went on, 'and, rather inevitably, the bus clapped out on the way. The next bus wasn't until the next morning. He offered me a room in a seminary overnight and we began to talk. I got him drunk, he sang like a bird.'

'Drunk?' I said, surprised.

'He's a priest.'

'Anyway, we, how shall I put it, bonded somewhat. It was rather like a confession in reverse. Seems everyone, even the clergy, needs a shoulder to cry on once in a while.'

Hilario passed Gladys, Ten and the doctor, glancing down quickly, before rising up on the little podium like a telescopic pole. I looked up at the giant beanpole, made more erect and rigid by the straight, narrow pulpit. 'Then you came back?'

'No, we stayed in the next village for a while.'

'Why is he late?' asked Maximo. 'Everyone else got here on time.'

'He's not. I had him hide outside. He was instructed to listen to what Gladys had to say before entering.'

'Very clever,' said Max, and shook hands with Jim. 'Ever considered military intelligence?'

Suddenly I felt marginalised and a little jealous. Maximo was mine. I wanted to be the one who saved him. I felt a little better, however, when Jim reached across to stroke MacArthur and he pecked him on the hand.

'Doesn't know you,' I said, smug, and leaned across to stroke him. The scrawny bastard pecked me as well.

'It's the heat,' said Maximo, grooming him. 'He gets irritated.'

'Talk about biting the hand that feeds you.'

Judge Lam cleared his throat with a roar, and said, 'OK, Jerry?'

Gladys was back in her chair, the doctor wafting a white flower under her nose. As soon as her eyes cleared and she saw the man on the stand she looked pale and drawn.

Jim coughed, put a hand on both our shoulders and stood. 'If I may, Your Honour, I'd like to question this witness first and Mrs Velasquez second.'

'Any order you choose, James, providing Miss Montellano doesn't object.' Maricel threw up her hands in abandonment.

The priest was sworn in using his own Bible, and Jim began simply, asking him his name and how long he'd been in El Refugio. If Jim wasn't a barrister he should have been. Or at least some kind of public speaker. For the next hour 300 people sat glued as he asked mundane questions and managed to make them sound interesting.

The padre's background, his parents, his early years in the church, his faith; we sat enthralled as the pair discussed the ins and outs of his life like old friends. They even had us all laughing, Lam included, at the stories of Hilario's missions to the outlying islands and the ways in which he'd converted people to Catholicism.

'And that's what I like about you,' Jim went on, stepping out from behind the desk into the centre of the ring for effect, the whole audience at his feet, 'your honesty. That most fundamental, most valued of human traits. That blessed gift that God gave us to help us through this life. *Totoo*.' (Being genuine.) He allowed the Tagalog to sink in, hands behind his back, head down, looking at his feet as he paced in thought.

Brenda and Annie were side by side, mouths open like everyone else at this performance. Brenda, I noticed, was wearing Jim's coral necklace.

Jim stopped in front of the priest. 'Did you hear Gladys's – Mrs Velasquez's – testimony, Father?' Hilario said he had. 'And what did you think?'

'I think–'

'Objection!' Maricel sprang up. 'Father Resurreccion's personal opinions are irrelevant.'

'Sustained.'

'I beg your pardon.' Jim pinched his nose in thought. 'Let's get to the point. Where were you on the night of the third and the morning of the fourth?'

'In my quarters.'

'Doing what exactly?'

Hilario looked at Gladys and said, 'Reading.'

'Alone?'

He hesitated.

'Who were you with?'

'I was with...' He glanced at Bernard. 'I was with Elsie.'

Everyone shifted, 300 bums sliding on wood with a 'shhh', like whispers.

'With Miss Rodriguez?' Jim looked up at him, then at Gladys, then him again, a bit like MacArthur would, jolty and bird-like.

Gladys looked at Hilario with pleading eyes and his name escaped her lips like a whisper.

'Yes. We were together.'

'Reading?'

He looked at Bernard again.

'Were you reading?'

'No.'

'What then?'

'We are...' Everyone leaned forward. 'We were...'

'What, Father? What were you? What were you doing that could take all night? Why wasn't Miss Rodriguez in the safety of her own home?'

'Because she was with me. At my home.'

'Doing what?'

'We... we were in bed together.'

The crowd erupted en masse, as if the home team had scored a goal. Lam hit his hammer with such force that the handle snapped and the end went flying across the desk, hitting the owl on the head. She held her temple and blinked.

The chief stood, decided he wouldn't be able to control the crowd, and sat again, head in hands. Ten stood and sat about ten times in succession, and Gladys, standing and gritting her teeth, picked up her handbag and flung it with full force.

Presumably it was aimed at the priest but Lam was seated between them and caught it in the forehead. There was an explosion of beauty products. The judge frowned, as though trying to remember something, and turned to face her.

The gathering was struck dumb.

'He's lying!' Gladys screamed.

Lam stared.

'He's talking rubbish! He would never sleep with that whore!'

'James!' Lam said, viciously glaring and pointing at Gladys with one hand, touching his forehead and checking his fingers for blood with the other. 'Any more questions?'

'Um, just one more if I may, Your Honour?' Jim smiled.

Doctor Jericho scurried behind the judge without him noticing and tried to examine his head. Lam jumped. 'Get off, man. There's nothing wrong with me. Chief, see to it that Mrs Velasquez stays in her seat.' He turned to Gladys, still holding his head. 'I could have you in court for that. But seeing as we're already here, and judging by the evidence piling up against you, I think I'll let justice take its course. I think you'll get your comeuppance.' He turned to Jim. 'Continue, James.'

The mob was still shell-shocked, mouths open at the revelations before them. The only people moving were the chief, who was now standing behind Gladys, hands on her shoulders (she absolutely refused to sit), and the old recorder owl who was searching the cockpit for the gavel head.

I looked down and noticed how tight my fists were clenched. Pride, revenge, fulfilment, justice, even salvation, it was a heady mix. I was actually shaking. Part of me felt sorry for Gladys, an old woman who looked like she was about to keel over, but as soon as I looked at Bernard, tears streaming down his face, I was reminded of what she'd done.

Jim rubbed his freshly shaven chin nostalgically and allowed everyone to settle before dropping his next bombshell. 'Father Hilario Resurreccion,' he said with soft amplification that filled every listening ear, 'have you ever had an intimate relationship with Mrs Velasquez? Gladys.'

The army of silent observers took a long intake of breath and held it. I wasn't breathing at all.

'Yes,' said the priest.

A gradual hubbub started as gossip and caught hold like a small brush fire. Lam raised his hammer, saw there was only a stick, and said, 'Continue. Quickly.'

'And were you still seeing Gladys intimately while you were seeing Miss Rodriguez?'

I looked at Bernard. He was staring at the roof, tears rolling off his cheeks.

'No.'

'Why not?'

'I broke it off.'

The brush fire caught hold, the flames fanned by intrigue, and the noise level went up to the point where Jim could be heard only by those of us in the ring.

'Would you describe Gladys as a jealous woman?' Jim shouted over the din.

'Objection!'

'Answer,' said Lam, ignoring the prosecutor.

'Yes. Insanely jealous. She would not accept it. She would not leave me alone,' bawled the Father over the racket.

'Enough to kill off her competition, would you say?'

'Objection!'

'Yes.'

'And isn't it true,' bellowed Jim, 'that Mrs Gladys Velasquez said she would kill Miss Rodriguez if you didn't stop seeing her?'

'Yes.'

'You fool!' Gladys tried to run to the priest. 'I did it for you!'

The chief held on to her for a moment but got dragged off his feet by her weight. There was a scuffle and both fell.

The noise rose to fever pitch but stopped abruptly when Gladys emerged from behind the desk clutching the chief's gun awkwardly in both hands. 'You're mine!' she screamed. There was a bright flash and a deafening bang as the gun went off, magnified ten times under the tin roof. Father Hilario slumped like someone who'd just received bad news.

Pandemonium followed. Three hundred people stampeded down the terracing like water flowing over rocks. Kids fell, men shoved, women clutching babies went down under the heave.

And then there was a sound like thousands of marbles hitting the corrugated-iron roof, a noise so bizarre it drowned out everything else. I looked out from my position cowering behind the desk through the open sides of the building. It was a hailstorm! Thirty-eight degrees centigrade and hail the size of marbles had been unleashed from God knows where.

As I knelt there, a glassy bead of ice bounced into the ring and rolled in the dust between my hands. I picked it up, relishing the paradox of its temperature. A tiny minnow was trapped within, preserved.

The last thing I saw when I looked up, before the curtain of bodies fell on the final act, is engraved on the inside wall of my memory. Gladys, a trembling woman with a blue perm, was still pointing the gun at the padre. Then, in a weird electric-grey light, Brenda came flying through the air, horizontal like a scud missile, arms outstretched. She cleared the desk and hit Gladys full in the chest, knocking her completely sideways.

The last thing to enter my ears was a second shot ringing out.

I ducked back behind the desk with Maximo. Something warm flecked across my face and I touched it. I then looked at the shocking red smeared across my fingers and palm.

A buzz ran through me; the same sensation you get before passing out, and then a feeling of being sick to the stomach. I went dizzy and broke into rivers of sweat, looking pleadingly at the old man beside me. He gazed into my eyes, grief-stricken, like the time my dad had to carry me off a schoolboy football field with a broken leg.

'Dad,' I said, confused, hardly able to breathe. 'Help me.'

He opened his mouth and said…

'Cock-a-doodle-doo!'

We both looked down at MacArthur.

The bird, once white, was now streaked a beautiful crimson. It looked up through its one dying eye, blinked once, gave a last feeble attempt at flapping its useless wings and flopped over in Maximo's arms. Dead as a dodo.

SOLE
MATES

1

'ANGEL SAVES BABY IN JEEPNEY CRASH!' That was the headline in *Imbestigador*, a tabloid that covered everything from the usual scandals and pin-ups to daily words of guidance from the Bible and '*52 Things to Raise Your Self-esteem*'. Now there's a paradox.

I flicked through it quickly (lingering on the consummate allure of a certain Filipina actress), then dropped it on the beach. I picked up *People's International Journal – Serving the New Heroes*. The headline: 'SENATOR ACCUSED OF FONDLING HOUSEWIFE.' Inside, nothing.

And so on through all the popular rags and broadsheets that Janet had delivered from Manila every day. Zilch. It had been the same every day since the trial. I don't know what I was expecting, but our trial seemed to me worthy, if not of front-page news, then at least page two or three. Failing that, a mention in the 'Dear Attorney Reyes' agony column. There was a whole page devoted to the benefits of a new push-up bra, entitled 'Big News!', and half a page dedicated to 'Mama Violetta's Recipes'.

I chucked them all on the sand and got comfortable on the beached outrigger. It was still early and the sun was just warming the eastward flank of Charlie's island. The boat was pulled up on the sand, still wet from the catch, and it made a nice place to be as the village woke.

A nice place to come and sit and go through the papers before breakfast at Janet's. I wanted to be the one who ran in saying, 'It's here! Front-page news!'

The funny thing about El Ref and the whole wreckage of the murder trial, I thought, was that Chinese whispers still applied. Here we were in a village where not only did everyone know everyone else, but they had all, every man woman and child, witnessed the events with their own eyes. In broad daylight.

And still the recounting of what had actually taken place that day had become more and more fantastic in the weeks since. Not just daily departures from the true events, but even the story as told by the same person.

At first the village was in a state of quiet numbness, as though everyone was waiting to see what would happen next. Most people seemed reluctant to get the prattle ball rolling in the beginning.

The floodgates seemed to open, however, when Gladys was taken away. The seeds of rumours were sewn, a generous helping of bullshit fertiliser was sprinkled over them, a watering can full of tittle-tattle was added, and within days we had a healthy grapevine.

Mrs Komprendio, the eatery owner, knew best, having been seated ringside throughout the trial. It wasn't the chief's gun at all, she insisted as she ladled soup from the caldereta pot into a customer's bowl. It was Gladys's own gun, inherited from her first husband, an American soldier who'd died under mysterious circumstances. 'Probably killed him too.'

And, she went on to anyone who cared to listen, she'd known about the affair with the vicar all along. Had seen them in a compromising embrace one night on the beach: 'At it like teenagers, they were. Course, it won't have been the good padre's fault; he was just the victim of an evil woman. Good against evil. More rice?'

'No, no, no, that's not the way it was at all,' insisted Francis the ladyboy, hands on hips, stamping his foot on the Hard Rocks earthen floor. Gladys hadn't fired the gun at all, it was the chief. He was the one. He wanted to silence both Father Hilario and Gladys to keep his own position of authority in El Refugio. It just looked like Gladys firing because she was standing in front of him. 'Huh,' he huffed, pouting. 'Wouldn't you shoot a woman with a haircut like that? Blue! Yuk!'

Even Elvis Presley Lam, the mayor, chucked in his two-penneth. 'Absolute rubbish,' he'd said during one of his rare appearances at Bernard's bar one night. 'Father Hilario had the gun under his tunic.' According to his theory, the good Lord had sent the good shepherd a gun in his sleep one night via a messenger to clean up what he saw as El Refugio's inevitable slide towards damnation. When I asked how that could explain Hilario's own wound he simply said that the gun had misfired.

'But you said it was a gift from God?'

'That's correct,' Elvis explained, 'but God wanted to remind the padre of his own sins.'

And so it went on, day after day, week after week, the only topic of conversation in every house, eatery, guest house, classroom, tricycle, bus and fishing boat in the vicinity. Gladys, the chief, Ten, Hilario, even Judge Lam and Jim were candidates for not-so-sharp-shooters over the coming weeks.

And, despite myself, I couldn't help but embroider the story in the telling either. Of all the people, I, having been seated in the ring, should have known better. But, caught up in the steady trickle of tourists in the run-up to the holiday season, both Filipino and foreign, I felt somehow compelled. Such eager earholes from incredibly mundane everyday lives. They were like sponges soaking up my aqueous tales of things turned upside down in an exotic land. They lapped it up. I lapped it up.

Night after night I held court in Bernard's bistro, taking each group of backpackers on an unforgettable journey through the heart of darkness; a land not known to guidebooks or maps. A place where the only law was the law of the jungle. I had them eating out of the palm of my hand while their freshly grilled king prawns à la Elsie went cold on the plate.

'John'll tell you about it,' became Bernard's standard response when another fresh-faced traveller came into town, having heard about the weird village at the end of the line. Of course I was reluctant. Every night.

It's fair to say I basked in the glorious heat of that inferno, and used it to light up other lives, fanning the flames of curiosity that lie at the heart of every traveller. Lots of free drinks, too.

The truth, however, remained simple and, if not exactly rational and clear-cut (affairs of the heart rarely are), then at least understandable. It was a crime of passion, *fait accompli*. And one that fed so much gossip simply because everyone could relate to it. Everybody could see themselves in the same position, but for the grace of God.

A few further facts about Gladys's hitherto unknown history had been passed from Hilario to Jim, and from him to me. They were most telling, and went a long way towards understanding Gladys's actions. Again, they were not so complicated.

She had, according to Hilario (who, let's face it, had got it from the horse's mouth), once been a low-flying dove herself in a place called Angeles, the old American military base in Luzon. Although at first stunned, most people upon hearing her secret realised very quickly that it was precisely her being a reformed prostitute that had made her so righteous. Rather like ex-smokers becoming such anti-smoking nags. It seems that we all pick the character flaws of others to express our own worst fears about ourselves, however harmless and minute those imperfections might be.

All of that had been in the early days when Gladys was young and beautiful and had decided, for whatever reason, to sell herself to American soldiers. She fell in love, dared to dream and it came true. She married an American. They moved as far away from her past as possible without leaving the country. To this remote village on the 'Cuckoo Coast', as Maricel so fittingly referred to it.

To cut a long story short, things turned sour, as they often do with mixed-race marriages, especially where ex-prostitutes are involved. Gladys was left with a guest house as alimony. Or, to be more insightful, irrecoverable beauty and a small business.

Time is a bastard to everyone, but to someone whose sex appeal has been her ticket to a better life, it is like slow death. Without the looks to find the kind of man she'd grown accustomed to over the years, and without grandchildren to care for, she changed her name and overripened into a sour old grape. One who kept the flame of love burning only in the form of candles and crucifixes.

And then Father Hilario came along, posted in by the church from Manila. It seemed her inner desire was awakened once more, and she dared to dream again. It didn't matter that he was a man of the church so long as he could love her, albeit secretly, and express kindness both in words and touch.

At first purely religious, a relationship based on scholarly biblical learning with him as her teacher, it slowly blossomed into a physical passion. Most people found it hard to believe that anyone would fall for such a gorgon but I'd seen the photo that night in her house. She had been beautiful. Some of it must have still been there.

The secret affair went on for years without anyone knowing. They would meet outside the village at night and creep back before dawn, never allowing him to come to her unless under the pretext of religious education.

And then, predictably with a growing economy, came the oldest profession on earth to El Refugio. It must have seemed like a sick turn of fate to Gladys when A Better Place opened. Hilario, Gladys's only reason for living, fell in love with one of the stunning young girls at confession.

And Elsie wasn't the first. Rose was. Gladys, very cleverly doing the best thing she could to avert the naughty padre's drifting gaze away from such intoxicating, alluring young flowers, tried to entice the girls away by showing them other options.

Thinking she knew how these girls' minds worked, she employed one of them as a maid. Her strategy, Jim speculated, was to introduce them to foreign tourists in the vain hope that they would see better prospects than those offered by a 50-year-old priest.

A nice idea, and it worked with Rose, but Gladys hadn't bargained on a whole flophouse full. And, more importantly, the allure of a gentle man in robes when it came to young girls who were desperate for the soft fatherly hand of redemption. Of all people, Gladys should have seen it coming.

Of course, none of that excuses her for taking someone's life. But it just goes to show how emotions, even those whose impulsive teenage years have long since vanished over the horizon, can get the better of reason. There could only ever have been one outcome with a man like Hilario, whose eye wandered constantly, but Gladys, like so many of us, failed to see it. Blinded by love.

'John!'

I peeled my eyes off the newspapers on the beach, the headlines now bleeding into each other as the tide crept in, and looked up. Janet was on the balcony of the cafe miming eating actions at me.

'Coming,' I shouted back.

'I thought you are leaving today.' Bernard was standing on the wall of his restaurant stretching his bones like a cat, his little pink pot belly glowing in the sun.

'I am,' I said. 'After the parade.'

'You have been saying that for weeks, my beautiful *kalbo* friend.'

'Yeah, but I was too hung over to get the bus last time. You keep giving me free beer!'

He laughed. 'This is my trick. This is how I trap Lord Jim for five years!'

I'd said all my goodbyes the previous night at the bistro. Still hung over from our last party, one day had merged into another to form a week-long binge that threatened to keep me locked within these limestone walls for the rest of my life.

I told Bernard I'd see him at the parade and turned towards Janet's place, the warm butterflies of sadness dancing inside. Sadness not at my leaving, but at Bernard staying.

I'd asked him numerous times over the previous weeks if he wouldn't like to come with me but he'd refused. Although he didn't feel good here without Elsie, he said, he wouldn't feel right anywhere else either.

Ever since the trial he'd been in a kind of limbo, utterly lost but somehow comfortable in that solitude. Gladys's confession

337

and subsequent removal to Manila had given him all the closure he needed on the subject, but still he remained.

He was no less the person he had been (he still spent a suspicious amount of time at the cemetery), but seemed to stare a lot more than before. He stared at the cliffs mostly. He was like a bird that wanted to fly over them, but had forgotton how, a bit like MacArthur. A sentiment I could fully understand; I'd spent years in Hong Kong doing the same, just substitute skyscrapers for cliffs.

El Refugio really is like a nest, protecting its human residents from the rigours of everyday living in the real world, a world that demands everything. This place asks for nothing. A comforting, motherly womb where weak hatchlings can fold up their wings and never use them.

You didn't even need money to live here. Jim and Charlie were proof of that. If you want out of the rat race, The Refuge is Nirvana. A world outside the world, where outsiders can get lost in a village full of outsiders.

'John!' Janet and her dog looked over the balcony. 'It is getting cold. Get up here, now! I need to prepare my costume.'

2

At first I thought MacArthur's grave had shifted, the earth's tectonic plates, centred on El Ref, having moved to the left in the past 2 hours. I stood at the front gate of Bonga's guest house, stomach full, and blinked, studying the layout. New signboard (painted by me), picket fence (painted by Max), hibiscus hedge (trimmed by Rose), the faint lingering odour from the cesspit (filled by Frank), and MacArthur's little square grave next to the flower bed.

But now, in the centre of the military-squared front lawn, dividing the path in two, was a rectangle of newly dug ground. The turf had been replaced but it looked like a badly fitting wig.

I looked at Maximo sitting on the veranda, pretending to polish his tin helmet, whistling tunelessly, then back at the ground. Then I had to look away to hide the grin creeping across my face. Did he really think I would fall for that old mantrap routine?

Since his release he'd redoubled his efforts, surpassing himself in ingenuity and the sheer scale of his hare-brained, oversized mousetraps. A front gate that came off its hinges when opened, a front gate with 220 volts going through it, front steps that had been half-sawn through. Chair legs unscrewed, table legs sawn, planks of wood over doorways, tripwires that set off fireworks. And, once, a wire tied to the manikin so that it was brought crashing down like some phantasm on me at two in the morning as I went through the restaurant to the toilet.

I opened the gate and entered.

He flicked his twinkling old eyes at me and rubbed away, whistling a falsetto version of 'Colonel Bogey March'.

I'll play along, I thought, it's my last day after all.

I crept towards the grass wig slowly. His whistling grew louder, more erratic. He sounded like MacArthur warbling. Here goes nothing. I stepped in.

The grass covering caved in, twigs snapped, and my smile of benevolence turned upside down as I sank up to my knees in...

'What the... is this?' I pulled myself out with a squelch. My bare legs were now thick with brown gunge and my flip-flops had been swallowed.

'Ha!' Maximo came quickly down the steps, hands on hips, looking down at me. 'Got you again, soldier! Filled it with excrement. You weren't expecting that, I bet.'

My stomach heaved at the stench. 'You're mental!'

'No, I'm sane. Gladys is radio rental,' he said, using my own slang as usual.

I lay on the grass and looked up at his smiling face. 'Please tell me it's not human shit.'

'Course not. MacArthur's.'

'MacArthur?'

'Yes.'

'There's no way a chicken can shit this much, especially not a dead one.' I sat up, wondering if the old man was so sad about the rooster he refused to acknowledge its passing. 'MacArthur's gone. We buried him over there, Max,' I said, nodding to a rose bush.

'Not that MacArthur. That one.' He pointed. 'MacArthur II.'

There, tethered to the fence beside a tree, was the sleepiest, greyest, most decrepit-looking old buffalo I'd ever clapped eyes on. Its nostrils had split so many times over the years from being led by a rope through its nose that it looked like a coke addict. It was now tethered by a rope through its one remaining ear instead. Its hip and shoulder bones stuck out like chairs under a table cloth, and its eyeballs seemed too small for their giant sockets. It looked like it was shrink-wrapped in its own skin.

'Bought it from a farmer,' Maximo said with satisfaction.

'You paid money for that? It's ancient! It's got grey hair!'

'I've got grey hair.' He went across and stroked the animal's nose. In return it burrowed its head lovingly into his stomach, pushing the old man to one side playfully. 'He's strong.'

'He's full of shit, I know that much.' I wiped my legs on the grass and stood, retrieving my flip-flops and throwing them to one side in disgust. 'That's the end of them. What on earth are you going to do with that old bullock, Max, seriously?'

'I'm going to ride him in the parade today. You coming?'

I could see by the way he nearly looked over his shoulder when asking the question that he was hoping for a yes. To him an affirmative reply would mean I'd changed my mind about leaving yet again.

'Course.'

He relaxed a little. 'So you're not going then,' he said sharply, not daring to look at me. He was like a small boy who behaves sheepishly when he doesn't want a kind relative to leave, too shy to say what he really means. None of us ever really grow up.

'You know I am.'

He went back to stroking the animal. 'Where are you going?'

'You know where.'

And he did know. I'd told him a thousand times; through the southern islands, then Sulawesi, then I don't know.

'With Arnie?'

'Brenda's staying with Jim. You mean Annie.'

He looked at me as though her name hurt him.

'You've got Rose,' I said. 'She'll take care of you. And Frank's still here to eat you out of house and home.'

'But she's…'

'What?'

'She's… um…'

'A woman. I know.'

'No, a…'

'A young woman?'

He shook his head, said, 'Ahh, you know, a um…' and snapped his fingers impatiently.

I sat on the grass. This could be a long one. Over the past few weeks, despite Rose's maternal instincts towards both father and unborn child, or perhaps because of it, Maximo's memory seemed to deteriorate.

It wasn't Rose's fault directly, but it seemed now that she was doing all the cooking and cleaning, giving Maximo so much free time, his mind wandered, untethered to reality. Every conversation held at least one 'Um… ahh… you know.'

Given our past I kept a safe distance from Rose. It certainly didn't seem prudent to make any suggestions regarding her lover's mental health.

'An Italian!' he suddenly said. 'See, I can remember things.' He patted the cow's rump heartily.

There was a grinding of gears in the distance and the chief's brand new four-wheel drive Pajero came down the road. His reward for 'solving' the crime. It had really bothered me at first, but when a visiting Spanish tourist informed me that 'Pajero' was Spanish for someone who masturbates I couldn't stop laughing. Now everyone knew the chief was a wanker except the chief himself.

'How many gears on an Italian tank?' Maximo said.

I humoured him. 'Don't know.'

'Five: one forward and four reverse. Hee hee.'

The shiny car, now sporting pompous presidential-style bonnet flags, ground to a stop in front of the gate.

'And did you know the Italian army has a new uniform? It buttons up at the back so it looks like they're attacking when they're running away. Heh heh.'

The mayor's head popped out of the car in a flustered sweat, a clipboard in his hands, greased teddy boy quiff on head. 'Your slot is at the back, Maximo, behind Janet,' he shouted. 'Have you got that?' Maximo said he had. 'Good. You're pulling the sleigh, remember, with your new buffalo. Remember what we said? NO ARMY UNIFORM! OK?'

'No uniform.'

'No guns, no military things of any kind. This is a pageant to showcase our wonderful village for the new tourist season.' His head went back in and the car roared off in a cloud of dust.

'No uniform.' Maximo put the helmet on his head and saluted. 'Whatever you say, Mr Mayor.'

3

It was like Piccadilly Circus. I pushed through the crowd to get a front-row position, still holding onto Annie's hand with a firmness that belied the butterflies raging in my stomach.

What a crowd. It was like Easter all over again. And it felt like a festival, with bunting draped between storefronts and kids with balloons.

We were standing at the junction of two streets with every other soul in town to get the clearest view, not only of the convergence of the parade but also the bus south. I didn't want to miss it.

It felt strange standing there with a packed backpack at my feet, and I wasn't even sure if I was just on a day trip somewhere. I really wasn't sure if, after the procession had passed, I'd simply pick up my bag and head back to Max's guest house again.

'You're hurting me.' Annie held up her blue hand, crushed within mine.

'Sorry.'

'You no want to leave.'

I forced a smile. 'I'm just a bit sad, that's all.' I looked back at the bus to hide my emotion. Annie gripped my hand.

'We stay another day?'

It was time to go, I knew. If anything I'd stayed too long, reaching that line that divides days filled with activities and sitting in a restaurant moping over a book. It's easy to spot travellers who are not having a good time; they're the ones who've travelled halfway round the world only to sit reading.

And, strangely, I'd begun to feel like an outsider again; outside the outsiders of The Refuge. As though, given my happiness with Annie, I no longer belonged to their particular lonely-hearts club. And that's what makes a true outsider, I think; a heart and soul that's terminally unsatisfiable.

I still belonged in that category but my current elation seemed to alienate me from the others. Happiness didn't belong here. It was a place to find yourself, cure your heartache. A place for people at odds with the world.

I didn't think Annie was my soulmate but that didn't matter, because they did. They, I think, mistook our laughing, happy faces – the elation that always comes with the high of new love, before the stagnation – as the beginning of a mating for life. Like all unconventional people, they could never find the right person because there is no right person for them to find. It's a search that only ever ends physically, often born out of the sheer weariness of looking.

Some of us simply get tired of searching the world over for a love that fits and end up staying with someone just because we don't want to be alone, putting up with a sincere, though ultimately counterfeit, affiliation.

It takes one to know one.

I gripped Annie's hand again and kissed her, unsure exactly what I was feeling at that very moment, but happily numbed by it.

'No,' I said. 'It's time to go.'

'You sure?'

'Not sure of anything, to be honest.'

There was the sound of music, rock 'n' roll, and everyone cheered. A moment later a bunch of schoolkids dressed in cheerleader outfits with pompoms turned the corner and marched towards us, in step with the beat.

'Sounds like The Rolling Stones,' I said.

'Juan dela Cruz Band,' said a denim-clad, middle-aged man next to me, his granddaughter on his shoulders. 'Better than The Rolling Stones. Our mayor is a big fan.'

Sure enough, right behind the dancing girls came the lead vehicle, a pick-up. And standing in the back playing his white electric guitar was our very own mayor, Elvis PresLam, majestically dressed in a white silk jumpsuit. Also in the back was Frank on drums, a bass player, amps, and a small generator powering it all.

'I wondered where Frank was,' I said, really wondering about his skills and why he hadn't said anything about his part in the parade. 'He's good.'

The bluesy rhythm reached its turnaround seventh, Frank hit the cymbal and Elvis came in with his trademark lisp, bringing everyone along with him.

'Everyone knows the words,' I said, feeling marginalised.

The same denim-clad man next to me said, 'A Pepe Smith classic,' by way of explanation, and sang along. Even the eight-year-old on his shoulders knew the lyrics.

As they passed by I waved to Frank. He was in the middle of a drum fill and missed me. Behind them came more kids dressed variously as flowers, farmers, fish, animals, and what looked to me like green clouds, but I was told were local vegetables.

Francis the ladyboy was next, dressed appropriately as a *dama de noche*. With his colleagues from Hard Rocks he came by in a riot of colour and hyperactive movement. He was flying everywhere, probably on speed as usual, going from one side of the road to the other sprinkling leaves and petals on the crowd. I got a big kiss.

Everyone had their turn, from the nurses at the clinic to the government employees, and Ten and Thomas, proud in their new Wankmobil. Bringing up the rear were the foreigners, the outsiders.

Janet was first of the last, dressed as a Swiss cheese. A wedge of yellow cloth and chicken wire with a head and legs. She held the hands of two local children who were dressed as bars of Toblerone.

The band played on and Bernard, Brenda and Jim rounded the corner. The bistro owner was disguised as a baguette. The happy couple were just hand in hand, their cloak of infatuation brighter than any costume.

Jim stopped and looked over his shoulder. He told Brenda to go on then turned back the way he'd come, frowning.

'Did Brenda say how long she's going to stay here?' I asked Annie.

'Until Jim leaves.'

'Could be a long time.'

'They are in love.'

I stood on tiptoes and looked over the heads. The bus driver was in his seat revving the engine, clouds of black diesel smoke rising into the air.

Jim came marching back out grinning from ear to ear, repeatedly glancing back and trying to keep a straight face.

Honk, honk!

Dressed as Santa Claus but looking like a garden gnome sitting in his sleigh was Ziegwalt, flinging handfuls of sweets to a stampede of kids.

The sledge was pulled by an ox. An old ox called MacArthur the Second. And on that ox was an old man. An old man called Maximo.

Maximo Bonga, Filipino, guest-house owner, World War Two veteran, alcoholic, womaniser, cockfighter, father-to-be at age 85. Maximo the good. Maximo the wise, the outcast, outsider, the accused, the victim, the victor. Maximo the Me in old age. Maximo my friend.

And now Maximo the comedian, the agitator, rebel and madman. Shell-shocked eccentric who wanted to shock everyone into looking at themselves in the mirror.

Maximo Bonga the totally naked astride a buffalo, wearing only a grin, his tin helmet strapped tightly to his head, and my battered old flip-flops on his feet. His skinny bum rocked from side to side with the rhythm of MacArthur the Second's swaying hips.

A collective gasp went up in the crowd. Mothers covered the eyes of their children, fathers laughed, and Maximo saluted like Lady Godiva.

Annie said, 'It's Maximo! Mamma mia!'

Maximo bowed politely and blew her a kiss.

Our eyes met, compassion among a sea of misunderstanding, before a nun ran on and threw a Philippines flag over him.

He looked at me still, gaze fixed, head turning to compensate for his progress. The look said, 'Don't be afraid. Don't be scared of the road, however long it is and however lonely, because there are others on it. And sometimes those solitary, unfrequented roads lead to the best rewards.'

He blinked and the look continued to speak volumes, much more than words ever could. It was nostalgic and looking ahead all at once, telling me that he knew I'd be back. That some day we would meet again, so not to worry about farewells.

But above all his dusty eyes said, 'I'm going to miss you.'

And that's what eyes are for; to say things from the heart and soul, those things too important for the mouth. Words get drowned in background noise. Looks travel across rooms, streets, huge noisy crowds. They say all the things men can't.

And he was gone. I blinked out the tears. When I closed my eyes he was still there though, forever the last image I'd have of him.

I picked up my bag without thinking and let Annie lead me out towards the bus stop in silence.

It took 10 minutes for the bus to get through the village; a distance of only 500 paces. My mind had already travelled around the world, from El Ref to Manila to Hong Kong, to Italy and London and back. From now to the past to the future.

Something in me had been renewed, and I think it was my faith. Faith in people, in the redemptive power of travel; in the broad spectrum of people it brings you into contact with.

Change, the result of physical movement, had shown me this place, and in particular a certain guest house and its owner.

The limestone cliffs, like the walls of a giant bird's nest, towered above us and we were in the damp of the their shadow. The village held its breath one last time and the bus was pushed out into brightness. We were greeted by the sparkling beauty of a brand new world.

And a bus coming the other way, squeezing itself between those rock faces. We slowed to a crawl so that it could pass by on the narrow road, our windows almost touching, and I looked inside at its occupants.

One tourist only, a woman about my age with a thousand-yard stare. Eyes again, I thought, and their inability to hide what's going through a person's mind.

We passed within centimetres of each other, separated only by dust and glass, and our bus stopped to take another passenger. I waited, looking at the side of her head.

She turned and opened her window. I opened mine. 'Long journey?' I asked.

She smiled, nodding, her muddied mind refusing to let go of the things that had driven her here. Down this long road right to the end of the line, right into the comfort of the refuge, away from the churning machine.

She picked up her brand new guidebook (as thick as a brick and about as useful, as Bernard would say), flicked a few pages and sighed, as though this place, this trip, was the last thing in the world she needed.

'How long are you here?' I asked.

'No time limit really. What's it like?'

There it is, I thought, that inevitable question.

'Like anywhere,' I said. 'Depends on the people you meet.'

She looked at Annie, her eyes full of conquered emotion.

'What are the people like?' she asked.

I thought a moment, flexing the soles of my stiff feet. 'You need to stay a while to get to know them. Stand in their shoes and walk around a bit,' I said.

She seemed to like that, and laughed.

The driver revved his engine.

'Recommend anywhere to stay?' she asked quickly. 'Any nice guest houses?'

Annie and I looked at each other.

'Yeah,' I said, leaning out the window and pointing back to the village. 'Ask for Bonga's Guest House. Bonga's.'

She flicked through her guidebook, frowning. 'It's not in here.'

I smiled.

'What's the owner like?'

'You'll love him,' I said. Then I found myself going into great detail about how best to draw water, where the power fuse was, what not to touch in the ammo boxes, before Annie elbowed me in the ribs. I couldn't help it, I felt as though I was being told by mum and dad that they had rented out my room.

'The vacant rooms are always open, take your pick,' Annie interrupted.

'Doesn't sound very secure.'

Annie grinned. 'Don't worry about security.'

The last passenger got on the bus and the driver started to move off slowly. I said 'good luck' and she thanked me as our buses drew futher apart.

A tear welled in my eyes and Annie put her arm around my shoulders, pulling me closer. I looked down at my feet, at Maximo's massive hobnail combat boots I was now wearing, and realised for the first time in years just how much lighter I felt.

Have you enjoyed this book?
If so, why not write a review on your favourite website?

If you're interested in finding out more about our books,
find us on Facebook at **Summersdale Publishers** and
follow us on Twitter at **@Summersdale**.

Thanks very much for buying this Summersdale book.

www.summersdale.com